"The game's afoot"

"The game's afoot"
A Sports Lover's Introduction to Shakespeare

CYNTHIA LEWIS

McFarland & Company, Inc., Publishers
Jefferson, North Carolina

ISBN (print) 978-1-4766-7006-5
ISBN (ebook) 978-1-4766-3191-2

Library of Congress cataloguing data are available

British Library cataloguing data are available

© 2018 Cynthia Lewis. All rights reserved

No part of this book may be reproduced or transmitted in any form or by any means, electronic or mechanical, including photocopying or recording, or by any information storage and retrieval system, without permission in writing from the publisher.

Front cover images © 2018 iStock

Manufactured in the United States of America

*McFarland & Company, Inc., Publishers
Box 611, Jefferson, North Carolina 28640
www.mcfarlandpub.com*

To my students

Table of Contents

Acknowledgments   ix

Preface   1

Introduction   3

1. "Ancient grudges": Rivalry in *Romeo and Juliet* and the Lakers versus the Celtics   13
   Inside Shakespeare: Pronouns in *Romeo and Juliet*   32

2. "Glory like a shooting star": *Richard II*, Over-Confidence and "The Miracle on Ice"   34
   Inside Shakespeare: Subtext in *Richard II*   52

3. "The uses of adversity": The 1988 World Series, Kirk Gibson and *As You Like It*   55
   An Interview with Coach Bob McKillop   74

4. "Even play of battle": *Henry V*, Agincourt and Super Bowl III   84
   An Interview with Kevin and Della O'Neill, Leicester City Soccer Fans   103

5. "I am the man!" *Twelfth Night* and Women of Prowess   113
   Interview with Shakespearean Actor Graham Smith   131

6. "Vaulting ambition": Team versus Self and *Macbeth*   142
   Inside Shakespeare: *Macbeth* and the Question of Emphasis   164

7. "Sea change": *The Tempest,* Andre Agassi and Second
Chances   166
    Inside Shakespeare: Over-Simplification in and of
The Tempest   184

Appendix: Professional Actors Comment on Parallels Between Spectator Sports and Shakespearean Performance   187

Chapter Notes   189

Bibliography   197

Index   203

Acknowledgments

This book wouldn't exist without the contributions of Zac Grant, who played with me intellectually to discover connections between athletics and theater, as well as between specific plays and sports examples. Alan Kaliski read each chapter as I drafted it and made invaluable suggestions for adding and revising. My colleague Steven Weinberg, who taught at Davidson College for a semester, kept up my spirits by reminding me often how much he loved the idea of the book. You were all key.

My student assistants over the last few years, all students at Davidson College, have helped me research, revise, edit, and proofread. From the start, Christine Noah, class of 2014, contributed the skills and wisdom of a mature colleague as she reviewed each newly drafted and each revised chapter. Able and amiable students who followed were Michael Van Hoose, Michael Meznar, Gabriella Barrier, Chelsea Alexander, and Casey Margerum, the last of whom painstakingly proofread and checked the accuracy of textual references and MLA formatting. English major graduate and former Davidson football player Preston Eldridge talked with me productively about the project as I began to think about researching and writing it. I'm indebted to each and every one of you.

Most of these students were supported by my stipend as Charles A. Dana Professor of English, funding from Davidson College for which I'm deeply grateful. Davidson also gave me a grant for photographs.

Fond thanks to the students in my "Sports and Shakespeare" class during fall semester 2016. You shaped my thinking. Danielle Rifkin signed on to help me teach the class through an independent study. I've borrowed liberally from your ideas for discussion and your own sports examples.

Davidson College colleagues Dick Cooke, men's baseball coach, and Matt Spear, men's soccer coach, graciously discussed sports with me in the early stages of drafting. Later, Pete Johnson helped me with additional sports examples.

Interviewees Kevin and Della O'Neill, Graham Smith, and Bob McKillop lavished me with their time and provided the book variety, thoughtfulness, depth, and pleasure. Graham Smith also generously canvassed his fellow actors for their thoughts, represented at the end of the book, about parallels between spectator sports and Shakespearean theater. Bob McKillop led me to a photograph of himself in action. I thank each of you.

Friends Nancy Gardner, Ann Marie Costa, Sally McMillen, Amy Weir, and Maryah Howell listened patiently over the months to reports on the book's progress. Amy Weir's son Bradford helpfully reviewed the interview about Leicester soccer. Best bud Thomas Mallon guided me along my way. Best friend Rob Johnson's steady personality, tech savvy, and abiding love saw me through. Love to you all.

Preface

Many people who have asked me about this book during the years I've been researching and writing it have misheard the title as "sports *in* Shakespeare" rather than "sports *and* Shakespeare." I explain that the book isn't about instances of athletic events in Shakespeare's plays, like the jousting tournament in *Pericles*, but, instead, about parallels between theatrical performance of Shakespeare's plays and spectator sports. Once people understand that concept, they're usually skeptical. What could Shakespeare and modern day sports possibly have to do with each other?

Production of the plays share numerous elements with athletics—an arena, an acting ensemble that works like a team, a combination of scripted and improvised performance, for example. In addition, individual plays find myriad reflections in sports stories about teams, events, and people, both heroic and flawed. And no wonder: stories about athletics, like those that populate the pages of Shakespeare's playscripts, arise from archetypal human relationships, experiences, and situations. An example from *Romeo and Juliet* is representative: the long-lived rivalry in the NBA between the L.A. Lakers and the Boston Celtics mirrors the "ancient grudge" between the Montagues and the Capulets (Prologue 3). The purpose of this book is to access the plays through such sports analogies, with the intent of making the plays more readily comprehensible and meaningful to beginning readers already interested in and knowledgeable about sports.

In fact, in response to people who wonder what sports could possibly have to do with Shakespeare, I wonder why no one has ever thought to bring the two together before. As far as I know, however, this is a first. It includes chapters on seven of Shakespeare's best known and most often performed plays, questions for discussion of each play, insider information on the plays, and personal interviews that elaborate on the parallels between Shakespearean theater and spectator sports. The sports analogies it comprises range across the 20th and 21st centuries, providing glimpses into sports history.

Teachers and students interested in honing interpretive skills should note that the discussion of each play models close reading as the basis for literary interpretation.

May the book engage many a potential fan of Shakespeare and prove of worth to students of all ages and types, whether still in school or long graduated and hoping to reconnect with a writer who, despite his daunting language and historical distance, is still as fresh and culturally significant today as ever.

Introduction

This is a book for readers who love sports and would like to love Shakespeare—or at least understand why so many others have loved him so much for so long. It's also an introduction to Shakespeare for readers who, so far, know more about sports than about the playwright. Maybe you're required to read a Shakespeare play—for a high school or college course—or maybe you'd like to round out your education in the spirit of a scholar-athlete. Maybe you have tried to tackle one of his plays before, but have been put off by the language or intimidated by Shakespeare's reputation. What you may not realize yet is that the world of Shakespearean theater teems over with stories, characters, and drama that, thrill for thrill, match the extraordinary events and big personalities in the world of sports. Both are worlds of performance, scripted and yet unpredictable, that draw from and illuminate what is most essentially human in all of us. Both worlds figure forth rivalry, triumph, loss, ecstasy, and misery. *"The game's afoot"* uses parallels between these two kinds of performance to show that Shakespearean drama can stir spectators' emotions as powerfully as the best of sports.

Sports and Shakespeare's plays are linked by their shared role in teaching, learning, and inspiring. The competition for the gold medal between the U.S. and the Japanese women's soccer teams in the 2012 London Olympics illustrates this concept. The rivalry between these two superb teams was especially intense because, one year earlier, Japan had narrowly defeated the U.S. in the World Cup final. The American women, though extremely respectful of the other team, sorely wanted the Olympic win. But so did Japan, for whom winning was about more than the Olympic gold: it was also about the process of recovering from the disastrous tsunami that had struck the country's shores in 2011. The coach of the Japanese team, Norio Sasaki, spoke through an English interpreter about the significance of a win to his nation: "All the people in Japan are still trying to come back from the disaster. And through our competition, all of the Japanese people will be able to obtain some encouragement, some energy from this team" ("U.S. Women's Soccer"). Japan's ultimate victory was a way of channeling grief and devastation into a productive, healing process.

In much the same way, characters in Shakespeare's *King Lear* crawl out of black despair in search of hope. The Earl of Gloucester, for instance, believes that his son Edmund loves him and that Edgar, his other son, is plotting against him. But Gloucester has it backwards: Edgar genuinely loves him, and Edmund is spreading vicious rumors about Edgar, who must flee the court or be executed as a traitor. Eventually, Gloucester is brutally blinded as a result of Edmund's treachery, and only then does he discover that Edgar is his loyal son. When Gloucester and Edgar are reunited, they have both grown from their mistakes and misfortunes. Gloucester's suffering has taught him compassion for the suffering of others, and he repents his unjust treatment of Edgar. When at long last he's reunited with Edgar, his old heart can't bear the joy: he dies from too much happiness.

Lovers of Shakespeare never tire of calling him the poet of human nature. If that's true of his plays, it's also true of athletics, which afford lessons about heroic action, failure, and relationships, whether on or off the field of play. Major athletes can assume iconic proportions on the order of Shakespearean heroes, both exemplary and tragic. O. J. Simpson has proven both. When he was a college football player in 1967, Simpson had everything on the line—a crosstown rivalry, the Rose Bowl victory, the Heisman Trophy, and the national championship—when he scored a game-winning touchdown with a 64-yard run that inspired famed *L.A. Times* columnist Jim Murray to write that he was "glad he didn't go to the opera after all." Simpson's feat makes every list of the greatest plays in the history of college football. But how far the mighty O. J. fell when, in 1994, he led Los Angeles police on a lengthy, low-speed chase following the murder of his ex-wife, Nicole Brown Simpson. Tom Brokaw called the tragic action an "event of Shakespearean proportions" ("June 17, 1994"). When we refer to Nicole Brown Simpson's death as "murder most foul," we owe the phrase to Shakespeare's *Hamlet*, as we do so many expressions that have melded with our common speech today. To think about Shakespeare's plays in connection with other forms of drama, whether fictional and staged or true and taken from the headlines, makes as much sense today as it did in Shakespeare's time.

* * *

In 1617, a year after William Shakespeare died, King James I of England issued his *Declaration of Sports*, making certain entertainments legal on Sundays and holy days. *Entertainments* is the operative word, since that's what *sports* meant during Shakespeare's lifetime. One popular form of such entertainment was drama. Another, which shared space with play productions in some theaters, was bear-baiting, a blood sport in which an enchained bear was repeatedly attacked by dogs.[1] Other activities termed "sports" included archery and dancing; all were frowned upon by Puritans, especially on Sundays, and beloved by less sober types, particularly in communities outside of London. Although we tend to think of Shakespeare's plays as high-brow culture—and therefore somewhat intimidating—drama was, in reality, but one kind of many popular "sports" in Shakespeare's time, all of them more or less equal in cultural stature.

What we mean today by the word *sport* is different in some respects, yet athletic spectacle still shares many traits with theater. Both offer shows, performed live before an audience, often in an arena. Both require extensive practice—rehearsal—and both start with scripts that, during performance, become subject to the players' improvisation. The word *play*, which sports and dramatic performance have in common, speaks to this phenomenon: once a *play* begins, the *players,* whether athletic or theatrical, shape—*play* with—their pre-scripted material as they go. What's more, to *play* means, at base, to interact with others, as in the case of children playing together. As actors and athletes *play* with one another, they also *play* with their viewers by interacting with them, even involving them. At the core of both athletic and theatrical performance lies a communal exchange through which the spectators are willing to project themselves into the action and invest themselves in its outcome for the sheer enjoyment of engagement.

Such was even truer in Shakespeare's day than in the current theater. Four centuries ago, spontaneous *play* was less the exception in the theater than the rule, as it can often be on the contemporary athletic field. Theatrical staging, in fact, took some of its cues from popular games and holiday celebrations that, like festive combat, involved spectators in a contest's outcome.[2] Unlike the carefully choreographed productions that today's theater audiences expect, the actors who originally performed Shakespeare's plays spent little time rehearsing together before opening a show. In addition, an acting company had between 20 and 40 plays in repertoire at any given time, and none of the players had read an entire play before they performed it. When they ventured on stage, then, they relied far less on previously memorized words and blocking than on listening to one another and responding accordingly—in the moment.

The players were physically closer to their audience than is now usually the case because viewers in public theaters were either standing around a stage that thrust into their midst or sitting in rows virtually stacked on top of one another around the stage's rim. In some theaters, audience members even sat on stage. The Elizabethan audience was also fully lit—by daylight, in roofless public theaters. These conditions invited *play* between spectators and actors, who were noticeably aware of their audience. They could unabashedly look viewers in the eye and address them directly, a practice rare today, since actors are currently taught to imagine a "fourth wall" dividing them from and preventing them from acknowledging the audience. Elizabethan players knew no "fourth wall."

The absence of a director in original Shakespearean performance also contributed to *play*ful, improvisational acting. The playwright was likely to attend at least part of a rehearsal and give notes, and actors might rehearse individually, but, otherwise, the acting company members were left to fend for themselves as an ensemble during performance. Their training as dancers and fencers allowed them to take risks and land on their feet.

The now familiar concept of a director, which we take as a given about any theatrical production, didn't take hold until the 19th century, anticipating the parallel evolution of the athletic coach, who nowadays is often observed shouting specific instructions to team members from the sidelines. Directorial involvement has imposed undeniable constraints on contemporary theatrical production, relative to its ancestral roots. But the best performances still, to this day, entail a significant element of free, unscripted, unanticipated *play*, as do sports events. Whether reacting to a game's changed circumstances or playing to an audience, highly trained athletes and actors in any era are prepared to adapt.[3]

Play in both sports and theatrics also involves spectators' investment in such features as character and narrative. Audiences in general eagerly await what will happen next and will pay to find out. The story of a particular drama or athletic match may capture attention for the moment, but added to that narrative is the long-term saga of a team, a rivalry, a playwright's career, a theatrical company's history—all overarching narratives that build game by game, performance by performance. Curiosity about how Shakespeare will top *Hamlet* with his next tragedy is on a par with the question of when the ghost of Hamlet's father will make his next appearance. The second question is answered during the course of a play, but to learn about the first, an audience has to come back to the theater.

Similarly, the drama featuring quarterbacks Tim Tebow and Peyton Manning spans across years of football history that traces game after individual game and shifting allegiances from season to season. Manning, a long-time member of the Indianapolis Colts and 11 years Tebow's senior, joined the Denver Broncos after they traded their recent recruit Tebow to the New York Jets. Both players are celebrities, Manning reputedly one of the greatest quarterbacks ever, and Tebow playing to mixed reviews of his skills and gaining notoriety for his religious observances during games. Fans, interested in the stars' professional and private lives, have attended their games or watched them on TV, anticipating the next episode in the story of how each quarterback's play affects his team's success or failure. Tebow's subsequent signing with the New England Patriots led to fresh speculation as to what position he would play and where he'd be positioned in the team's hierarchy. The saga continues.

The well-established fervor of some contemporary sports fans knows no bounds. Jersey-wearing, face-painted, wig-topped enthusiasts shout into the camera during any televised match. By all accounts, Elizabethan playgoers were every bit as rowdy and demonstrative as the most rabid followers of today's athletic teams. Rivalries among sports spectators, whether involving loyalties to local favorites or to alma maters, grow out of competition among teams—competitions that, in turn, reflect rivalries among Elizabethan theater companies. Shakespeare's company was constantly engaged in such bids for paying customers. That company—called the Lord Chamberlain's Men until Queen Elizabeth I's death and then named the King's Men when James I acceded to the throne in 1603—competed with many other theatrical groups.[4]

Certain actors—for example, Shakespeare's leading man Richard Burbage—were, like Tebow and Manning, their own draw. Much as Elizabethan staging conditions invited audience members to project themselves into the drama's action, so featured actors must have eventually seemed, to regular theater-goers, a part of their world, the world beyond the stage. In both athletics and theater, boundaries between those watching and those being watched can become porous. When Louisville's Kevin Ware suffered a severely broken leg in the 2013 NCAA Tournament game against Duke, his agony entered into the audience's space in image after brutal image. Such artificially constructed intimacy can seem convincingly real; when it does, it elevates the ardor of fans and the celebrity, if not downright cult status, of athletes and actors alike. Ware's selfless words to his teammates upon being injured—"I'm fine, just win the game"—made him an instant national icon. "It makes you feel really good," Ware said about the public's attention.[5]

In this instance and untold others, athletics serve as a medium for growth, change, and self-actualization. Countless readers, spectators, and performers of Shakespeare can say the same about one play or more. They have discovered a welcome companion in Shakespearean drama, offering comfort, provocation, wisdom, and challenge, to say nothing of the pride of mastery that goes along with reading or seeing it, and getting it.

* * *

If you've tried to read or watch a Shakespearean play before and have come away discouraged, think back to the first time you saw a particular sport being played—soccer, for example. You didn't know all the rules of the game at first, and you didn't know all the subtleties of play or the technical language experts use when they talk about wall passes, overlap, or an indirect free kick. But you didn't have to know everything about the game in order to understand the basic objective—to get the ball past the other team's goalkeeper without using your hands. As you continued to watch games, you gradually comprehended more about strategy and rules, about stakes, about each player's role, about team rivalries. Whether or not you became an actual expert, you evolved as a spectator, and your growth in understanding enhanced your appreciation for the sport.

The same is true of Shakespeare. You don't have to get everything all at once about a play in order to enjoy it. But, over time, with repeated exposure, your familiarity will grow and, with it, your enjoyment. Like any given sport, a Shakespearean play is a complex of meaning, involving a wide range of interpretive skills. Some of its mysteries resolve with greater familiarity, but others are never completely settled. Getting to know a play is always an incomplete task, a work in progress. But from the very start, if you love a good story and are interested in ideas, a play, like a sporting match, rewards the attention you give it. The discussion questions following each chapter in this book are meant to prompt thinking and discovery that will enhance a reader or viewer's engagement in a play.

The learning sequence for a play, moreover, has much in common with that for a sport. To read a play is a beginning, analogous to reading an account of a game in the newspaper, hearing a recap on TV, or listening to people discuss how to play a sport. To watch is better. Seeing a theatrical performance or an athletic match first-hand instantly explains matters that an indirect exposure leaves unclear. To participate, though, is best. Theatrical performance, like playing in a sporting event, is a supremely illuminating way of studying Shakespeare or gaining inside knowledge of athletics. The experience of taking a two-dimensional page of Shakespeare to a three-dimensional staging, requiring speech and bodily movement, is, like actually participating in a sport, instantly and immeasurably enlightening.[6] Some spectators of sports or theater who once were participants—on a high school team, for instance, or in a college theatrical production—report that they so strongly identify with the players or actors they're watching as to take vicarious pride in their accomplishments and feel personally disappointed by their mistakes.

Experience playing a sport, or considerable time spent following one, yields an insider's knowledge that more casual fans can only envy.[7] Knowing the significance of matters like time of possession in football, man-to-man versus zone defense in basketball, and drawing the infield halfway during a baseball game has its parallel in Shakespearean drama. People who've not only read his plays, but have long attended performances or even played a role in production, have accumulated their own insider information. Such awareness can clarify points in the text that would otherwise seem to defy explanation. Examples would include the use of prose or verse by certain characters in certain situations; the insertion of a play within the larger play;

the introduction of a character by hearsay, rather than in person; and the death of a character offstage, versus in the audience's view.

This book makes a special effort to point out inside-drama details because of their strong analogy with inside-sports information. In fact, some chapters are followed by a brief "Inside Shakespeare" commentary. Perhaps the most important principle to bear in mind is that, when you don't immediately understand an element of a Shakespearean play, the problem isn't necessarily that the playscript is corrupt or is making things difficult for you. Chances are, you need a little extra knowledge to figure out what that part of the script meant—or *how* it conveyed meaning—to Shakespeare's original actors and audience. Not all textual difficulties can be clarified, of course. Contrary to popular belief, Shakespeare wasn't perfect, and his texts have come down to us in forms that suggest a great deal of tampering by various others.[8] But many aspects of a 400-hundred-year-old play that at first seem strange or downright wrong may avail themselves of perfectly reasonable explanation in the light of insider information.

* * *

Because this book is intended as a bridge from an initial reading of a Shakespeare play to a more advanced level of understanding, it won't substitute for actually reading the play. It isn't on the order of *Cliff Notes* or *Spark Notes*, but is, instead, a collection of discussions that read rather like class lectures. It assumes a basic familiarity with a play for which it presents a coherent reading. In each chapter, a sports example frames the discussion of the play and reappears intermittently throughout the chapter. The focus, however, remains on the play itself, while the sports example serves as a point of entry into and a lens on the play. Each chapter has its own approach and organization, but every discussion follows the action of the play more or less chronologically.

In some cases, the sports analogy is surprisingly—even startlingly—apt, especially for those who, like most of us, haven't given much prior thought to correspondences between Shakespeare and sports. In other cases, the analogy holds up to a point, but then the play goes in a separate direction from the athletic example. In those instances, additional comparisons to other sports may be introduced to augment or supplement the original example. The aim of the book isn't to force a comparison between Shakespearean drama and spectator sports beyond reasonable and convincing bounds. Rather, it's to show a way to jump into a play and to start thinking about it.

In addition, the number of examples and plays discussed here is limited in view of the countless possibilities. The athletic examples included are intended to represent a wide spectrum of sports and levels of play, as well as a diverse group of athletes and time periods. The majority of these examples, having occurred before many of the book's readers were born, concern now famous moments in sports that contribute significantly to modern cultural history. As for the plays selected, they are some of Shakespeare's most read and performed and range over the four genres in which he worked: comedies, tragedies, histories, and romances. Readers will likely come up with dozens of their own connections between a sports story, figure, or issue and a play. In that event, the book will have accomplished one of its purposes: to spark awareness of how the drama enacted in the theater is embedded in—and taken from—everyday social structures and situations.

Contemplating Shakespeare's plays in terms of key sports events and figures works both ways. If Shakespearean drama is taken as a starting point, in other words, it can elucidate athletics from various perspectives, some of them unexpected. Sports commentators and writers often take their phrasing and analogies from Shakespeare's plays, as in the popular comparison between the Montagues and Capulets in *Romeo and Juliet* and the rivalry between the L.A. Lakers and the Boston Celtics, the subject of Chapter 1. Henry V's inspiring St. Crispin's Day speech before the Battle of Agincourt, as discussed in Chapter 4, surely shares rhetorical features with rousing pre-game talks by the likes of Green Bay Packers coach Vince Lombardi and Lou Holtz, coach of multiple college football programs and, later, of the New York Jets. Shakespearean soliloquies, in which a character speaks alone onstage in an effort to persuade—or recruit the loyalties of—the offstage audience, have much in common with recruiting pitches. The three interviews in the book—one with sports fans, one with a Shakespearean actor, and one with a college basketball coach—all illustrate and augment the parallels between athletic games and stage plays.

Sports journalism has also engendered its own eloquent writers, well worth the attention—among them, George Plimpton, Dick Schaap, George Will, Roger Angell, Keith Olbermann, and Frank Deford, who, incidentally, wrote a fanciful piece on the 2008 Super Bowl that begins, "The Super Bowl has grown so big that we can think of only one man to cover it: William Shakespeare." What follows that sentence is a mini-play, rendered in rough and ready iambic pentameter, in which Deford spoofs the drama played out between the New York Giants and the New England Patriots. The Patriots' defeat was an upset of major—one might even say Shakespearean—proportions. Stunning linguistic performance is on a par with the most elegant, graceful maneuvers of a figure skater.

The very title of this book, "*The game's afoot*," speaks to the intersection of theatrical performance and other kinds of *play*. The Latin word for both a game and a play—*ludus*—suggests a long-lived connection between sport, whether a card game or a hunt, and the interaction between actors and audience during a dramatic production. That such a connection was vital in

Shakespeare's imagination becomes plain simply by observing the number of games within his plays—Puck's trick on the lovers in *A Midsummer Night's Dream* (2.2, 3.2), Hamlet's attempted use of "The Mouse-trap" to "catch the conscience of the King" (2.2.605), and the game of chess between the newlyweds in *The Tempest* (5.1.171 s.d.), to cite but a few. Such games can yield amusement to those with the upper hand, like the revelers in *Twelfth Night* who get the better of Malvolio and the theater audience who enjoys Malvolio's comeuppance (2.5). But characters who, like Malvolio, are forced to forfeit control don't just play a game; they become game—game in the sense of prey. Augustus Caesar, for instance, stalks Mark Antony, described as a "pluck'd" bird in *Antony and Cleopatra* (3.12.3). Dramatic situations in which a game turns vicious remind the audience that the notion of *play* encompasses vying for all manner of emotional, psychological, political, and social supremacy.

Sports writer George Plimpton on HBO, 1986.

"*The game's afoot*" is a line from Shakespeare's history play *Henry V*—the subject of Chapter 4—spoken by King Henry himself (3.1.32). The English have invaded France in hopes of conquering it, and Henry is rallying his men to attack the French city of Harfleur with courage. In referring to a city as "game," Henry may seem to trivialize the citizens of Harfleur and a high-stakes battle for an entire kingdom. From another perspective, however, he's comparing the assault on Harfleur and the invasion of France to a sport in the sense of a contest for superiority. Much as any sport—whether swimming, basketball, lacrosse, or badminton—is a competition for dominance, so do all of Shakespeare's plays, in one way or another, concern power. Who has power from moment to moment? Why does a given character want power, and how is that character plotting to get it? What do the characters do with it when they have it?

These questions emerge not just in plays about contests over entire kingdoms, but also in comedies, where women and men make marriage bargains, and in tragedies, where power becomes mishandled, ill-used and ill-gained. At almost any juncture, in any staged drama, one character is making a *play* for power over at least one other. In this sense, as well as others, a Shakespearean play is as much a sport—a game—as a round of golf, a tennis match, or a cross country race. When the pursuit is romantic, as in the wooing of women in *As You Like It*—the chase is similar to a hunt, much as courtship in the 1988 movie *Bull Durham* is analogous to a game of baseball. But when Henry V describes his soldiers as "greyhounds in the slips, / Straining upon the start," he's comparing the British army to dogs that are eager to ravage their French prey (3.1.31–32). "The game's afoot!" Henry cries, relishing the sport of conquest (3.1.32).

1
"Ancient grudges"
Rivalry in *Romeo and Juliet* and the Lakers versus the Celtics

The Roots of Rivalry

The 2010 NBA finals, between the L.A. Lakers and the Boston Celtics, were the most watched, according to sports journalist Charlie Duerr, in "recent history." A headline from the *Detroit Free Press* reads, "Lakers-Celtics Big Now Because It Was Big Then." Although today's younger fans may view this rivalry in terms of Kobe Bryant, Kevin Garnett, and Rajon Rondo, journalist Michael Rosenberg sets the record straight. "If you are 35, Kobe-Kevin Garnett cannot possibly be as important as Magic-Bird," he writes. "But if you are 55, Magic-Bird was not nearly as important as Wilt Chamberlain-Bill Russell. And if you are 15 and this doesn't make sense to you ... well, wait until you are 35." Asked recently if this enduring competition is good for the NBA, reporter Fran Blinebury remarked, "Are we seriously even asking this question? Lakers vs. Celtics, Hatfields vs. McCoys, Montagues vs. Capulets, Cain vs. Abel, Jennifer Aniston vs. Angelina Jolie. Anytime, anywhere, we're watching" (qtd. in "Ball Talk").

William Shakespeare, himself a marketer of entertainment, was well aware, even in the late sixteenth century, of Rosenberg's point. Rivalry sells. For whatever reason the feud between the Montagues and Capulets began—and part of the point is surely the triviality of an enmity whose origins no one remembers—*Romeo and Juliet* brings it to life from the first moments of performance. Does the audience pay attention to which servants ally with Capulet and which with Montague when Sampson, Gregory, Abram, and Balthasar angle for a fight (1.1.31–63)? Probably not. More important is how Prince Escalus characterizes the "Three civil brawls" that have lately broken out merely because of an "airy word"—for no good reason (1.1.89).

Unlike the Lakers-Celtics rivalry, that between Montagues and Capulets has virtually nothing to recommend it. The competition between Russell and Chamberlain and then between Earvin "Magic" Johnson and Larry Bird not only advanced the growth and popularity of the NBA, but it often positively affected the game of those individual players. "When the new schedule would come out each year," Magic has confessed, "I'd grab it and circle the Boston games. To me, it was The Two and the other 80." Bird admits the same: "The first thing I would do every morning was look at the box scores to see what Magic did. I didn't care about anything else" (qtd. in Kilduff, Elfenbein, and Staw 943).

While sports and business rivalries can spur players and employees to perform better, serious competition can also stymie them (Kilduff, Elfenbein, and Staw 960). According to sports historian Aram Goudsouzian, the latter was often the case when Chamberlain tried to outdo Russell, who was known for his "agility, brains, and a fierce competitive ethic" (240). "The frustrations of losing twisted Chamberlain into convoluted excuses and bizarre psychology," writes Goudsouzian (241). Russell knew how to psych out his opponent, "sticking a hand in his face, flicking at the ball, and once blocking a shot straight down" (240). Chamberlain's statistics could portray him as the most gifted basketball player ever. Take, for example, the 100 points he scored for the Philadelphia Warriors in 1962 against the New York Knicks, still the record high. But his dazzling accomplishments couldn't prevail against the Celtics' center. "Every season, it seemed," says Goudsouzian, "Chamberlain set records and Russell won championships" (240).

The parallel rivalry in *Romeo and Juliet* does nothing to uplift the characters, but only degrades them. It unleashes passion, which quickly leads to violence, which then spreads rapidly in 1.1 from servants to citizens to masters, as both the elder Capulet and Montague enter the fray (1.1.72, 74, 75–79). When Prince Escalus addresses all involved as "you men, you beasts!" he makes a crucial distinction that runs throughout the play and reflects early modern thinking about human beings, as distinct from animals (1.1.83). The faculty of reason was believed to elevate humanity above "beasts" by enabling people to control their passions and behave civilly. Friar Lawrence echoes this concept in his first scene, 2.3, where he compares the medicinal and poisonous properties in one flower to human nature: "Two such opposed kings encamp them still / In man as well as herbs, grace and rude will" (lines 27–28). "Grace" is as angelic as "rude will" is savage.[1]

In Shakespeare's culture, the fact that human reason provided for speech meant that the use of language also distinguished human beings from beasts. *Romeo and Juliet* reflects this thinking frequently through its references to and emphasis on eloquence, clear communication, and literacy. Characters who use language to forge peaceful relationships and communities raise

The Boston Celtics' Bill Russell and coach Red Auerbach, 1964.

themselves, whether socially or morally, above those who don't or can't read or speak to "graceful" effect. "I pray, sir, can you read?" inquires Capulet's servant of Romeo when he can't decipher the names written on the guest list to Capulet's ball (1.2.57). Similarly, the Nurse asks Romeo, "Doth not rosemary and Romeo begin both with a letter?" (2.4.206–07). Because she is illiterate, the Nurse can make out only the same *R* sound at the beginning of both words. As much as Romeo's social rank ensures that he can indeed read, even some of the most upright and learned members of the privileged classes in the play also abuse language and mangle communication to tragic effect.

The Los Angeles Lakers' Wilt Chamberlain at Madison Square Garden, 1965.

How well characters in *Romeo and Juliet* both use speech and read the world determines whether they strive for "grace" or succumb to "rude will." As the play unfolds, members of both houses prove capable of either alternative. Such is also true of the Lakers/Celtics divide, which lends itself to simplistic, black and white terms, as in Duerr's dichotomy of "Hollywood glamour versus East coast working class grit."[2] Humorist Chuck Klosterman ridicules such rigid characterization. "As I have grown older," he writes, "it's become clear that the Lakers-Celtics rivalry represents absolutely *everything*: race, religion, politics, mathematics, the reason I'm still not married, the Challenger explosion, ... and everything else. There is no relationship that isn't a Celtics-Lakers relationship" (97).

True, certain generalities seem to separate the Lakers and Celtics. The latter have historically been more white than L.A., for instance, and the element of sexual scandal threads through the Lakers' generations: Wilt Chamberlain boasted about having slept with 20,000 women; Magic Johnson, who is now an activist for safe sex and AIDS awareness, tested positive in 1991 for the HIV virus; and Kobe Bryant was accused in 2003 of raping a nineteen-year-old hotel employee in Colorado. From Russell and Chamberlain's days until the present, moreover, the Celtics have stressed team play over star power. Russell was known for pulling together his team, in contrast to Chamberlain's pursuit of his own glory, suggestive of Tybalt's constant need to prove himself in Shakespeare's play. Later in Boston's history, the "Three Amigos"— Kevin Garnett, Paul Pierce, and Ray Allen—formed a tight-knit unit of players, analogous to Romeo, Benvolio, and Mercutio. A similar trio—Isiah Thomas, Bill Laimbeer, and Vinnie Johnson—bonded at the core of the Detroit Pistons, beginning in 1989. They led their team, who became known as the "Bad Boys of the NBA" for their brand of defense-centered play, from rock-bottom performance to championship triumph during the early '90s. Such team coherence is opposed to the Lakers' singular Kobe Bryant.

But such patterns aren't absolute, and they can mislead. When Len Bias died in 1986 of a cocaine overdose, the Celtics forfeited the player they expected to be their next Larry Bird. That staggering loss illustrates the vulnerability of any professional team to the sort of impulsive, self-destructive behavior that ultimately topples the houses of both Montague and Capulet. Nor are Shakespeare's "Three Amigos," however bonded together, immune to such ruin. Mercutio dies feeling victimized by "both houses"—Romeo's Montagues and Tybalt's Capulets—and no amount of loyalty among the friends can prevent two of their deaths (3.1.91). Similar estrangement resulted when Celtic Ray Allen switched to a rival team, the Miami Heat, in 2012, reportedly despite a reduction in financial compensation. The transition cooled relations between Allen and Garnett, who appears to have taken it personally.

Promising Love

If any factor stands to keep Verona's civil strife at bay, it's the budding, young love of the tragedy's twin protagonists. Students of the play, however, may understandably question the validity of that love. For one thing, before

Romeo lays eyes on Juliet, he's pining for another woman, Rosaline (1.1–1.2). His tangled, self-indulgent language about love points to its emptiness. He is less in love with a real woman than in love with love and with such extravagant language to describe it as "choking gall" and "preserving sweet" (1.1.194). How, then, can he possibly be truly in love with Juliet, as he attests upon first meeting her, upon marrying her, and upon dying rather than living without her? How can the audience take Romeo and Juliet's love seriously?

The most straightforward answer to that question is itself a paradox— Romeo and Juliet are deeply in love and not yet deeply in love. To rephrase, the promise of true love roots between them, but is robbed of the chance to flourish. The very youthfulness that often makes them seem like precocious but foolish middle-schoolers is also inspiring, especially to older people who fondly remember their first love, however juvenile it was. Although Friar Lawrence repeatedly urges the pair to "love moderately: long love doth so," he too is struck by the opportunity to mend the rift between Montagues and Capulets through their children: "this alliance may so happy prove / To turn your households' rancor to pure love" (2.6.14, 2.3.91–92). Everyone, even a cloistered friar, dreams of "pure love" and its power to heal. By comparison, sports fans eagerly await the arrival of promising new players each season on a favorite team. This could be their best season ever!

Such purity about Romeo and Juliet's feelings for one another is implied in their first meeting, at the Capulets' feast in 1.5. Rather than merely worship Juliet from afar, as he does Rosaline, Romeo approaches her soon after glimpsing her. Initiating a sonnet they create together in alternating speeches, he claims two kisses from her (1.5.93–110). The sonnet's ornate structure and sophisticated figures of speech mirror the social harmony that, through their children's union, might result between their families.[3] When Juliet follows up the highly formal sonnet by telling Romeo, "You kiss by th' book," her playful insult establishes her impatience with the sort of predictable formulas that Romeo tosses off in 1.2 regarding Rosaline (1.5.110). She prefers authentic expression of feelings. Even as early as this first encounter, Romeo and Juliet's attraction—flirtatious and physical, while refreshingly innocent— hints of something real and lasting. Because Romeo is crushed when he hears of Juliet's family ties just after their first encounter, his interest in Juliet appears genuine (1.5.117–18): Rosaline is also a Capulet, a fact that doesn't concern Romeo, probably because he doesn't believe they'll ever wind up together.[4]

That impression endures in the famed "balcony scene," 2.2. Here Juliet appears to be learning about love at an accelerated pace. In 1.3, when Lady Capulet engages her before the ball in an awkward conversation about marriage, she seems thoroughly unprepared to consider "the County Paris" as a lifelong partner (lines 63–99). Lady Capulet herself is clearly uncomfortable

Romeo (Douglas Booth) and Juliet (Hailee Steinfeld) meet at the Capulets' ball in the 2013 film *Romeo and Juliet*.

discussing marriage with a daughter she doesn't know as well as Juliet's Nurse does. She first dismisses the Nurse, then nervously calls her back when faced with the prospect of being left alone with Juliet to discuss intimate matters (1.3.7–9).[5] Juliet, only thirteen years old, is too young, even for the time, to know much of anything about love and marriage, especially with a mother who avoids these subjects. But obviously eager to please the older two women in the scene, she readily agrees to give Paris a "look" (1.3.97).

In 2.2, though, Juliet's obliging youthfulness begins to give way to more adult independence. Her society dictates that she shouldn't be forward with Romeo, yet she brushes away "compliment"—social convention—and asks him outright, "Dost thou love me? I know thou wilt say, 'Ay,' / And I will take thy word" (2.2.89–91). She also feels emboldened to correct and edit Romeo's thinking and speech. When Romeo tries to "vow" his fidelity "by yonder blessed moon," she interrupts him to point out that "th' inconstant moon" is a poor choice by which to pledge his faithfulness (2.2.107–11). She continues to reject Romeo's clichés, advising him, "Do not swear at all" (2.2.112). Given the chance, Juliet claims control of herself, her feelings, and her newfound love. She already barely resembles the passive, agreeable girl of just hours before and seems more at ease with romantic love than her mother does.

Her joy in Romeo is also infectious. Despite her recognition that her affection for him is "too rash, too unadvis'd, too sudden," she puts no limits on her feelings: "My bounty is as boundless as the sea, / My love as deep; the more I give to thee, / The more I have, for both are infinite" (2.2.118, 133–35). When she compares Romeo to a pet bird on a string that she might "kill" with too "much cherishing," she intertwines her almost comical tendency to take charge in this relationship and her endless longing for someone she treasures (2.2.176–83). As Friar Lawrence conveys in the next scene, Romeo has a crush on Juliet (2.3.65–88), and the crush is mutual. Even so, three scenes later Lawrence consents to marry them, urging them to "love moderately" and praying the "heavens" will "smile … upon this holy act" (2.6.14, 1).

Boys on the Loose

If *Romeo and Juliet* were principally about the title characters, the play would be far less accomplished and interesting, and the roots of its tragedy would be plain: "A pair of star-cross'd lovers," in their youthful impetuosity, "take their life," as the Chorus announces in the Prologue (line 6). While this explanation leaves open the intriguing question of whether ill fortune or the protagonists' bad judgment is more to blame, the matter of tragic cause in *Romeo and Juliet* is infinitely enriched because it is an ensemble play.

As such, it brims with juicy supporting roles—most notably Mercutio, Lord and Lady Capulet, the Nurse, and Friar Lawrence, but also Benvolio, Tybalt, and cameos by the servant Peter (especially in 2.4) and the Apothecary (immortalized in 1998 by the great actor Tom Wilkinson as a stage-frightened stutterer in the movie *Shakespeare in Love*). In the end, Romeo and Juliet are no more singly responsible for their tragedy than would be Magic, Bird, Kobe, or Garnett for a win or a loss. Much as star basketball players depend upon role players to achieve their ends, so do Romeo and Juliet fall prey not only to their own weaknesses and inexperience, but also to the failure of other characters whose support the young lovers desperately need. Where tragic responsibility is concerned, this play has plenty of characters to share it.

Mercutio's actions surely hasten the tragedy. Until his slaying in 3.1, the play might have resolved into comedy. Beloved by generations for his vitality and often scurrilous wit, Mercutio, whose name indicates his "mercurial" nature, is given to bouts of cynicism and belligerence.[6] His great speech on the fairy Queen Mab, which he delivers in his first scene, swipes at folk who, like Romeo, put faith in dreams and swats at various character types who dream about fulfilling their selfish fantasies—lovers, lawyers, parsons, and soldiers (1.4.53–94). Mercutio's colorful language is both dazzling and peppered with scorn; he is especially contemptuous of lovers like Romeo, whom he portrays as effeminate and silly. For him women are less to be loved than used; images of raw sex pervade his sarcastic speeches objectifying women, whether Romeo's "mistress" in 2.1 or the Nurse in 2.4 (2.1.34–38, 2.4.109–39).

Mercutio reserves his sharpest criticism for Tybalt, perhaps because Tybalt's ultra-manly posturing threatens him. Romeo, Mercutio, and Tybalt are all adolescents with raging hormones—whether manifested in love or in picking a fight. Hearing the news in 2.4 that Tybalt has sent Romeo a challenge, Mercutio moves quickly from ridiculing Romeo for his love-sickness to portraying Tybalt as a sissy. When Mercutio calls Tybalt "Prince of Cats," in reference to Tibalt the cat in the fable of *Reynard the Fox*, he alludes to Tybalt's lack of ferocity, however tough he may try to appear (2.4.19). Calling Tybalt the "courageous captain of compliments," Mercutio labels him a courtly show-off, a "duellist" who excels merely at fancy fencing, but not real fighting (2.4.20, 24). Tybalt and his fellows are "fashion-mongers," says Mercutio, too delicate, affected, and precious to sit on a wood "bench" without whining in discomfort: "O, their bones, their bones!" (2.4.33, 35).

Mercutio obsesses over cutting Tybalt down to size with insults, resembling modern day "trash talking" among aggressive athletes on high-profile teams. Add to that preoccupation the young men's restlessness on a hot summer day in 3.1, and you have a recipe for catastrophe. As the scene opens, Benvolio is well aware that the teenagers' "mad blood stirring" could easily lead to a "brawl," but he can't convince Mercutio to vacate Verona's open streets (3.1.1–4). Mercutio is so contentious that he tries to ruffle Benvolio, accusing him of habitually "quarrelling" over nothing (3.1.5–30). As Benvolio points out, Mercutio is actually describing himself (3.1.31–33). All the incentive Mercutio needs to quarrel for real is Tybalt's entrance (line 34).

Tybalt, though, is in search of Romeo, who has offended him by crashing the Capulets' feast in 1.5 and who is now, unbeknownst to Tybalt, related by marriage to his former enemy. For Tybalt, Mercutio is a distraction from his prey, a gnat to sweep aside as he hunts down Romeo, but Mercutio isn't about to be dismissed. He taunts Tybalt repeatedly, inciting him and inviting brutality. When Tybalt asks to speak with Mercutio or Benvolio, Mercutio introduces violence: "make it a word and a blow" (3.1.38–40). Mercutio is the first to refer to his rapier, his "fiddlestick," by his side and the first to draw his weapon (3.1.48, 74). He repeatedly mocks Tybalt for using over-refined language like "consort" and for being "King of Cats," nothing more than a "rat-catcher" (3.1.45–49, 77, 75). An audience may wonder whether any harm would have come about in this scene if Mercutio had only left Tybalt alone to act big and tough around Romeo.

The melee that erupts is on the order of rough-housing among a bunch of physical boys that gets out of hand before they know what's happened. In the moment that Mercutio is slain under Romeo's arm, several of the tragedy's most prominent themes come into focus. Tybalt's brutish attitude and

Mercutio's relentless stalking represent the "rude will" associated with the beastly capacity of humanity (2.3.28).

Romeo, for his part, misreads the scene he enters. Although motivated by the best of intentions, that of patching up his relationship with his new cousin and keeping his friend Mercutio from harm, Romeo views the situation he comes upon through the lens of his own happiness and hopefulness, rather than realistically. As he later tells Mercutio, "I thought all for the best" (3.1.104). His failure to prevent injury by coming between Tybalt and Mercutio is on the order of an "own goal" in soccer, hockey, or, occasionally, basketball—both produce an effect disastrously other than the one desired. When Mercutio is mortally wounded not just *despite* Romeo's action, but *because* of it, Romeo has been defeated by his momentary illiteracy (3.1.90).

Mercutio's reaction to his wound—cursing "both houses" for their feud—augments his immaturity (3.1.91). He rejects responsibility for his condition, though his gallows humor about it—"Ask for me to-morrow, and you shall find me a grave man"—may endear him to the audience (3.1.97–98). Racked by guilt and grief, Romeo demonstrates his own immaturity by identifying his love for Juliet, not as the solution to further enmity, but as its cause: it has made him "effeminate," he now complains, echoing Mercutio (3.1.114). All rationality is lost. Tybalt reenters, "furious" as an animal, and Romeo sinks to his level, abandoning his original mission of peace and killing him to avenge Mercutio's death (3.1.121, 131). Romeo's recognition that he is now "fortune's fool" is both belated and, like Mercutio's avoidance of responsibility, tinged with denial of his own responsibility (3.1.136).

The frenetic aftermath of this tragic climax raises many questions, none more pressing than the whereabouts of these boys' parents. In 1.1, they join the fighting in the streets. At the end of 3.1, they try to persuade the Prince that the other family's child is to blame. But where is a single guiding hand on the part of a parent who could set a good example or rein in an offspring's violent behavior?

The same question repeatedly applies to athletes, both collegiate and professional, who run afoul of the law or of mere decency: where are the coaches, mentors, and parents who could provide preventive advice? The gun-wielding, locker-room showdown in 1999 between Washington Wizards players Gilbert Arenas and Javaris Crittendon took then coach Flip Saunders by surprise and led to Arenas' suspension—which effectively ended his basketball career. Crittenton is serving a 23-year prison sentence for killing a woman in Atlanta. In the last 20 years or so, Washington has completely rebuilt its team, absent the two trouble-makers. In the case of Latrell Sprewell, a coach was the victim. In 1997, when Sprewell was playing in the NBA for the Golden State Warriors, he choked then coach P. J. Carlesimo for suggesting he improve his passes. After a 68-game suspension and a few years playing for the New York Knicks, Sprewell was traded to the Minnesota Timberwolves, where he made a name for himself in 2004 by complaining that the three-year, 21-million-dollar contract extension he'd been offered wasn't enough to feed his family.

In fact, the threat of violence and actual violent skirmishes among teammates and between teams is an entrenched feature of sports culture, especially baseball culture. Players fight; fans watch. And as in the case of the older generation in *Romeo and Juliet,* sometimes the coaches and managers join in. Some of the conflicts are relatively minor, though their effects may linger for years afterwards. When, in 1993, veteran Texas Rangers pitcher Nolan Ryan grazed Chicago White Sox batter Robin Ventura on the arm, Ventura went after him, held him in a head-lock, and pummeled him. Moments later, the dugout had emptied onto the field, and even the White Sox' manager Gene Lamont was ejected from the game, while Rangers' coach Mickey Hatcher sustained a gash above his eye. (The six-minute fray is archived on a YouTube video: https://www.youtube.com/watch?v=VIZB9O24BEE.) Similar scuffles have broken out between Nationals team members Bryce Harper and Jonathan Papelbon, in 2015, and the Milwaukee Brewers' Carlos Gómez and the Atlanta Braves' Freddie Freeman, in 2013.

Ryan and Ventura got over their animosity to interact without incident in years to come. The Nationals' manager Matt Williams downplayed the outburst between Papelbon and Harper—referred to by one sports reporter as the best baseball player in the world at the time. Williams referred to the altercation as a "family affair" that would heal quickly, as it did in fact seem to do. Other instances of sports-related violence aren't so easily repaired. "Football hooliganism"—that is, fans' gang-like bad behavior at soccer games—emerged in Britain in the 1960s and, though tamped down by the government in the UK, spread to other European countries later in the century. Thriving on the rivalry between fan clubs, hooliganism mimics the longstanding conflict between the Montagues and the Capulets, threatening serious physical harm to people and darkening the reputation of the sport in locations where it goes uncurbed.

Self-Centered Adults

Lord Capulet qualifies as a loving, responsible parent even by today's standard when he explains to Paris that his approval of any marriage prospect for Juliet is "but a part" of a fuller picture that includes her choice as well (1.2.16–19). He begins as a rational father fulfilling his social role for a prized daughter who is even more precious to him because "Earth hath swallowed all my hopes but she"—all of the Capulets' other children have died (1.2.14).

Sagely, in 1.2 Capulet advises Paris not to marry too quickly, but to attend the ball and measure Juliet's attractions against those of other women (lines 20–33).

That night, at the ball, Capulet is also the consummate host. Later scenes—4.2 and 4.4—suggest his knack for and relish in entertaining. He clearly wants his party guests to have a good time. He chats and banters with them as they enter, and he counsels "patien[ce]" to Tybalt, who rages at Romeo's attending the feast uninvited (1.5.16–40, 60–74). When Tybalt refuses to be ruled by Capulet, the patriarch lets him know who's boss. "Am I the master here, or you? go to!" he berates his nephew (1.5.78). Much as a coach discourages players from letting their personal quarrels and competitions interfere with the team's cohesion, so Capulet wants nothing akin to a "mutiny among my guests" (1.5.80). As he tries to snuff out Tybalt's fiery temper, he continues to wear a welcoming public face, calling for "More light, more light!" and urging his guests, "Cheerly, my hearts!" (1.5.82–88).

As warranted as Capulet's suppression of Tybalt in this situation may be, it doesn't quell Tybalt's "willful choler"—his uncontrolled anger over Romeo's "intrusion"—which he vows will eventually reemerge as "bitt'rest gall" (1.5.89–92). In fact, Capulet's treatment of Tybalt backfires. Twice he belittles Tybalt by addressing him as "boy," a demeaning reference to a teenager posing as a tough guy (1.5.77, 83). Tellingly, when Tybalt finally confronts Romeo in 3.1 over his perceived trespass at the ball, Tybalt derisively calls him "wretched boy" (3.1.129). In this case and in others, the way the adults treat and speak to the younger generation models how the younger characters behave and speak.

From the turning point in 3.1 onward, whatever self-control the adult figures in the play may have displayed gives way increasingly to irrationality by which the younger generation is doomed. A synopsis of events after Mercutio's death reads like a radio announcer's breathless narration of a game that's taken on a life of its own. In basketball parlance, following 3.1, the play goes into transition. While basketball players may welcome, even wish for, such an occurrence, the characters' inability to hold their emotions in check causes traumatic unraveling, often apparent in their failure to communicate clearly. Juliet's stunning soliloquy in 3.2, anticipating her marriage night with Romeo in gorgeous, erotic language, is juxtaposed against the Nurse's inept wording as she struggles in the same scene to announce Tybalt's death and Romeo's banishment. Her panic-stricken line "I saw the wound, I saw it with mine eyes" seems to Juliet to mean that Romeo, rather than Tybalt, has been killed (3.2.52).

In this scene, Juliet, all of thirteen, begins to appear more mature than the adults in her midst. Once she understands the harsh truths about Tybalt and Romeo and retrieves her bearings, she calls herself a "beast" for ever denouncing Romeo and rededicates herself to her "husband" (3.2.95, 97). She instills enough calm in the Nurse to go forward with her wedding night (3.2.138–41). Juliet's fortitude contrasts sharply with Romeo's emotional collapse in the next scene, 3.3. First the Friar, then the Nurse, urge Romeo, who's groveling tearfully on the ground, to "Stand up, stand up" like a "man" (3.3.88). When Romeo threatens to kill himself rather than face the consequences of his actions, the Friar condemns his self-loathing as "desperate" and "womanish"—versus cool and manly—but even more disgracefully, resembling the "unreasonable fury of a beast," language earlier applied to Tybalt (3.3.108–11, 3.1.121). As the play continues, Juliet's growth progressively separates her from Romeo's moral degeneration, which reflects the older generation's influence.

The glimpse of the couple on the morning after their wedding night together shows that Romeo is capable of real concern for another person. He nearly agrees to linger in bed with Juliet and risk death because she begs him to (3.5.17–18). The couple's loving exchange in 3.5 recapitulates the now dwindling hope of the balcony scene, 2.2. If not for the interference of reckless parents and other adults, Romeo and Juliet may well have thrived.

Capulet's bargain with Paris in 3.4 exemplifies such interference and predicts the disasters to come. It is a "desperate tender" of Juliet's hand in marriage, terms that mirror Romeo's childish "desperat[ion]" in the Friar's cell (3.4.12, 3.3.108). Gone is the even-tempered father of 1.2 who was content to let his daughter choose a husband. In his place is a man now ruled by "haste," a word appearing ever more frequently in a play whose characters become undone by impulsiveness (3.4.22). That same "desperate" father enters Juliet's chamber in 3.5 expecting gratitude from her for his care-taking (line 125).

What he finds instead is a daughter racked by grief, but not, as Lord and Lady Capulet suppose, over Tybalt's death. Before Capulet's arrival, Juliet has held up remarkably well with her mother, accessing enough self-control, even after Romeo's wrenching departure (3.5.59), to pull off verbal irony. In response to her mother's thirst for revenge on Romeo, for example, Juliet manages to seem in agreement with her mother, but to convey the polar opposite to the audience. "I never shall be satisfied / With Romeo," she tells Lady Capulet, "till I behold him—dead— / Is my poor heart, so for a kinsman vex'd" (3.5.93–95). Such verbal command dissolves, however, when Lady Capulet informs Juliet of her father's imminent marriage plans for her (3.5.112–15).

In the following bout between daughter and father, Juliet's hysteria springs from her combined fear of marriage to Paris and separation from Romeo (3.5.126–203). Capulet's outsized anger stems from his frustration over failing to make his daughter happy. Much as Capulet wants nothing more in 1.5 than to entertain his guests, now he yearns to cheer up Juliet. In the resulting dynamic, the harder Capulet pushes his "decree" that Juliet marry Paris, the more uncontrollably she weeps; the more she sobs, the more Capulet copes with his feelings of inadequacy by abusing her verbally and threatening her physically. Calling her "green-sickness carrion" and "tallow-face" and preparing to strike her—"My fingers itch"—he forfeits whatever sympathy the audience once had for him (3.5.156-57, 164). If Lady Capulet, who herself shows scant tenderness to Juliet, questions how "hot" he's become, he must be boiling over (3.5.175).

His final tirade, which his wife and the Nurse both fail to curb, reveals his controlling ego:

> And you be mine, I'll give you to my friend;
> And you be not, hang, beg, starve, die in the streets,
> For, by my soul, I'll ne'er acknowledge thee,
> Nor what is mine shall never do thee good.
> Trust to't, bethink you, I'll not be forsworn [3.5.191-95].

Treating her like personal property, he'd rather force her to marry Paris than go back on his word to another man. When Lady Capulet follows her husband off stage, the audience may suspect that she's seen this sort of scary outburst before from a husband she's afraid to contradict. She herself would rather desert her daughter and protect herself than confront her husband and risk his wrath. "Do as thou wilt," she tells Juliet, "for I have done with thee" (3.5.203).

In dire need of support, Juliet turns to the one adult left on stage who can help her. "Comfort me, counsel me!" she begs her Nurse (3.5.208). In the scene's third and last betrayal, the Nurse, in her own way, also abandons Juliet. "I think it best you married with the County," she advises Juliet (3.5.217). Never mind that Juliet is already married! Although the Nurse presents her opinion as if it's in Juliet's best interest, her motive too is tainted by selfishness. What would become of her if she were exposed as an accomplice in Juliet's secret marriage? From the Nurse's perspective, her life and livelihood would stay intact if Juliet would only forget about Romeo and marry Paris. According to the Nurse's bottom-line mentality, Juliet should move on from Romeo, because, as an exile, he's no longer of "use" (3.5.225). Disheartened by such crass self-interest, Juliet once again masks her true feelings with irony. "Well, thou has comforted me marvellous much," she tells the Nurse to her face, reserving what she really thinks until the Nurse's exit: "Ancient damnation! O most wicked fiend!" (3.5.230, 234-35).

Earthy and practical, the Nurse hints at her self-interest in her earlier meeting with Romeo, in 2.4. When he tries to pay her for her services, she at first refuses, then relents and pockets his gratuity (lines 182-86). Romeo promises further monetary reward to her for setting up his wedding: "I'll quit thy pains" (line 192). The Nurse, apparently (and ironically) named "Angelica," mirrors the parents who would sacrifice their daughter to serve their own ends (4.4.5).

Things Fall Apart

At the end of 3.5, Juliet realizes she has one option left. "I'll to the friar to know his remedy," she says, comparing her situation to a disease requiring a cure (line 241). Indeed, the sleeping potion the Friar provides in 4.1 resembles a medicine, but turns out to be an ironic inversion of one. Nearly everything about the Friar in his meeting with Juliet proves ironic. In particular, the even-keeled counselor who once warned against "haste" and promoted "lov[ing] moderately" loses his grip on rationality (2.3.93, 2.6.14). As vulnerable as the Nurse for his own involvement in Juliet's secret marriage and reeling from Paris' expectation of imminent marriage to Juliet, the Friar confesses that the situation "strains me past the compass of my wits" (4.1.1, 47). Rather than take a deep breath and contemplate reasonable options, Lawrence gets caught up in the general panic. Not only does he urge a "desperate" measure on Juliet—an alarming word, at this point—but he unconscionably plays on Juliet's desperation to escape a marriage with Paris (4.1.68–70).

A responsible adult who hears a young person's willingness to "leap … / From off the battlements of any tower" rather than marry someone, would proceed with caution, as the Friar in fact does when Romeo earlier threatens suicide (4.1.77–78, 3.3.108–58). Now, however, Lawrence virtually goads Juliet into discarding caution, challenging her to embrace the very choice she ought to question. When Juliet says of the potion, "Give me, give me! O, tell me not of fear!" a reasonable person would dissuade her (4.1.121). Instead, the Friar sends her home with the potion and proposes a plan that hinges on, of all unreliable instruments, some "letters"—an action about as responsible as a coach's urging a player to use a performance-enhancing drug (4.1.113–17). In this additional ironic inversion, a letter, the very embodiment of literacy, reveals Lawrence's *illiteracy*, his inability to read the practical world. Petulantly, but aptly, Romeo earlier observes about the Friar that his cloistered life has left him ignorant of the real world, where letters, delivered on horseback from city to city, are likely to miscarry (3.3.64–70). "Thou canst not speak of that thou dost not feel," Romeo says to Lawrence when the Friar tries to use philosophy to comfort him (3.3.64).

An analogy between the Friar as spiritual/life counselor and an athletic coach is not farfetched. A coach enters the life of a player and a team not exactly as a parent, but as a guide whose objective is to improve everyone's performance. Phil Jackson, coach of the L.A. Lakers from 1999 to 2004 and from 2005 to 2011, saw himself in terms strikingly similar to the Friar's when the audience first encounters him in act 2. As Jackson attempted to "get Kobe [Bryant] under control" for the good of the team in 2000, he approached him not as a "father" or even a "mentor," but as an advisor allowing Bryant sufficient "liberty" to improve his play and yet not enough to hold the Lakers "hostage" to his "stardom" (x, xii). Much as the Friar urges "philosophy" on Romeo in 3.3.55, Jackson recommended models for Bryant, like Celtics great Bill Russell and *Corelli's Mandolin*, a novel about achieving freedom within restraints (xi, xv). Although in 3.3 the Friar ultimately manages to steady Romeo with his reasoning, in his later scene with Juliet—4.1—his self-absorption takes over.

As he loses his head and as Capulet ramps up the frenzy by moving the wedding ahead to the next day, Juliet, alone of all the characters, tries to read her future clearly (4.2.24). In her gripping soliloquy before she swallows the potion, she calibrates—brilliantly—everything that could go wrong (4.3.14–58). "What if," she wonders, "this mixture do not work at all" (4.3.21)? "What if" the Friar has given her poison to protect himself (4.3.24–27)? "How if" she wakes up before Romeo arrives (4.3.30–35)? Ironically—tragically—the only possible outcome she doesn't consider is what actually happens: that Romeo will arrive early and, never having received the Friar's letter, mistake her for a corpse. The youngest character in the play is also, at this point, the most valiant and rational, but not enough to save herself.

Juliet (Hailee Steinfeld) contemplates drinking the sleeping potion in *Romeo and Juliet*.

The contrast between Juliet's efforts to take care of herself and the reactions of others to her presumed death in 4.5 widens the dichotomy between "grace" and "rude will." As the Nurse, the Capulets, the Friar, and Paris enter Juliet's bedchamber to discover her cold body, the lamentations of each appear strained, self-centered, and competitive with the others.' A line like the Nurse's "O woe! O woeful, woeful, woeful day!" approaches comedy (4.5.49).[7] In a verbal muddle, all the characters wail at once, paying no attention to anyone else, but only to their own expressions of grief, which hardly seem related to the girl lying dead, as they believe, on her bed. At the scene's end, the quarrelsome musicians' concern only for filling their stomachs with food meant for the wedding feast underscores the decline of virtually all the characters into selfishness (4.5.145–46).

Ultimately, the young people in *Romeo and Juliet* learn "rude," selfish behavior from their elders. Lady Capulet, afforded the opportunity to sway Juliet toward her own good, instead succumbs to self-concern and, like some athletes' agents, and even family members, puts herself first. The Nurse, a kind of coach for Juliet, reveals herself to be equally self-centered, capable of using Juliet for her own purposes. Everywhere Romeo turns, he encounters a negative role model, whether his vengeful parents or his own inadequate coach, Friar Lawrence, who also resembles a zealous sports fan with unrealistic fantasies. Lawrence's ambition for Romeo and Juliet—to repair the rift between Montagues and Capulets—leads not only to foisting unreasonable expectations on them, but also to neglecting what they themselves desire—only to be together. Like athletes who are manipulated by self-promoters and wind up destitute, Romeo and Juliet are eventually drained of life itself.

No wonder, then, that, in the last act, Romeo has degenerated, his "intents" having become "savage-wild, / More fierce and more inexorable far / Than empty tigers or the roaring sea" (5.3.37–39). His purchase of poison from the impoverished apothecary, although often cut from performance, is crucial for showing his descent into beastliness (5.1). At word of Juliet's death, he again misreads the situation, never pausing for a moment to consider that the news might be a miscommunication. Instead, he impulsively, cynically, and illegally purchases poison from a druggist whose hunger he exploits. "Desperate," he uses the apothecary's need, bribing him with "gold" and telling him to "Buy food" (5.1.36, 80, 84).

When Romeo reaches Juliet's tomb, he has become "desperate" enough to threaten both his man Balthasar and Paris with death if they dare to interfere with him (5.3.33–39, 59–70). Although Paris might seem unsympathetic at this point because of his desire to marry Juliet, an audience should remember that he isn't aware, as we are, of Juliet's marriage to Romeo. He's at her tomb to pay his respects and mourn her death. When he's surprised by the man who, for all he knows, caused Juliet's death from grief over Tybalt, he has reason to question Romeo's presence at the Capulet monument and even to apprehend him as a declared criminal (5.3.49–57, 68–69).

But Romeo slays Paris because he's in Romeo's way (5.3.70). At that moment, Romeo calls him "boy," the same insulting term Capulet once used with Tybalt and Tybalt then used with Romeo (5.3.70, 1.5.77, 83, 3.1.130). The demeaning language introduced by a parent has found its way into one murderous episode after another, representing disregard for human dignity, even human life. Still, Romeo honors Paris' dying request to be laid with Juliet in the tomb, proving that his conscience survives in some form and providing a fitting prelude to his moving death speech, which pays final tribute to his love for Juliet (5.3.88–120).

Friar Lawrence's words and actions at the tomb complete his characterization as an adult whose myopia and cowardice utterly fail the young couple he meant to protect. Too afraid to enter the tomb where he has, in effect, placed Juliet by urging the potion on her, he tries instead to coax her out with the offer to "dispose of" her "Among a sisterhood of holy nuns"—hardly an attractive enticement to a love-struck teen (5.3.135–36, 156–57). Paralyzed by fear of being found guilty, he leaves her in the tomb to die alone, calling out, "I dare no longer stay," possibly the most selfish act of many in this play (5.3.159).

A "glooming peace"?

As coach of the Lakers, Phil Jackson assigned himself the role of team-builder. He understood that, although rivalry with the Celtics might enhance his team's unity, rivalry within his team—centered particularly on Kobe Bryant and Shaquille O'Neal—would destroy it. "No matter how great the player, or players," he writes in *More Than a Game*, "it takes a team to win. Everyone must be willing to sacrifice and give of themselves to be the champions" (xviii). Such understanding led to the famed re-match between Lakers and Celtics in the 2010 NBA play-offs.

But rivalry need not become, or remain, enmity. After retirement, Magic Johnson and Larry Bird became close friends—so close, in fact, that their relationship became the basis of a Broadway play in 2012. Not a box-office success, the show closed shortly after opening. But the friendship endures. In a similar display of generosity, Jackson writes admiringly about Bird as the Celtics' coach. "Bird's ego was never at stake," Jackson says. He merely wanted his team to win (261).

Throughout *Romeo and Juliet*, the prevalent imagery of light and dark corresponds with the "grace" and "rude will" of human nature. While the dark side of humanity finally smothers the light of innocent love, the Capulets and the widower Montague apparently reconcile in the play's final lines, each offering to build a statue in honor of the other family's child (5.3.298–304). But is Montague's offer to construct a "figure" of Juliet in "pure gold" more a display of his wealth than of sorrow over Juliet's loss? And does his language hint of competitiveness with Capulet, who asks for his hand (5.3.296)? "But I can give thee more," replies Montague to Capulet's gesture of peace (5.3.298). Has this rivalry truly been subdued for good? Or could what the Prince refers to as a "glooming peace"—neither black nor white, light nor dark—go either way (5.3.305)?

Discussion Questions for *Romeo and Juliet*

- What other sports team rivalries do you think match up well with the ongoing competition between the Montagues and the Capulets? What individual athletes, coaches, or other sports figures match up with individual characters like Mercutio, Tybalt, Benvolio, Friar Lawrence, and others?
- Hope Solo, the gifted U.S. goalkeeper, was suspended from U.S. Soccer for comments she made about the Swedish team that beat the Americans at the Olympics in Rio. An article on her suspension "U.S. Soccer Suspends Hope Solo and Terminates Her Contract" ran in the *New York Times,* August 24, 2016. As hot-headed as Solo may have been, was a suspension and loss of contract justifiable in this case? Do you think a man would have been punished for making the same comments?
- Take a close look at Mercutio's long speech about Queen Mab in 1.4.53–94. If you were the actor delivering the speech, how would you want your internal audience—Romeo, Benvolio, and other young men in the party—to react to you? Do you think the internal audience reacts differently from the external audience—the theater audience? If so, why? Is Mercutio's aim, in your opinion, more to get attention than to make a serious point about dreams? How would you back up your viewpoint?
- When Romeo is gearing up to slay Tybalt in 3.1, he uses the excuse that his love for Juliet has made him "effeminate" (3.1.114). He's worried about what other men will think of him if he doesn't avenge his friend Mercutio's murder. Similarly, Lord Capulet bullies Juliet into marrying Paris so that he won't be "forsworn"—that is, found to be untrustworthy by other men (3.5.195). What other instances do you see in the play when men act out of concern over how other men will judge them?
- Many characters in the play see themselves ruled by the "stars," to quote Romeo, or "A greater power than we can contradict," to use Friar Lawrence's words (5.1.24, 5.3.153). To what extent are the play's events determined by forces outside of human control? How much do characters' actions and choices matter to the play's outcomes?

- In the 1968 film of *Romeo and Juliet,* directed by Franco Zeffirelli, Juliet's stunning soliloquy at the opening of 3.2 was cut: "Gallop apace, you fiery-footed steeds...." Zeffirelli couldn't coach his Juliet, played by Olivia Hussey, to deliver the speech to his satisfaction. What is the soliloquy about, and what would make it so challenging to a young actor?
- Does Romeo's slaying of Paris in 5.3 detract from his portrayal as a hero? If so, to what degree? Could you argue that Romeo's unnecessary violence in that case makes him more interesting and human by virtue of being flawed? Or does the act compromise the audience's sympathy for him too much for comfort?
- A few characters in the play retell action that the audience has already witnessed: Benvolio recounts the opening brawl at Montague's request (1.1.104–15); the Prince solicits Benvolio's account of the fight in 3.1 after Mercutio and Tybalt are killed (3.1.151–75); at the end of the play, Friar Lawrence reviews the entirety of Romeo and Juliet's tragic fate, including his own role in their deaths, in response to the Prince's demand to explain what he knows about what happened (5.3.228–69). Ordinarily, a playwright would avoid such long narration in a play, since it could easily bore the audience. Why do you think Shakespeare employs various instances of it in *Romeo and Juliet*?
- What role does Friar Lawrence's recapping of events play in resolving the play's action? Overall, how resolved do you think this play is?

Inside Shakespeare: Pronouns in *Romeo and Juliet*

Contemporary audiences of Shakespeare's plays are used to hearing characters address one another as either *you* or *thou* and *thee* without so much as thinking about the difference. But for Shakespeare's original audience, the difference was well known and important. *You* and its various forms—*your* and *yours*—were formal. *Thou, thee,* and *thine* were informal. Romance languages preserve this difference. In French, the formal *vous* and informal *tu* signal different kinds of relationships. Similarly, in Spanish, *usted* (singular) or *ustedes* (plural) and *tú* represent the formal and informal, as do *lei* (singular) or *voi* (plural) and *tu* in Italian.

When do Shakespeare's characters use formal pronouns, and when do they use informal pronouns? Normally, formal pronouns are used in formal situations between characters who aren't intimate—who aren't, say, friends, lovers, or family members—and who are maintaining a respectful distance from one another. By contrast, informal pronouns appear between familiars, especially in relaxed situations. Often, a person of high social standing will address an inferior—a servant or a commoner—with the informal *thou*. Thus, when Capulet tells his servant to "go hire me twenty cunning cooks" for purposes of preparing Paris and Juliet's wedding feast, the servant responds, "*You* shall have none ill, sir, for I'll try if they can lick their fingers." Capulet responds, "How canst *thou* try them so?" The servant tells Capulet that a bad cook won't lick his own fingers (4.2.2–8). He can joke with his master, but he must refer to him in the formal mode.

As we might expect, Romeo and Juliet reflect their true love for each other by using the informal pronouns quickly and consistently in their conversation. Whether Juliet is addressing Romeo in the morning after they've consummated their marriage—"Wilt *thou* be gone? it is not yet near day"— or before she swallows the sleeping potion—"Romeo, Romeo, Romeo! ... I drink to *thee*"—or as she tries to die by finding traces of poison on Romeo's lips—"I will kiss *thy* lips..."—she shows her romantic bond with him (3.5.1, 4.3.58, 5.3.164). Similarly, Romeo begins addressing Juliet in the informal manner as soon as he meets her and first kisses her: "Thus from my lips, by *thine*, my sin is purg'd" (1.5.107). In the play's final scene, Romeo also refers to Paris in the familiar—"Wilt *thou* provoke me? Then have at *thee*, boy!"— expressing both contempt for Paris and his sense that he's older and more manly than this "boy" (5.3.70). Paris has already shown similar condescension to Romeo: "Condemned villain, I do apprehend *thee*" (5.3.56). Romeo's address to the absent apothecary who has provided him with poison—"*Thy* drugs are quick"—bespeaks his higher social standing, as well as a conspiratorial connection he's formed with a man he perceives as his ally (5.3.120).

Tellingly, Juliet speaks to her mother in the formal—"Madam, I am here, / What is *your* will?"—while she refers to the Nurse in the informal—"And stint *thou* too, I pray *thee* nurse, say I" (1.3.5–6, 58). She indicates not only her social superiority to the nurse, but also her greater emotional attachment to her than to her own mother. Granted that children were more respectful of parents in the early modern period than is often the case today, and granted that even husbands and wives were likely to address each other in the formal, the contrast between how Juliet thinks and feels about her mother and her nurse emerges in her use of pronouns. She is simply closer to the woman who nursed her and cared for her than she is to the woman who gave her birth.[8]

2
"Glory like a shooting star"
Richard II, Over-Confidence and the "Miracle on Ice"

Power Shifts

At the 1980 Winter Olympics in Lake Placid, New York, the Soviet hockey team was believed to be the world's best. No one trusted in their untouchable supremacy more than the Soviets themselves, and they had ample evidence. Just thirteen days before the Olympic Games, the Soviets had trounced the U.S. team in an exhibition game at Madison Square Garden, 10–3. In the opening round of Olympic competition, the Soviets had humiliated opponent after opponent—beating, among others, Japan, 16–0; the Netherlands, 17–4; and Poland, 8–1.

So confident was Soviet coach, Viktor Tikhonov, that he excused his best players from practice before the Medal Round and told them to go review plays, the equivalent of a theatrical director's excusing his cast from dress rehearsal and advising them instead to study their lines. In contrast, Herb Brooks, the U.S. coach, kept subjecting his players to notoriously demanding practices. As accomplished as the Soviets were, their conviction in their invincibility became a chink in their armor: Team USA, a group of college students, defeated the Soviets, all hockey professionals, when complacency and panic left the Soviets open to mistakes of which the Americans took full advantage.

In 1399, English history took a sharp, monumental turn that shares several attributes with the 1980 "Miracle on Ice." King Richard II, who considered his rule sanctioned by God and therefore unassailable, was nevertheless deposed by Henry Herford, the Duke of Lancaster, who thus became King Henry IV. Shakespeare portrays Henry, also known in the play as Bullingbrook (or Bolingbroke), as an opportunist whose practical gift for politics enables him to rally both nobles and commoners around his cause. In contrast, Richard's over-confidence in his divine anointment blinds him to his vulnerability and leads to a series of mistakes that virtually invite Bullingbrook to seize the crown.

Richard's deposition was a drastic action, generating a dangerous precedent. Bullingbrook and his heirs, of the royal house of Lancaster, represented an altogether new concept of kingship from Richard's medieval model of divine right, in which subjects owed loyalty to a lord in exchange for land and protection. In Shakespeare's portrayal, the Lancastrian kings give lip service to such traditional values. But in reality they lay claim to rule through power, which they aim to consolidate and expand, as Henry IV's son does when he invades France in *Henry V*. The disruptive political reversal in *Richard II* is reflected in forms both sweeping and minute, as through the frequent *un*-words that call attention to a meaning and its polar opposite— "undeaf," "unking'd" and "unkiss," to cite a few (2.1.16, 4.1.220 and 5.5.37, 5.1.74).

These two styles of ruling have their analogy in the opposing coaching styles of Tikinhov and Brooks. Like Richard's, Tikinhov's mentality was that of entitlement, of someone ordained to dominate. Brooks, resembling Bullingbrook, led according to the precept that the players, like the commoners, should endorse the mutual cause.

Shakespeare remains characteristically noncommittal as to whether such sweeping change as Bullingbrook represents is positive or negative: he alternates perspectives on the deposition, King Richard, and Bullingbrook. But as he and his audience were well aware, the Bishop of Carlisle's prophecy of civil war to follow the deposition—"The blood of English shall manure the ground, / And future ages groan for this foul act" (4.1.137–38)—had come painfully true. Indeed, Henry IV's reign was constantly vexed by insurgency and his grandson's by full-blown civil strife. Theater-goers of the time had already seen the Wars of the Roses (c. 1455–85) portrayed in Shakespeare's earlier works about the reigns of Lancastrian Henry VI and Yorkist Richard III. The action of *Richard II* ignites a century of unrest before the Tudor monarchs, blanketing England in peace, could proceed politically from where Bullingbrook had begun.[1]

Over-Confidence, Incompetence, Consequences

In the first act of *Richard II*, the King displays majesty, but is actually insecure, operating from a wobbly power base. Some historical details of the play's complicated opening situation are obscured in the text, especially to modern audiences—who, for instance, don't recognize a name like Thomas of Woodstock, Bullingbrook's murdered uncle. But not even historians can draw definitive conclusions about all of the specifics, including who killed Woodstock (also referred to as the Duke of Gloucester). The death order almost certainly came from Richard and was likely carried out by Thomas Mowbray, the Duke of Norfolk. Bullingbrook's motive for publicly accusing Mowbray, though, isn't clear (1.2.35–42). Is it loyalty to the King, as he implies? Alternatively, is he trying to win the King's favor away from Mowbray, given the King's long-standing wariness toward both Mowbray and Bullingbrook? Or is he hoping to expose the King's murder of his uncle through Mowbray, the King's probable henchman? Gloucester's death remained a source of grief and hostility within his family, as illustrated in 1.2, where Gloucester's widow and brother, John of Gaunt, debate options for revenge.

In the opening scene, Richard bears himself royally, but fails to curb either Mowbray's or Bullingbrook's aggression. When neither man follows the King's order to put down the gages they've already exchanged, the King ironically reasons that, since they're unwilling to obey him, he has no choice but to give up, rather than negotiate. "We were not born to sue [ask]," he says, referring to himself with the royal *we*, "but to command" (1.1.196). In the follow-up scene, 1.3, when the contenders are scheduled to settle their dispute in mortal combat, Richard seizes power through the theatrical, high-handed gesture of interrupting the battle just as it's starting (1.3.118). He then executes his power by banishing both Mowbray and Bullingbrook (1.3.139–90). In so doing, Richard rids himself of two liabilities—an assassin and his would-be avenger. As an athletic coach or team owner may see fit to remove an able player from the field because the player is perceived as disruptive, Richard tries to smother accusations of his misconduct to secure his position. Because Richard realizes he's on shaky ground with John of Gaunt, his powerful uncle and Bullingbrook's father, he cautiously reduces the length of Bullingbrook's banishment from ten years to six (1.3.140–43, 209–12).

But in the next scene, 1.4, Richard abandons such prudence at Green's instigation. Citing a private reason for banishing Bullingbrook, Richard describes his cousin's threatening popularity, which Bullingbrook cultivates through "courtship to the common people" (1.4.24). When Green assures the King that Bullingbrook is out of the way and turns attention to the Irish rebels, Richard ill-advisedly resolves to "farm our royal realm" for income, since he's overspent on entertaining friends at "court" (1.4.37–52). Richard's notion of England as a "farm" to "supply our wants" repeatedly affirms his misunderstanding of his royal responsibility to his people, who do not exist exclusively for his pleasure, convenience, and exploitation, any more than a hockey team exists solely to benefit a coach, an owner, or a nation (1.4.51). Gaunt reprises Richard's metaphor on his deathbed, when he compares England under Richard's abuse to "a tenement or pelting [paltry] farm" (2.1.60).

Richard's sense of entitlement knows no bounds. In 1.4, he proposes to issue "blank charters" by which his officers can levy "large sums of gold" from the "rich" (ll. 48–50). While the dying Gaunt attempts in 2.1 to educate the King on effective ruling, Richard's egoism persists. Gaunt's tribute to "this realm, this England," one of Shakespeare's most familiar and admired monologues, expresses sentiments that fail to interest Richard once he enters the chamber (2.1.31–68). Cruelly, he calls Gaunt a "lunatic lean-witted fool" (words better suited to himself), brushes off Gaunt's death with "so much for that," and immediately confiscates Gaunt's "plate, coin, revenues, and moveables," all of which rightfully belong to the banished Bullingbrook (2.1.115, 155, 159–62). York's warning to his nephew that, by seizing Bullingbrook's property, "You pluck a thousand dangers on your head" essentially repeats Gaunt's line to Richard that he is about to "depose" himself (2.1.186–208, 104–08).

Richard's recklessness is characteristic of a reigning regime like the 1980 Soviet hockey team, whose choices repeatedly undercut their own position. Chief among the Soviets' missteps was their oblivious, seemingly arrogant exit from the ice several seconds before the end of the first period, leaving legendary goalkeeper, Vladislav Tretiak, alone in the net. When American Dave Christian shot the unprotected puck, Tretiak prevented a goal. But then, American Mark Johnson, the game's high scorer, collected the rebound and scored, tying the first-period score 2–2 at the buzzer.

To begin the second period, Soviet coach Tikhonov, writes sports analyst Kevin Allen, "stunned one and all by removing Tretiak and replacing him with [Vladimir] Myshkin." Tiknonov's deliberate humiliation of Tretiak proved self-defeating, as the U.S. scored two more goals, dethroning the Soviets with a final score of 4–3. In another self-defeating instance of either paralysis or ego, the Soviets spent the game's last minute in possession of the puck without pulling their goalie to gain the extra man in play. While the Soviets' blunders mounted, Team USA capitalized on its players' strengths, including the sharp shooting of Mark Johnson, Buzz Schneider, and Mike Eruzione, and the brilliant play of goaltender Jim Craig, whose college coach remembers that the net seemingly "disappeared behind him" (qtd. in Allen).

Of all the factors conspiring against the Soviets and in favor of the Americans, the greatest was, arguably, that of over-confidence. "Years after the event," asserts Allen, "it's easier to see that the Soviets badly underestimated the Americans' talent." Team USA had been dealing with its own confidence issues leading up to the Olympics, a period of less than stellar performance for them. But individual players like Craig had reserves of self-assurance, and the whole team, inspired by Brooks' leadership, had become convinced they could win. "The players had big egos," Brooks has said of Team USA, "but they didn't have ego problems" (qtd. in Allen). By contrast, the documentary film *Do You Believe in Miracles?* refers to the Soviets' "overflowing confidence."

The Unites States Olympic Hockey team celebrates their victory over the Soviets, 1980.

Upsets of powerful teams by determined teams in smaller leagues regularly snatch headlines, as in examples involving Football Championship Subdivision teams who prevail over the supposedly mightier Football Bowl Subdivision teams. The most notable such win occurred in 2007, when FCS-affiliated Appalachian State University beat then number 5-ranked University of Michigan, a team in the FBS, for a final score of 34–32. National rankings went haywire: the Appalachian Mountaineers won the favor of sports analysts and fans, much as Bullingbrook claims favor with the masses. More recently, in 2016, North Dakota State, in the FCS, beat six FBS teams, finally triumphing over Iowa, ranked number 13 in the nation at the time. Whether or not the FBS teams' over-confidence left them vulnerable to North Dakota State isn't clear, although it was surely something of a factor. Those in power have difficulty imagining that someone can take power away from them.

At the close of 2.1 in Shakespeare's play, the nobles who linger onstage to underscore Richard's violation of Bullingbrook's birthright accentuate the King's "overflowing confidence." That Richard is "basely led / By flatterers" may explain his arrogance, but doesn't excuse it (2.1.241–42). The frivolity of his lavish court is characterized by the Queen's elaborate repartee with the courtiers in 2.2. The conceit of her "unborn sorrow" is so highly wrought that it virtually trivializes her actual grief in the audience's view (2.2.10). The setting of the garden is symbolic of England; Bushy, Bagot, and Green, parasitical courtiers, are, in Bullingbrook's words, "caterpillars of the commonwealth" he seeks "to weed and pluck away" (2.3.166–67).

In acts 2 and 3, as Bullingbrook returns from exile and advances on the King and his corrupt court, Richard's confidence remains steadfast, despite signs that it is unwarranted. It's fed by the likes of the Bishop of Carlisle, who assures him, "Fear not, my lord, that Power that made you king / Hath power to keep you king in spite of all" (3.2.27–28). Richard follows suit, describing himself as an "anointed king," the "deputy elected by the Lord," whom the "breath of worldly men cannot depose" (3.2.55–57).

Such an outlook, though, becomes increasingly unrealistic, especially when, in 3.2, Richard receives one blow after another to his weakening power. So may Coach Tikinhov have felt his team's sense of anointment slip away as Team USA increasingly seemed capable of winning. In rapid succession, Richard learns that, because he arrived in Wales later than expected, the Welsh have assumed he's dead, have disbanded, and "are gone to" Bullingbrook; that Bullingbrook has mustered a general rebellion among Richard's subjects; that several of Richard's court favorites have been executed; and that Richard's uncle, the Duke of York, has, after long remaining loyal to Richard, finally "join'd with Bullingbrook" (3.2.71–74, 106–20, 138–40, 200–03). Richard's penchant for self-pity and cloying poetry in the face of such disappointments dampens whatever sympathy from the audience his woes might earn him. In response to laments like "For God's sake let us sit upon the ground / And tell sad stories of the death of kings," even his defenders like Carlisle recommend action (3.2.155–56, 178–82).

If Richard earlier underestimates his vulnerability, he grows ever more self-defeating in his pessimism. The King, once so unjustifiably self-assured, suddenly seems to cave in—to will, rather than predict, Bullingbrook's success. The tendency to make bad matters worse through rash or unconsidered decisions also marked several of the 1980 Soviet hockey team's actions. In particular, when several players exited the ice with seconds of play left, they opened themselves up to a U.S. goal. But when Coach Tikhonov reacted by benching his star goalkeeper, he let his frustration get the better of him and made a U.S. victory all the more likely.

Bullingbrook's Brand

Richard's apparent cooperation in his deposition raises the major question of whether he, in effect, abdicates or Bullingbrook truly deposes him. Although the King's talent for morose reflection makes him an easy target for a modern audience's impatience, it can obscure the large degree of influence Bullingbrook exerts over Richard.

Bullingbrook's countervailing talent for decisive, direct action offers an attractive alternative to Richard's moping and floundering. The political savvy and rousing rhetoric that allow him to raise a formidable army against Richard characterizes leaders like U.S. coach Herb Brooks. Played by Kurt Russell in the 2004 movie *Miracle,* Brooks says to his players of the Soviets, "The rest of the world's afraid of them. Boys, we won't be." Such bravado is compelling.

But Bullingbrook's political rhetoric also involves an ambiguity that masks the full extent of his ambition and aggression. Perhaps most ambiguous of all is what, exactly, he means when he promises the lords who back him and Richard himself that he's returned from banishment "But for his own"— that is, to reclaim only the property belonging to him, which Richard has seized (2.3.149). While everyone in Bullingbrook's hearing obviously understands his reference to "mine own" in this way, the climax in 3.3, when Bullingbrook takes Richard prisoner, indicates that "mine own," in Bullingbrook's mind, includes the crown (3.3.196).

Richard II is so theatrically and poetically formal that it can seem stiff, though its characterization, particularly of Bullingbrook, is often remarkably subtle.[2] Before Richard surrenders to him in 3.3, signs emerge of Bullingbrook's sizable ambition. One of the more visible of these is his treatment of the King's flatterers like Bushy and Green, whose execution he orders in 3.1. Bullingbrook justifies this act by citing how these so-called "caterpillars of the commonwealth" have "fed" upon his inheritance through their parasitical misleading of Richard (2.3.166, 3.1.16–27). But in seizing judiciary power to prosecute these men, no matter how severely they've offended him and the state, he is overreaching. Richard's earlier mocking reference to the banished Bullingbrook as "high Herford" implies the same (1.4.2).

Further suggestions of such arrogance arise as the play calls repeated attention to titles and terms of address. While Bullingbrook is quick to correct

Lord Berkeley when he uses a lesser title, "Lord of Herford," instead of "[Duke of] Lancaster" in addressing him, Bullingbrook's supporter Northumberland soon refers to Richard without the title of "King" (2.3.69–73, 3.3.5–6). The Duke of York, although having recently committed his support to Bullingbrook, still regards Richard as king. He rebukes Northumberland for an oversight that appears disrespectful at best. "It would beseem the Lord Northumberland," he says, demonstrably using the lord's title, "To say King Richard" (3.3.7–8). A verbal scuffle follows, in which Bullingbrook essentially cautions York against blowing a detail out of proportion and York warns his nephew against sedition (3.3.10–19).

A close reading of the play yields even earlier signs of Bullingbrook's intent to win the crown. In 1.4, after Richard has banished Bullingbrook, Aumerle refers to him as "high Herford," and Richard reports on how he and his cohort—Bushy, Bagot, and Green—"Observ'd his courtship to the common people, / How he did seem to dive into their hearts / With humble and familiar courtesy" (1.4.3, 24–26). Richard, in fact, believes Bullingbrook already to be angling for the backing of the populace, whom he courts with doffing his hat to "an oyster-wench" and bending on his knee to two "draymen"—men who haul with carts—and flattering them with "Thanks" and calling them "my loving friends" (1.4.31, 34). In a later play—the first part of *Henry IV*—Bullingbrook, now the king, reprimands his son, Prince Hal (eventually Henry V) for not practicing political theatrics with the skill he himself used as a younger man who would be king (3.2.39–59).

Hints of Bullingbrook's high aims resurface during 3.3 in the verbal confusion over whether he's kneeling before Richard as a subject would be expected to do. When Bullingbrook first approaches the King at Flint Castle in Wales, Northumberland acts as go-between. According to the stage direction, Richard "*appeareth on the walls*"—that is, atop the castle's walls, on the battlements—while Bullingbrook hides on the edge of the surrounding woods. Bullingbrook has instructed Northumberland to tell Richard he's come "On both his knees" and that he "doth kiss Richard's hand, / And sends allegiance and true faith of heart / To his most royal person" (3.3.36–38). Northumberland is referring to Bullingbrook's coming "on his knees" only for his inheritance, not the kingship (3.3.105–18). But Northumberland himself apparently neglects to kneel before Richard, an omission not lost on the King, who scolds Northumberland for his lapse—"how dare thy joints forget / To pay their aweful duty to our presence?"—but to no avail (3.3.75–76). Nowhere does Northumberland explicitly oblige him by kneeling.

At the same time, Bullingbrook and his lords are backed by an army in the woods of Flint Castle. Although Northumberland swears that the army will back off if Richard restores Bullingbrook's inheritance, Richard's understanding of the situation as a hostile usurpation may be correct. Once Richard has descended from the battlements to meet Bullingbrook face-to-face, he sizes up his competition, who is finally kneeling to him, with sarcasm that may well speak the truth about Bullingbrook's motives. "Up, cousin, up," he commands Bullingbrook to stand, "your heart is up, I know, / Thus high at least [*touching his crown*], although your knee be low" (3.3.194–95). When Bullingbrook responds, "My gracious lord, I come but for mine own," the ambiguity of the phrase has peaked (3.3.196). Whether Bullingbrook is referring only to his inheritance or to the crown is anybody's guess.

Despite this protest, royal power has transferred from Richard to Bullingbrook during 3.3 as surely as power shifted from the Soviets to the Americans on Lake Placid. The scene ends as Richard concludes, "What you will have, I'll give, and willing too, / For do we must what force will have us do" (3.3.206–07). Richard's perception that Bullingbrook's army stands ready to use "force" unless he surrenders the kingship gains credence, not only because Bullingbrook doesn't contradict him, but also because, two scenes later, Bullingbrook is prepared to step into Richard's position. "In God's name I'll ascend the regal throne," he announces (4.1.113).

The irony of Bullingbrook's invoking God's authority for his deposition of a king who himself claimed divine right is as obvious as it is historically accurate. Scholar Peter Saccio explains Henry IV's dilemma in defending his usurpation at the time:

> Commissions of lawyers and officials were set to work to formulate a justification for Henry's accession. For their consideration Henry first advanced a claim to the crown on grounds of lineal descent (through his mother) from Edmund Crouchback, the first earl of Lancaster.... Henry next attempted a claim by conquest, but the implications of this horrified the commissioners. Such a precedent could justify future seizure of the crown by anybody who had the strength to take it. He finally "challenged" the crown "through the right that God of his grace hath sent me, with the help of my kin and friends to recover it," a magnificently ambiguous formula [31].

Henry's signature ambiguity takes its cue from Machiavelli's advice to rulers in *The Prince*, one of the most prominent works of political theory in Shakespeare's time and surely a prime basis for characterizing Henry IV and his son, Henry V. Machiavelli urges a ruler to present a sterling public image, whether or not it's backed up by reality, and he stresses that, of all the virtues a ruler should seem to have, none is more important than religion (66).[3] Many a modern day athletic coach has practiced such good public relations by expressing great belief in his or her players.

As the process of deposing Richard continues in 4.1, evidence mounts that Bullingbrook is orchestrating matters so as to displace responsibility. When Richard challenges Bullingbrook to "seize the crown" from him, Bullingbrook turns the tables, making Richard the agent of his own abdication (4.1.181). "I thought you had been willing to resign," he responds to Richard's taunting (4.1.190). By indulging Richard's request for a mirror, one of the play's most suggestive metaphors, Bullingbrook allows him to view himself objectively, whereby he'll acknowledge his own flaws, rather than blame Bullingbrook for his predicament (4.1.263–68). When Bullingbrook commands members of his new court to "convey" Richard "to the Tower," Richard

The deposed Richard II studies his face in a mirror in the stage production directed by Michael Kahn, 1993.

calls him on the euphemism, another instance of Bullingbrook's politically shrewd ambiguity (4.1.316). "O, good! convey!" mocks Richard, remarking both on the meaning of *to convey* as *to steal* and on what Bullingbrook actually means by *convey*, which is to *imprison* him (4.1.317–18).[4] Richard peels back Bullingbrook's sanitary exterior to reveal a darker underside to proceedings that Bullingbrook is striving to attribute to Richard's errors alone.

The friction between Bullingbrook's carefully crafted public image and his underhanded dealings with Richard becomes more obvious as he assumes power and as Richard, for all his weaknesses, gains sympathy from an audience aware of the deposition's far-reaching costs. The contest between these two rivals is like a hockey match only up to a point: the play makes taking sides easy at first, then far more difficult as the action progresses. Just when an audience feels sure about rooting for the oppressed and against the oppressor, Richard turns out to be less like the Soviets, and Bullingbrook less like Team USA, than previously seemed to be the case.

The complicated interplay between judgment and sympathy toward Richard and his rule is concentrated in the Queen's second scene, 3.4. Here she learns what even the commoners know about her husband's being "seiz'd" by Bullingbrook, until now a relative nobody on the order of the amateur U.S. hockey players (3.4.55). The Queen's ladies attempt to distract her with "sport" at the scene's opening, recalling the Queen's frilly word play in her first scene, 2.2, and reinforcing the portrayal of her court as superficial, even decadent (3.4.1). The dialogue between the Gardener and his helper, moreover, ennobles the plain-speaking, literally down-to-earth viewpoint of the common man and casts shame on the "wasteful King," who failed to cultivate his country with care comparable to theirs for the garden (3.4.54–66). The audience's appreciation for the Gardener's simplicity likely continues as the Queen, "press'd to death through want of speaking," steps out of hiding to chastise the Gardener for his insubordination and to curse his "plants" (3.4.72–101). Her sense of superiority, based on class and licensing her insults, may offend a modern audience more attuned to democracy than social hierarchy.

But the Gardener's final empathy for the distressed Queen leavens what would otherwise be the play's harsh view of her. Although certainly part of the court that has spiraled out of decent bounds, she's also virtually impotent in the power play that Bullingbrook has waged against her husband, a maneuver that, until this point in history, was hardly imaginable. When the Gardener defies the Queen's curse through the kindness of planting "rue, sour herb of grace" in her "remembrance," his charitable response to her outburst not only increases his appeal, but also sheds understanding on the plight of the "poor queen" (3.4.102–07). As Bullingbrook becomes Henry IV, the Queen's honest expression of genuine emotion may, in retrospect, even seem refreshing.

Henry IV's "new world"

To compare and contrast the rules of Richard and Henry, Shakespeare relies partly on parallel dramatic structuring. In the most pointed example, the quarrel in 4.1 between Bagot and Aumerle parallels that between Mowbray and Bullingbrook in act 1 over the very same subject: "noble Gloucester's death" (4.1.3). As Henry now finds himself wading through accusations on both sides, he must be reminded of his earlier entanglement with Mowbray and probably recognizes, along with the audience, that all kings inevitably have to judge between competing claims. Although Henry seems in charge as Bagot and Aumerle hurl challenges back and forth, he actually proves no more effective in settling the dispute than Richard did in act 1. He delays judgment until "Norfolk be repeal'd," referring to Mowbray's being allowed back in England to serve as a witness (4.1.86–90). When Henry learns that Mowbray can't testify because he's died in banishment, however, the King drops the matter and turns his attention to York's announcement of Richard's submission (4.1.91–112).

In this second round of challenges, though, the contenders' motives are more obvious than in the first, as the men involved in act 4 are all remnants of Richard's court and, as such, flatterers who drained Bullingbrook's inheritance while he was banished. Once King Richard's favorites, they're now fighting for survival. Henry has cause to banish them all, or worse, and flattery will no longer serve their purposes. But the man who can identify Gloucester's murderer has a shot at the new king's favor. The lords' recognition that they stand precariously on untested political ground surfaces especially starkly in Fitzwater's declaration, "As I intend to thrive in this new world, / Aumerle is guilty of my true appeal" (4.1.78–79). The statement is illogical, even absurd: Aumerle can't be guilty of Gloucester's death simply because Fitzwater wants to "thrive," and Fitzwater's accusation of Aumerle isn't "true" just because he says it is. But Fitzwater's wording shows he'll say anything necessary to "thrive."

That readiness to manipulate language for the sake of political self-advancement, a trait of Bullingbrook's from the start, comes to characterize his regime—or at least Shakespeare's picture of it (as it does, incidentally, modern politics). Eventually, in the first part of *Henry IV,* one of Henry's original supporters, now disaffected with what he perceives as Henry's verbal slipperiness, disparages him as a "vile politician" (1.3.241). "Vile" or not, Henry fulfills the role of politician to a degree that Richard never approached—principally, through extending the ambiguity of his speech to full-fledged theatricality. To be sure, King Richard is theatrical, flamboyantly so. Henry, by contrast, is a method actor, so slick in his performances that he rarely appears to be acting. But Shakespeare drops hints that, as Machiavelli advises in *The Prince,* Henry's public face often obscures his private agenda.[5]

Henry's education in theatricality may well begin in 1.3, when he's about to leave England in exile. His father tries to lift his spirits by encouraging him to role-play, imagining himself not as banished and unhappy, but as in control and blissful. "Think not the King did banish thee," Gaunt instructs him, "But thou the King" (1.3.279–80). Inadvertently, the father coaches his son to think of himself as a usurper. In teaching Bullingbrook to fancy himself as more powerful than the King, Gaunt plants the notion that such a reversal isn't just theoretical, but entirely possible.

The son is a quick study. Returned from exile and making his way across England to Wales, Bullingbrook is intercepted by his uncle York, who is scandalized by the air of "gross rebellion and detested treason" about his nephew's reappearance (2.3.81–112). To reassure York and gain his trust, Bullingbrook shrewdly persuades York to role-play as Gaunt once taught him. Specifically, he asks York to think of himself, not as his uncle, but as his father:

> You are my father, for methinks in you
> I see old Gaunt alive. O then, my father,
> Will you permit that I shall stand condemn'd
> A wandering vagabond, my rights and royalties
> Pluck'd from my arms perforce—and given away
> To upstart unthrifts? [2.3.117–22].

Flattering York by calling him his father does not pay off immediately: York insists that Bullingbrook's bearing arms against the king is treasonous under any circumstances (2.3.143–47). Bullingbrook's method of persuading York through role-playing, however, ultimately yields success. Even here, York concedes that Bullingbrook has legitimate grievances against the King and, before long, he sees himself as his nephew sees him—a supporter (2.3.140–42, 3.3.200).

Although Northumberland describes Bullingbrook's verbal facility as "fair discourse" that, like "sugar," makes their difficult journey together "sweet and delectable," King Henry's speech often masks a hardened, unsentimental realism (2.3.6–7). By the time he confronts Richard at Flint Castle (3.3), he is focused on gaining, consolidating, and maintaining power, regardless of how polite or passive he may seem. Such theatricality in the service of public image may well have tinted the 1980 U.S. hockey team's humility, relative to the Soviets' arrogance, which surely helped the Americans gain favor among crowds. Several passages in *Richard II* attest to Bullingbrook's charismatic wooing of the populace (e.g., 1.4.23–36).

The actual political landscape behind such charm, however, is subtly and colorfully figured forth in the Queen's final scene, where she and Richard bid each other farewell (5.1). While the emotion of their parting can seem a little much, Shakespeare endows this couple with the tenderness and mutual caring of a true marriage, a love relationship of the sort that Henry, in Shakespeare's portrayal, lacks. Although the real Henry IV was in fact married, the three Shakespearean plays in which he's featured—this one and the two parts of *Henry IV*—never once refer to his queen. He may as well be a bachelor, except that he has a son, Prince Hal, who is mentioned briefly in *Richard II* and is arguably more central than his father to the two plays about Henry IV (5.3.1–12). Richard's made plenty of mistakes as king, but at least an audience can see he has feelings. Henry, on the other hand, seems to live for and through his crown.

Acting as Henry's representative in 5.1, Northumberland calls indirect attention to the King's callousness. When the Queen asks Northumberland to "Banish us both, and send the King with me," he responds by finishing the couplet, "That were some love, but little policy" (5.1.83–84). The witty rhyme undercuts the scene's emotion, belittling the Queen's anguish and spelling out that, in this regime, "policy"—political prudence—is top priority. Although at this point the Queen may be paying for her earlier courtly levity, Northumberland's sarcastic reminder of it in his curt rhyme trivializes her pain.

Equally telling in this scene is Richard's astute prediction that Northumberland's days of security under Henry are numbered. Richard first prophesies Northumberland's dissatisfaction with Henry's lack of gratitude for his help, then Henry's fear that the nobles who helped him depose Richard may well come after him next (5.1.59–65). A kingship beginning with a "usurped throne" is like a marriage originating in adultery: none of the principal players can trust one another (5.1.65). As Shakespeare's original audience knew, Richard's vision of Northumberland's future, which Northumberland brushes off, is destined to become true, as depicted in *1 Henry IV*. Once content to be the "ladder wherewithal / The mounting Bullingbrook" came to power, Northumberland, his son Hotspur, and his brother the Earl of Worcester will feel threatened and dissatisfied enough under Henry IV to mount a rebellion against him (5.1.55).

Full Circle

The last act of *Richard II* explores the intersection of the deposed King Richard and the newly crowned Henry IV as they continue to crisscross in the audience's sympathies. Henry's exploitation of verbal ambiguity is both the substance of comedy—in the episode involving Aumerle's attempted treason (5.2, 5.3)—and, when employed to produce Richard's assassination, a cause of horror. Richard, for his part, grows in character from his humiliation at Henry's hands. If U.S. citizens could have seen the aftermath of the Soviet hockey team's humbling, their sympathies, too, might have been swayed.

The mini-narrative involving the Yorks constitutes an early challenge to

Henry's rule that tests his judgment and satirizes his strategic reliance upon verbal ambiguity. During the time that has intervened offstage between acts 4 and 5, Henry has dropped the matter of Gloucester's death and treated Fitzwater, Aumerle, and others mercifully, only stripping them of the noble titles Richard had awarded them. As York reminds his wife in 5.2, their son is no longer a duke, but has been demoted to his previous rank of Earl of Rutland (5.2.42–45), an advisory the Duchess ignores by insistently referring to "Aumerle" (e.g., 5.2.81).[6] Henry's clemency toward the son, possibly a gesture honoring his father York's support of Henry's take-over, turns out to be a miscalculation when Aumerle is discovered in 5.2 to be plotting a rebellion against Henry.

York's reaction to the discovery foregrounds his dominant character trait—loyalty to the existing king so devout as to border on amusing. Despite having remained steadfastly true to Richard long after the other nobles, York would now rather sacrifice his son as a traitor than put the new king at risk. Such faithfulness is a luxury for Henry, enabling him to secure his reign. But to the Duchess, it's beyond reason. "Why, York, what wilt thou do?" she questions her husband as he prepares to inform the King of Aumerle's plot. "Wilt thou not hide the trespass of thine own?" (5.2.88–89). "Is he not like thee?" she persists, "is he not thine own?" (5.2.94). Her wording—*thine own*—is richly resonant. The Duchess' interest in protecting her *own* child mirrors the very self-interest that characterizes Bullingbrook/Henry IV, who once vowed, misleadingly, to claim only his *own*, then wound up on the throne. The phrase both humorously and cynically speaks for "this new world."[7]

When York, the Duchess, and Aumerle descend upon Henry in 5.3 to make their individual cases to him, the dark comedy abides, especially through the Duchess' fervent pleas to the King. As all three kneel to Henry to beg him in turn, they parody the earlier situation in 3.3, in which Northumberland's and Henry's willingness or failure to kneel is at issue (5.3.91, 97, 98). No doubt uncomfortable at the sight of his aunt's kneeling on a hard floor, Henry commands her three times to "stand up," but she refuses unless he grants Aumerle pardon (5.3.92, 111, 129–30). Henry obliges, but with notably vague language. "I pardon him," he says of Aumerle, "as God shall pardon me" (5.3.131). As if calling the audience's attention to the question of exactly what that statement means, the Duchess forces Henry to repeat his pardon and at last to state clearly, "With all my heart / I pardon him" (5.3.132–36).

This light handling of Henry's potentially treacherous ambiguity finds its more serious counterpart in the play's final scenes, in which (the eerily named) Exton carries out Richard's assassination. The short exchange between Exton and a servant again underscores Henry's deliberate use of ambiguity to accomplish his ends while eluding responsibility for his questionable acts. The purpose of the first man's presence in 5.4 is to validate Exton's perception of an earlier interaction the man observed between Exton and the King. The man confirms that Henry asked—not once, but "twice"—"Have I no friend will rid me of this living fear?" (5.4.1-5). The audience likely agrees with Exton that the King is indirectly asking him to be the friend who will "rid" him of the still "living" Richard. Eager to be that friend, Exton takes it upon himself to "rid" Henry of his "foe" (5.4.11). His use of Henry's own word, *rid*, emphasizes many points at once: Exton's care in listening to the King, his desire to follow the King's wishes to the letter, and the King's clear message about what he wants done, despite his subtle way of asking for it.

When Exton appears before Henry in the last scene with Richard's corpse in tow, however, Henry reviles him for it, accusing Exton of ruining his regal reputation (5.6.34-36). Exton defends himself by reminding the King, "From your own mouth, my lord, did I this deed," but Henry wriggles out of being blamed (5.6.37). "They love not poison that do poison need," he responds to Exton, "Nor do I thee" (5.6.38-39). In essence, Henry tells Exton that, as much as he may have wanted Richard dead, he can't sanction the murder.

With supreme ambiguity, the King adds about his predecessor, "Though I did wish him dead, / I hate the murderer, love him murthered" (5.6.39-40). His hatred of Exton is plain enough, but in reference to Richard, is Henry saying he loves him or loves the fact that he's murdered? The line, which could read either way, beautifully illustrates Henry's thorough-going deceptiveness, which also marks his promise to visit the Holy Land "To wash this blood off from my guilty hand" (5.6.49-50). Although Henry repeats this promise several times in subsequent plays, he never finds time to expiate Richard's death by making the promised pilgrimage to Jerusalem.

This unfulfilled vow becomes yet another instance of Henry's unreliable words, which, in turn, assume an aspect of the very parasitism identified with King Richard's wastefulness. If Henry's broken his word to the nobles by returning to England from exile for more than just *his own*, then he's been feeding on their trust and good will as Richard once fed on Bullingbrook's birthright. This is how the rebellious nobles see Henry in *1 Henry IV*: England has simply exchanged one "shameful conquest of itself," to use Gaunt's phrase, for another (2.1.66).

Richard manages, however, to shed a great deal of his shame in his final moments. His long soliloquy in Pomfret Castle, where he's imprisoned, is one of the most accomplished in all of Shakespeare's plays. The speech is introspective, rather than egotistical—a new direction for him. His conscience fully engaged, Richard analyzes his situation and how he got there. He takes responsibility for his imprudence. "I wasted time," he admits to himself and the audience, "and now doth time waste me" (5.5.49).

The Groom who visits Richard in his last living moments elevates the fallen king even more. His role resembles that of the Gardener in 3.3, who solicits sympathy for the humiliated Queen. The Groom's loyalty to Richard outlasts even York's, and he delivers one last punch to Bullingbrook's arrogance as he describes how Bullingbrook usurped Richard's former horse, Barbary, "So proudly as if he disdain'd the ground" (5.5.83). The *he* in that sentence technically refers to the horse, but the wording also allows it to suggest Bullingbrook.

Richard fulfills his role as a tragic hero completely when he confronts his assassins. This man, whose deposition resulted from his bad judgment, has suffered and recognized his faults; in the end, he discards self-pity and defends himself. He kills two henchmen who try to murder him, leaving Exton to perform the deed (5.5.106–07). Even Exton praises Richard's courage. "As full of valure [valor] as of royal blood!" he remarks of the slain monarch (5.5.113). Exton's immediate pang of guilt for having "spill'd" such blood further renews Richard's nobility.

Shakespeare invites the audience of *Richard II* to consider whether England benefited enough from a sitting king's deposition to justify the upheaval. The signs are highly mixed. Audience members must sort out whether, to the extent Henry IV proves substantially different from King Richard, the difference is positive. Bullingbrook, who once seemed the golden alternative to Richard, loses at least some of his luster—how much remains an open question.

In 1980, the U.S. climate was as politically ready for a triumph over the Soviets as England was to accept Bullingbrook's conquest, despite the thorny issues the defeat raised. The contrast in cultural meaning between the 1980 "Miracle on Ice" and an earlier "Miracle," in 1960, when the U.S. took its only previous gold medal in hockey, illustrates the importance of public perception at a time of shifting power.

At the 1960 Olympics, in Squaw Valley, California, the U.S. defeated the Canadians, the Soviets, the Czechs, and the Swedes. The stupendous victory was, by Kevin Allen's estimation, "every bit as remarkable, if not more so," than the second. Yet the 1960 gold medal is commemorated in a documentary whose title, *Forgotten Miracle*, says it all. Compared with the 1980 Miracle in Lake Placid, which was greeted by Americans as a phenomenon of global proportion, the 1960 Miracle in Squaw Valley barely registered with the public. The difference owes not only to the growth of professional hockey and interest in the sport, but also to a significant cultural transition during the twenty years between the two wins. While the 1960 Olympics involved negative Cold War sentiment between the U.S. and the Soviets, the 1980 games took place against an added backdrop of American demoralization in the face of a recession at home and military aggression in the Middle East, where the Ayatollah Khomeini imprisoned Americans and the Soviets invaded Afghanistan.

The U.S. saw the Soviets as the "red menace" and "very, very intimidating," recalls 1980 Olympic forward David Silk in *Do You Believe in Miracles?* Of the match between Team USA and the USSR, the same documentary says, "It was freedom versus communism" and of the Soviet team, "Technically, they were soldiers in the red army." Allen concludes that the "Americans loved the 1980 hockey team and their victory over the Soviets. They made America feel like it was back in control." The Soviet players returned home to the shame of constantly being asked in the street why they'd lost. They considered their silver medals such a disgrace that they never engraved them. They were, in effect, as exiled as King Richard and his Queen. The American conquest, on the other hand, was cause for extraordinary jubilation and national pride—so much so that, in 1999, *Sports Illustrated* cited it as the Top Sports Moment of the 20th Century.[8] As a character named Edgar observes in Shakespeare's *King Lear*, "Ripeness is all" (5.2.11).

In a similar instance of this principle, although the 1980 hockey players were regarded as heroes largely because they were college amateurs who felled a group of overly confident Soviet professionals, subsequent U.S. teams, unwilling to forfeit perceived competitive advantages, also turned professional. Under the compelling pressure to win, Team USA discarded the very attribute that once made its feat miraculous while, incidentally, ignoring the definition of Olympic sport as competition among amateurs. Like the audience of *Richard II*, today's Olympic fans are left to evaluate the relative glory of winning under changed circumstances.

Discussion Questions for *Richard II*

- *Richard II* includes very few women's roles and even those are very limited. Of course, when Shakespeare could avoid writing numerous women's roles, his job became easier, since the women were played by boys. But in his earlier comedies, he didn't shy away from writing plum roles for women. Katherina in *The Taming of the Shrew* and the French Princess and Rosaline in *Love's Labor's Lost* are examples. If Shakespeare isn't shying away from excluding women from *Richard II* because doing so takes some pressure off of his acting company, why else would he make that choice?
- How are the Duchess of Gloucester (1.2) and Queen Isabel characterized?
- Many of the characters in this play refer to and invoke God as an ultimate judge or power. Are they all sincere, or are some giving lip service to the divine, all the while relying only on human power?
- The mirror ("glass") that Richard breaks on the ground in 4.1.288 is one of the play's most suggestive metaphors. What is its significance?

What other stage properties or literary symbols appear in the text, and what do they signify?

- Many audiences believe that Richard comes across as a changed person through his soliloquy as a prisoner in Pomfret Castle in 5.5. Do you agree? How has he changed? Or is he as self-indulgent and self-pitying as ever in that speech?
- That soliloquy is a common choice for an actor's audition. What would draw an actor to it? What about the soliloquy might show off an actor's ability? What are the speech's most difficult challenges to an actor?
- Is Bullingbrook ultimately a better king than Richard? Why or why not? What is your standard of "better"?
- For all of the serious actions and questions throughout act 5, it also offers a great deal of humor, especially in 5.2, where the Duchess of York assails Henry IV about her son, Aumerle. What is the role of the humor in act 5? Where else do you see humor at work in the play?
- Make a list of all the unanswered questions you can think of in *Richard II*. What do you think is the purpose of the ambiguity about each?
- The end of Chapter 2 raises the question of whether the Olympics should have remained all amateur, rather than allow professionalism to creep in. What is your viewpoint?
- The interview with Kevin and Della O'Neill that follows Chapter 4 (on *Henry V*) suggests that Leicester City's Premier soccer team win in 2016 paralleled Henry V's triumph over the French at Agincourt in 1415. But it might also parallel the deposition of Richard II by an adversary who took advantage of Richard's overconfidence. What signs do you see in the case of the 2015–16 British soccer season that the complacency of the teams who were considered the only possible winners helped Leicester City to defeat all or some of them?

INSIDE SHAKESPEARE: SUBTEXT IN *RICHARD II*

Do Shakespeare's plays have subtext? This is a debated question in the realm of theater. If subtext is defined as "the implicit or metaphorical meaning" of a literary text, then, yes, all of Shakespeare's plays have subtext, since each has the capability of being interpreted metaphorically in multiple ways. *Richard II* can implicitly refer to the reign of Elizabeth I in at least two ways. It can suggest Elizabeth's danger of being deposed in an aborted rebellion attempted by the Earl of Essex in 1601. Shakespeare's company performed the play just days before the rebellion was to occur. Together with the other plays about Lancastrian kings—in particular the two parts of *Henry IV* and *Henry V*—*Richard II* also alludes to the Tudor dynasty, which, in addition to Elizabeth, also included her grandfather Henry VII and her father, Henry VIII. Through British history of the fifteenth century, Shakespeare can explore his own monarch at a politically safe distance.

But another aspect of the question about subtext is whether Shakespeare's characters ever literally say one thing, but implicitly mean something else or something in addition to their literal meaning. Some theatrical directors say no: Shakespeare's characters always say explicitly what they mean. They do so in soliloquies, in asides, and even when speaking to one another. They may indulge in poetic expression, as in Macbeth's line to Lady Macbeth, in which he expresses anguish about the uncertainty of a kingship begot by murder and treachery: "O, full of scorpions is my mind, dear wife!" (3.2.36). But even with such metaphorical language, Macbeth is clearly and directly describing his troubled state of mind.

Literary critics, however, are more inclined to believe that Shakespeare's characters may not express all of their inner thoughts and meanings overtly, but, rather, imply meaning that the astute audience member will pick up on by listening carefully. One example of possible subtext in *Richard II* might be Richard's motive for exiling both Thomas Mowbray and Bullingbrook in 1.3. While the King cites the enmity between the two men as a threat to civil peace (1.3.123–39), he has the added, unstated motive of getting rid of two nuisances to his royal stability. If Mowbray was indeed responsible for Thomas of Woodstock's death at Richard's behest, then permanently eliminating Mowbray from the kingdom would help protect Richard from being exposed and subject to retaliation—retaliation that Gaunt says he would like to have for his brother's murder in 1.2. Bullingbrook is scarcely more in Richard's graces. Not only was he one of the Lords Appellant that for a time intercepted Richard's failing rule, much to Richard's chagrin, but he is also beloved by the people, as Richard makes explicit in 1.4, and therefore poses a current threat to the King's position. In other words, Richard fears being displaced and perhaps even deposed by Bullingbrook.

Another example of subtext, which is mentioned in Chapter 2, is Bullingbrook's misleading promise that he is violating the terms of his exile and returning early to England only to recover "mine own"—that is, the property he has legally inherited from his father, John of Gaunt, which Richard has illegally been seizing for himself. In the crucial scene where Richard descends from the battlements of Flint Castle to surrender to Bullingbrook's forces, Bullingbrook overtly reassures him that he doesn't intend to take the crown, only what rightfully belongs to him. "My gracious lord," says Bullingbrook,

"I come but for mine own" (3.3.196). Richard, however, understands Bullingbrook's intents differently, which is to say correctly. Bullingbrook appears ready and willing to fudge on the meaning of "mine own": if he can claim the throne as his own, he will. That the play alludes repeatedly to the phrase "mine own" encourages the audience to think about its implicit meaning. In 5.2, where the Duchess of York scolds her husband for his willingness to reveal their son's treason to the newly crowned Henry IV, she echoes Bullingbrook by urging York to "hide the trespass of thine own," his son Aumerle (5.2.89).

Intriguingly, Henry IV's subtext is the very subject of Exton's conversation with his servant in 5.4. Exton is certain that Henry was covertly asking him to assassinate the imprisoned deposed king with the words "Have I no friend will rid me of this living fear?" (5.4.2). Exton verifies the words themselves by asking his servant if he heard them correctly (5.4.4–5). When the servant agrees, Exton continues to interpret Henry's unstated meaning: "I would thou wert the man / That would divorce this terror from my heart"— (5.4.8–9). He understands Henry to be urging him to get rid of Richard, an understanding that, in the play's final scene, Henry will deftly and dishonestly deny.

3
"The uses of adversity"
The 1988 World Series, Kirk Gibson and *As You Like It*

Overcoming Adversity

"I don't believe what I just saw! ... I don't **believe** what I just saw!" Sportscaster Jack Buck repeated his disbelief when Kirk Gibson won the first game of the 1988 World Series for the L.A. Dodgers against the Oakland Athletics with a two-run, pinch hit, walk-off home run. Every home run is cause for enthusiasm, but this one was especially remarkable—"unbelievable," as Buck famously said.

In the bottom of the ninth, the Dodgers trailed, 4–3. The A's' formidable right-handed closer, Dennis Eckersley, had struck out two Dodgers and strategically pitched around left-batting pinch hitter Mike Davis, putting him on first. Eckersley wanted to reach the pitcher's spot in the order, assuming the Dodgers had exhausted all available bench power and every left-handed pinch hitter. Meanwhile, the left-handed Gibson had spent the entire game in the training room, suffering from injuries to both knees and a pulled hamstring. Early in the game, he and coach Tommy Lasorda were so convinced that his injuries would prevent him from playing that he hadn't so much as ventured outside to tip his cap to the home crowd gathered at Dodger Stadium for Game 1. During the fifth inning, Gibson had told his wife she could go home, so sure he was that he wouldn't be playing.

But at the last minute, assessing the situation and feeling he could contribute, Gibson signaled to Lasorda that he was ready to bat. In a personal interview with this book's author, Lasorda recalls that Gibson took everyone by surprise, including himself. "The big thing is," he now says, "Gibson never came out for the introductions." While Lasorda worried during the ninth inning about what to do next to help his ailing team, Gibson sent a locker room attendant to tell the coach that Gibson needed to see him. At first Lasorda said, "I don't have time for that now. I need to do something." Then he found out that Gibson had gotten dressed on the spur of the moment. Gibson told him, "I think I can hit for you."

When Eckersley finally delivered a 3–2 pitch, Gibson struck the home run that won the game and gave the Dodgers the momentum to win the World Series. Too hobbled to run around the diamond, he limped the distance, pumping his fist in celebration and, at home base, reaching the arms of his joyful teammates. "It paralyzed the other team," remembers Lasorda. "They couldn't believe we'd won the game."

Many athletes and fans would say that all sports are essentially about overcoming difficulty. But some triumphs over adversity shine more than others. Gibson's home run, often cited as one of the most exciting moments in baseball history—and sometimes in all sports history—is one of them. It's number one, in fact, on the official list of the greatest sports moments in Los Angeles. At this point in the season, the Dodgers appeared finished, the A's were highly favored to beat them, and Gibson was seemingly injured beyond hope. But Gibson, with the instincts of a hero, seized the opportunity he saw before him. "Lucky or whatever it was," he has since said in an interview, "I was determined to try and do it. It worked out well"—so well, in fact, that it has all the ingredients of great theater. The breathless Jack Buck announced at the time, "I've seen a lot of dramatic finishes to a lot of sports, but this one might top almost every other one.... I am stunned!" In the interview for this book, Lasorda said much the same about the crowd. "They were stunned. Nobody left.... Not one person left before the game's end."

In an equally stunning move, Shakespeare's romantic hero Orlando, a talented and daring wrestler, fells his highly favored opponent, Charles, in the opening act of *As You Like It*, much as Gibson took down Eckersley. The play's first lines portray Orlando as the victim of his older brother Oliver's injustice. Although Oliver is morally obligated to use their father's inheritance for educating both of his brothers, he keeps Orlando at home and treats him like a servant. Later, Oliver explains why: "my soul … hates nothing more than he. Yet he's gentle, never school'd and yet learned, full of noble device, of all sorts enchantingly belov'd, and indeed so much in the heart of the world, and especially of my own people, who best know him, that I am altogether mispris'd" (1.1.165–71). To quell his jealousy of Orlando, Oliver urges Charles to "break his neck," but, by the time Orlando is finished with Charles, the unseated champion is too battered to speak (1.1.146–47, 1.2.220). In turn, Orlando's triumph fuels Oliver's wrath, forcing Orlando to flee for his life into the Forest of Arden.

The theme of one brother's burning envy of another traces to the biblical story of Cain and Abel, the sons of Adam and Eve, as related in the book of

Genesis (4). When God withholds the favor from Cain that He has bestowed on Abel, Cain slays his brother in a jealous rage. In *As You Like It*, Oliver's animus toward Orlando reflects that of their sovereign, Duke Frederick, toward his older brother and rightful ruler of the kingdom, Duke Senior.[1] Duke Frederick has not only usurped and exiled the adored Duke Senior to the Forest of Arden, but he also resents the people's love of Duke Senior's daughter, Rosalind, the cherished friend and cousin of Frederick's daughter, Celia. Fearing that Rosalind's popularity will disadvantage Celia and believing that Celia will thrive only if Rosalind is eliminated, he banishes his niece from court (1.3.77–84).

But all these attempts on the part of a jealous character to suppress a beloved character misfire. Members of court voluntarily exile themselves to accompany their Duke Senior into Arden, while Duke Frederick only succeeds in bringing shame to himself and his rule. With a seasoned wisdom reminiscent of Duke Senior and the adages to go with it, Tommy Lasorda reminds college baseball teams, "Leave a legacy. Don't embarrass [your] institution." In the end, selfish actions turn inward on aggressors. Even Celia deserts her father's court to join her dear friend Rosalind in the forest, where Orlando and Rosalind, who will eventually marry, rise above their circumstances through their talents and virtue. Thus, *As You Like It* concerns how these characters, all congregated in the Forest of Arden, overcome adversity. The forest corresponds with a baseball field: both are arenas in which characters are tested and in which they grow. Over a long sports season, whether in baseball or any number of other sports, lows will inevitably interrupt highs and threaten to bring down morale. At those low points, the willingness and ability of a team to work together and summon resources of persistence and integrity can transform a dreadful situation into a winning streak.

A Positive Outlook

As in sports and life in general, one element of the prevailing characters' success is attitude. The diversity among the characters' outlooks is true to life. Some, like "the melancholy Jaques," willfully choose discontent (2.1.26). Jaques is, in fact, a character type known as a "melancholy malcontent." Others find contentment in the most challenging situations. When we meet Duke Senior and his entourage in the Forest of Arden at the beginning of act 2, the contrast with Jaques becomes immediately apparent. "Sweet are the uses of adversity," proclaims the Duke about the lessons of hardship (2.1.12). He extols nature, which, although it can be harsh and violent, offers "tongues in trees, books in the running brooks, / Sermons in stones, and good in every thing"

(2.1.16–17).² While Duke Senior regrets killing deer for food, Jaques "grieves" at the prospect in the extreme (2.1.26). He protests that the displaced courtiers "usurp" the deer's rightful territory, as Frederick has stolen Duke Senior's throne, and he "weep[s]" over a slaughtered stag (2.1.22–63, 65–66).

The various personality types in Shakespeare's Arden find their parallels on sports teams. Every player has at least one role to discharge, one position to play. While some team members may call attention to themselves and indulge in fanfare to fulfill their roles, others simply do their jobs without demanding excessive recognition. Kirk Gibson may well have displayed elements of both attitudes on the night of his famed home run. By performing through his pain, he made a notable self-sacrifice for the sake of the Dodgers, a self-sacrifice that also made him an enduring legend.

Although Shakespeare doesn't overtly choose sides between the viewpoints of Duke Senior and Jaques, he privileges the duke's by giving him an eloquent speech at the scene's opening. What's more, by introducing Jaques to the audience, not in person, but through the subtle irony of a Lord who reports on having observed Jaques at a distance, Shakespeare slightly subverts him (2.1.26–66). Such disparate means of introducing the audience to a character is a tactic that theater-insiders understand, much as baseball-insiders appreciate details that inexperienced viewers miss. Still, the audience eventually comes to appreciate both the pros and cons of each character's outlook: Duke Senior's attractive optimism might seem candy-coated, for example, and Jaques' sourness tangs of realism that might have stood the Duke in good stead when his brother deposed him.

In any case, by allowing each perspective to play out naturally, so that an audience can see the likely consequences of both, Shakespeare gradually shows the benefits of the Duke's open heart and the limitations of Jaques' running critique of others. For example, when the desperately hungry Orlando arrives in the Forest of Arden brandishing his sword and demanding food from the exiled courtiers, Duke Senior needs only to "welcome" Orlando to his "table" to defuse the violent encounter (2.7.104–05). "Speak you so gently?" Orlando asks in amazement (2.7.106). In the same scene, Jaques delivers his famous speech about the seven ages of man, beginning with the words "All the world's a stage, / And all the men and women merely players" (2.7.139–40). In context, Jaques' speech cynically reduces every period in a man's life cycle to its least desirable traits, whether the "Mewling and puking" of a baby or the false bravado of a soldier (2.7.143–44, 149–53). Immediately after Jaques describes the final stage of life, old age, as "second childishness, and mere oblivion, / Sans teeth, sans eyes, sans taste, sans every thing," Orlando walks in carrying his old servant, Adam, who is fainting from hunger (2.7.165–66). Adam, possibly played by Shakespeare himself in 1599, may indeed lack teeth, sight, taste, and other youthful faculties. But as critics of the play have pointed out, by embodying the vital loyalty that the play holds up as the highest good through unflagging service to Orlando's family (2.3), Adam silently undercuts Jaques' dyspepsia.

In other passages, Jaques' intolerance is intolerable, as when Rosalind responds to his pride in his melancholy by calling it excessive and affected (4.1.5–7, 33–38). Orlando, for his part, grows "weary" of "Monsieur Melancholy" (3.2.284, 294), and Duke Senior, who is actually fond of Jaques' quirkiness, exposes him when Jaques announces in 2.7 that he wants to become a court fool, like Touchstone the clown. This instance most clearly points up Jaques' actual folly, in contrast with Touchstone's wise folly, which harbors truths beneath a joking or seemingly nonsensical surface. When Jaques and Touchstone earlier talked in the woods, Touchstone spoke mock-philosophically about the mundane passage of time: "It is ten a' clock," Touchstone said, "'Tis but an hour ago since it was nine, / And after one hour more 'twill be eleven" (2.7. 22, 24–25). The admiring Jaques, however, fails to see that, by stating the obvious as if it were a revelation, Touchstone is actually ridiculing Jaques' overblown language and self-importance. In addition, Jaques misunderstands Touchstone's license to speak his mind, which Jaques covets only because he wants "liberty" to correct human folly—to "Cleanse," as he says, "the foul body of th' infected world" (2.7.47, 60). But Duke Senior points out Jaques' hypocrisy. "Most mischievous foul sin, in chiding sin," the Duke reproves Jaques, "For thou thyself hast been a libertine" (2.7.64–65). Jaques wants freedom to scour everyone's faults but his own.

The positive thinking of Duke Senior, Orlando, and Rosalind enhances their resourcefulness, which is the main reason for their ultimate success. Likewise, the L.A. Dodgers' Tommy Lasorda, although never a gifted player himself, epitomized the encouraging coach, often helping his players achieve more than they thought was possible. In a romantic comedy like *As You Like It*, younger characters will be forced in various ways to mine their inner strength and develop their natural abilities, maturing into independent adults ready for marriage and resilient in the face of opposition from those like Duke Frederick, Oliver, and Jaques. Similarly, rookie athletes must endure tests and undergo trials before reaching their full potential as either amateur or professional players. Their testing ground, the playing field, is a kind of sanctuary removed from the outside world, where they have freedom to experiment, explore, and mature. Shakespeare's Forest of Arden, a pastoral environment set apart from court and therefore offering escape from some toxins of civilization, is its own sanctuary. It provides the ideal place for Orlando's and Rosalind's self-reliance, sexual awakening, and growth in confidence to occur.[3] The play centers on their romantic relationship as a core that will result not only in a healthy marriage, but also in a reformed society, where dysfunction is rebalanced into community.

Orlando's Fear, Rosalind's Power and Self-Discovery

Shakespeare focuses most on Orlando, the gifted athlete who in Charles' presence knows no fear, but who, in Rosalind's midst, melts into a puddle of anxiety. When he wins the wrestling match handily, Rosalind, already love struck, admiringly and affectionately places a chain around his neck (1.2.245). But Orlando, suddenly tongue-tied, can't even thank her or respond to her when she again tries to speak with him. "What passion hangs these weights upon my tongue?" he asks himself (1.2.257).

Why, indeed, is Orlando "thrown down" by Rosalind as he has "overthrown" Charles (1.2.250, 254)? One reason is his lack of education and practical experience, brought out at the play's opening. Orlando continually displays his social naiveté, whether by posting insipid love poetry on the trees in Arden or by materializing for an appointment with his beloved an hour late (3.2, 4.1). Often, he simply doesn't know how to conduct courtship, a gap in his background that Rosalind, as his future wife, fills while they're in the forest.

But another, less obvious cause of Orlando's apparent ineptitude as a suitor lies in the chain that Rosalind drapes around his neck in 1.2. It suggests commitment, even entrapment, and commitment can be terrifying. Oliver, after all, was committed by his father's will to provide for Orlando, but instead turned on his sibling, broke the bonds of brotherhood, and sought to take his life. How can a young man who has lived through such betrayal ever trust anyone again, much less a woman, a member of the alien sex? In a play preoccupied with men's dread of emotional and sexual betrayal, Orlando's major obstacle to overcome is his fear of commitment, bred by both his experience at Oliver's hands and his inexperience with real, versus idealized, women. Rosalind guides him toward addressing his anxiety up to a point, but he alone is ultimately responsible for vanquishing his insecurity and choosing to trust again. As for so many athletes, defeating adversity involves defeating fear.

Rosalind can access Orlando's private thoughts about love, of course, because she's disguised in Arden as a boy named Ganymed.[4] (The name is spelled *Ganymede* in many editions of Shakespeare, but the edition cited throughout this book uses the early modern spelling *Ganymed*.) When she first encounters him in the forest, resolving to "speak to him like a saucy lackey," she pretends to doubt his claims about being genuinely lovelorn (3.2.295–96). Citing his lack of a "lean cheek," "a blue eye and sunken," "a beard neglected," incomplete dress of all sorts, and a generally "careless desolation," she pokes fun at his self-seriousness, accuses him of self-love, and lures him, unawares, farther under her influence (3.2.373–84). He asserts his sincere love of Rosalind. "Fair youth," he says, "I would I could make thee believe I love" (3.2.385–86). When, in turn, she proposes to cure him of love's "madness" through methods she's learned from a mysterious "religious uncle" in the woods, he declines: "I would not be cur'd, youth" (3.2.400, 344, 425). Presumably, he prefers to wallow in his passion.

But when Ganymed promises to role-play with Orlando as if he/she were Rosalind, Orlando accepts (3.2.426–29). He can't pass up the chance to imagine

A leggy Katharine Hepburn plays a barely disguised, ultra-feminine Rosalind/Ganymed on Broadway, 1950.

himself in Rosalind's presence and to "woo" her (3.2.427). In subsequent scenes, then, Rosalind/Ganymed, playing the role of Rosalind herself, will exploit her proximity to Orlando to coach him in love and show him the kind of husband she wants him to be. Initially driven to don her disguise by the dangers confronting unaccompanied women on the open road, she remains disguised long after those dangers have passed (1.3.108–22). One reason is likely the social mobility she now enjoys as a virtual man, including the freedom to speak her mind. What begins for her as a gesture of self-protection transforms into a means of empowerment, one of the play's many illustrations of adversity's eventually proving "sweet."[5]

Rosalind's newfound control extends beyond Orlando and into relationships between other characters in the play, including Silvius and Phebe. The purpose of that plot element is one of the most fascinating questions about the play. What are these courtly lovers, sighing and dying for love, doing out in the country, anyway? A corresponding question is why Rosalind/Ganymed interposes herself in the relationship, apparently coaxing Phebe to fall in love with her. Why does she follow up her warning to Phebe *not* to fall in love with her by telling Phebe where she lives, in case Phebe wants to find her (3.5.74–75)? The answer to that question may well be that Rosalind has discovered a taste for her unaccustomed power and is exercising it whenever and however possible. Upon hearing about Silvius' fevered chase of Phebe through the woods, Rosalind/Ganymed decides to "prove a busy actor in their play" of courtship (3.4.59). In doing so, she seems to relish her ability to manipulate them.

Although at points Rosalind could be charged with enjoying her power over others a little too much and at their expense, the intertwined scenes featuring her interaction with Orlando and with Phebe and Silvius confirm her intent to effect the best outcome possible for all. Phebe is clearly attracted to Ganymed's scorn more than to Silvius' worship. She seems motivated to desire what she can't have.[6] Gradually, and through ample irony, Rosalind/Ganymed denounces both Phebe's proud rejection of Silvius and Silvius' self-defeating idolatry of Phebe. To Phebe, she delivers the famous put-down, "For I must tell you friendly in your ear, / Sell when you can, you are not for all markets" (3.5.59–60). She also ridicules Silvius' insipid fawning over a woman who mistreats him. "'Tis such fools as you," she scolds, "That makes the world full of ill-favor'd children" (3.5.52–53).

Rosalind/Ganymed's intervention in the drama of Phebe and Silvius culminates in 4.3, one scene in particular that a live performance helps to clarify more readily than reading. As the scene opens, Phebe has misled the doting Silvius into believing that the letter she's written to Ganymed, which Silvius now delivers, rebuffs Ganymed for insulting her. In fact, the letter is intended to woo Ganymed behind Silvius' back, as Rosalind/Ganymed insinuates by reading portions of it aloud for Silvius to hear first-hand. Rosalind/Ganymed awakens Silvius to Phebe's cruelty toward him through ironically commenting upon the letter's contents. When, for example, Rosalind/Ganymed reads a line of Phebe's letter like "Art thou god to shepherd turn'd, / That a maiden's heart hath burn'd?" and ironically refers to it as Phebe's "rail[ing]," Silvius finally gets it (4.3.40–42). Phebe isn't railing at or "chiding" Ganymed; she's coming on to him (4.3.64).

Celia, herself disguised as Ganymed's sister Aliena, expresses pity for the duped Silvius that Rosalind/Ganymed rejects. "No, he deserves no pity," Rosalind / Ganymed asserts, because he's at fault for wasting his passion on "such a woman," who will "play false strains" upon him (4.3.65–68). Calling him a "tame snake," she sends him back to Phebe with Ganymed's injunction to love Silvius instead (4.3.69–74). Rosalind/Ganymed thus inaugurates the final process of Phebe and Silvius' education as lovers.

A young Helen Mirren plays a gender-ambiguous Rosalind/Ganymed on television, 1978.

By the play's end, Silvius' devotion to Phebe has not appreciably toned down any more than Phebe's ardor for Ganymed has cooled. Still, when Phebe discovers in the closing scene that Ganymed has been a woman all along, she keeps her earlier promise to transfer her affection to Silvius if she decides not to marry Ganymed (5.4.13–15). Does her acceptance of Silvius ring true? "I will not eat my word, now thou art mine," she says. "Thy faith my fancy to thee doth combine" (5.4.149–50). Some audiences believe Phebe's conversion to be sincere, and others doubt it. In either case, the twists and turns of Phebe and Silvius' story prove the play's general rule, as Touchstone wittily expresses it: "We that are true lovers run into strange capers" (2.4.54–55).

Rosalind's Education of Orlando

While Rosalind/Ganymed attends to the relationship between Phebe and Silvius, she is centrally concerned with fashioning her desired relationship with Orlando. Convinced (however naively) that Rosalind is indeed a boy named Ganymed who is playing the role of Rosalind, he avails himself of Rosalind/Ganymed's instruction. Far from curing him of love's madness, though, Rosalind is teaching him about the commitment he fears. His most grievous mistake in courtship is arriving merely "within an hour" of his date with the so-called "Rosalind," as if that's close enough (4.1.42). It isn't, as "Rosalind" informs him: "Break an hour's promise in love! ... Nay, and you be so tardy, come no more in my sight" (4.1.44, 51–52).

In response to Orlando's broken promise, Rosalind/Ganymed introduces a threat. Her comparing Orlando to a "snail"—identified by his "horns"—is the first of many implications in 4.1 that men who take commitments lightly should expect the same treatment from women (4.1.54, 59). Rosalind/Ganymed alludes to the horns of a cuckold, the legendary sign of a husband whose wife has humiliated him by cheating on him. S/he temporarily deflects the seriousness of this moment by flirting with Orlando as "Rosalind": "Come, woo me, woo me; for now I am in a holiday humor, and like enough to consent. What would you say to me now, and I were your very very Rosalind?" (4.1.68–71). Orlando again missteps. "I would kiss before I spoke," he ventures (4.1.72). The same Orlando who couldn't speak a word to "very very Rosalind" in 1.2 now avoids civilized conversation by resorting to a kiss before attempting to talk with her.

Repeatedly, Rosalind/Ganymed corrects Orlando's misconceptions about wooing and wedding. When Orlando acts like a courtly lover who might "die" from unrequited love, she deflates his self-indulgence with perhaps the most famous speech in the play, including the line "men have died from time to time, and worms have eaten them, but not for love" (4.1.93, 106–08). Rosalind is out to reform Orlando's idealization of love and lovers, especially Rosalind, whom he insistently places on a pedestal. Idealizing women and marriage can lead only to disappointment, jeopardizing a couple's commitment in the very way Orlando fears. If Rosalind can disabuse Orlando of his fantasies about women and teach him to see wives as real and fallible, she can bring him closer to a realistic understanding of marriage and increase their chances of a stable, lasting union. That's why she warns him that "maids are May when they are maids, but the sky changes when they are wives" and why she tells him to expect generally bad behavior from the actual Rosalind (4.1.148–56). By predicting difficult times ahead, she is preparing him for the "worse" in "for better and for worse."

Characteristically, even as Rosaline teases and teaches Orlando, she marries him. The ceremony uniting them may be a mock marriage in which Celia/Aliena acts as the priest without even knowing the ritual's wording (and in which the groom doesn't know exactly whom he's marrying), but most scholars think that saying the vows before a witness is nevertheless as binding as a full-fledged ceremony conducted by an ordained cleric (4.1.124–39). Once she has taken Orlando as her husband, she continues to instruct him. Playing with the bawdy overtones of "wit," Rosalind/Ganymed warns that a woman is just as adept as a man at cheating on her spouse and will likely do so if he's cheating on her (4.1.160–71). She also informs him that a woman worth her salt can hold her husband responsible for any "fault" she herself commits (4.1.173–76).

Orlando must feel bewildered when he quickly exits, saying, "For these two hours, Rosalind, I will leave thee" (4.1.177–78). Rosalind/Ganymed has poked holes in every aspect of womanhood Orlando could possibly idolize, and she appears to be confirming his worst fears about betrayal. By the end of act 4, however, he will have worked through those fears. In more instances than just Orlando's, *As You Like It* bears out a view that Touchstone, characteristically, expresses in clownish terms: "Courage! As horns are odious, they are necessary.... Horns? even so. Poor men alone? No, no..." (3.3.51–52, 56–57). Marriage, in other words, involves the risk of being cuckolded, but the gift of companionship is worth the risk. In a similar vein, the horn song in 4.2 encourages men to "Take ... no scorn to wear the horn" (13). Accepting a man's vulnerability is, in this play, a manly thing to do. Learning to trust one's partner is perhaps the chief way of overcoming adversity, much as trust among members of a sports team is crucial to top performance. Tommy Lasorda's generous trust in Kirk Gibson certainly paid off.

Conquering Fear

As narrated in 4.3, Orlando offers Oliver his renewed trust. No sooner has Rosalind/Ganymed dispatched Silvius to confront Phebe than Oliver enters to announce that Orlando has been delayed (4.3.74). By this gesture, the audience and Rosalind understand that Orlando has taken seriously her injunction to be on time. When he can't make it himself, he sends a substitute, proving his trustworthiness. But at this point the audience must wonder why the substitute is Oliver. Has he hurt Orlando? What's the meaning of the "bloody napkin" in Oliver's hand (4.3.93)?

The reason for Orlando's tardiness is just as important to his relationship with Rosalind as his efforts to be prompt. Oliver reports how, in the woods, Orlando has battled a lioness to save Oliver himself from the beast, unworthy though he is of such courage and affection. That Orlando "Twice did ... turn his back" with the intent of leaving Oliver to die by the lioness, but then rescued him out of "kindness," resolves the enmity between the siblings (4.3.113–32). Orlando's decisive moment recalls Gibson's in 1988; both are turning points with major effects. For one, Orlando's self-sacrifice changes Oliver utterly. "'Twas I," he says of himself before Orlando saved him, "but 'tis not I" after his "conversion," a conversion to virtue owing to his brother's saving him even though he didn't deserve to be saved (4.3.135–36).

But the symbolism of the story—suggestive of a dream—seems to relate as much to Orlando's relationship with Rosalind as it does to that between him and Oliver. Taken literally, the story is implausible. How likely is a lioness to be roaming the Forest of Arden? But, figuratively, the gender of both the lion and the snake that Orlando first sees threatening Oliver links females with aggression and hostility. In fact, the snake coiling around Oliver's neck and targeting his mouth recalls the chain that Rosalind placed on Orlando's neck in 1.2, an act that, by freezing Orlando's tongue and reducing him into a "liveless block," made him impotent (1.2.251).

Like the "Barbary cock-pigeon," the "parrot," the "ape," and the "monkey" that Rosalind/Ganymed connects with "Rosalind" in 4.1, the snake and the lioness embody Orlando's fears (lines 150–53). In the first instance, the animals associate Rosalind with imposing speech ("parrot"), masculine power ("cock"), and sexual promiscuity ("ape" and "monkey"). In the second instance, "snake" and "lioness" imply female treachery (in contrast to the "tame snake" that Rosalind/Ganymed has just called Silvius in the same scene [4.3.70]). Orlando's choice to save Oliver is a choice to risk being betrayed by him again. As such, it opens the door to the risk of marriage. In wrestling the lioness to the ground, as he once overthrew Charles, Orlando symbolically tames his fears of treachery. Rosalind's capacity to dominate him, reflected in her male disguise, will no longer deter him.[7]

Reading a scene like 4.3 in figurative, versus literal, terms parallels an "inside-baseball" understanding. An experienced audience of Shakespeare's drama follows apparently illogical action and symbolism involving animals in much the way that knowledgeable sports fans unravel the deeper meaning of a tricky play. For example, once Tommy Lasorda knew that Kirk Gibson was prepared to bat, he was keenly aware that he must not produce Gibson from the clubhouse until after the A's had finished pitching to Mike Davis. When Lasorda sent a light-hitting, right-handed utility infielder to the on-deck circle instead, he encouraged the A's' belief that the Dodgers had no remaining quality hitters to fill the upcoming pitcher's spot in the order. Had Eckersley and the A's known the left-handed clutch hitter Gibson was on stand-by, even injured, they would never have pitched around Davis.

A healthy skepticism about the appearances shown by one's opponent makes equal sense when contemplating a seeming inconsistency in one of Shakespeare's plays. Many a first-time audience of *As You Like It* is confused by the curious entrance of a lioness and may consider Oliver's sudden reversal toward Orlando to be a gimmick. But insiders realize that at precisely those moments when the action seems surreal or contrary to ordinary reasoning, they should look carefully for meanings that go beyond the immediate. As in sports, the needling questions, confusions, and frustrations for a novice turn out, for the more advanced participant, to be cues and clues toward more sophisticated interpretation.

Resolutions

Although no Shakespearean play ends without leaving some questions unanswered, the final act of *As You Like It* represents one of the most resolved and least problematic in the canon. Rather like the 1988 World Series, in which Gibson's home run in the first game led naturally to a Series win, the play's satisfying conclusion is determined by adversity's being overcome in the middle acts.[8] Through making honorable choices, the characters survive "trial" and keep their word, as Rosalind/Ganymed insists upon with her repeated, elaborate commands in 5.1 to her father, Orlando, Silvius, and Phebe (1.2.187).

The happy ending is also furthered by the fairy tale element of Duke Frederick's sudden spiritual conversion, through which Duke Senior is rightfully restored, and by the fantastical appearance of Hymen, the mythological god of marriage (5.4.154–66, 107). Accompanied by the now undisguised Rosalind, Hymen ensures the proper arrangement of couples in a quadruple wedding (5.4.125–46).

Yet even these extravagant features of fiction capture something true to life. The eventual revelation of steroid abuse by Oakland A's players Mark McGwire and Jose Canseco painted them in terms nearly as black as those portraying Duke Frederick before his conversion, styling them as villains relative to the more reputable Dodgers. And the multiple weddings in *As You Like It* are coincidentally mirrored by Kirk Gibson's own double ceremony, in which his wife's sister married one of his teammates from the Detroit Tigers, for whom both were playing in 1985.

But the most compelling correspondence between the play and this slice of baseball history is an individual's heroic action that simultaneously stems from and overrides hardship, thus advancing an entire group, whether a team or a royal court. In a phrase that Orlando might have uttered when he stepped up to save his brother's life, Gibson says of his risky, bold decision to bat, "This is what it's all about. It's what you play the game for." Gibson stepped in and stepped up, much as Orlando does in numerous dramatic moments, whether rescuing Old Adam from starvation or Oliver from predators. In words that reflect not only Gibson's fortitude, but also the strength of Shakespeare's lead characters in *As You Like It*, Tommy Lasorda advises college baseball players, "Some people make it happen. Some watch it happen. Some wonder what happened." Clearly, Gibson made it happen.

The opportunity to make a crucial difference is fleeting, but the results linger. "I was an average player in my career," says Gibson, humbly, "but I did some exceptional things at some very important times." Those exceptional things include seizing an opportunity when he stood to make a crucial difference and consequently being named the National League's MVP in 1988. Lasorda's self-description is remarkably similar. "I'm just an ordinary person," he said in the interview for this book, "who had the good fortune to do what he loves." As the wise fool Touchstone might say, not just about peace-making, but also about seizing the moment, "much virtue in If" (5.4.103).

Epilogue: Conquering Fear II

At the end of *As You Like It,* Rosalind says that "a good play needs no epilogue," then adds that even "good plays prove the better by the help of good epilogues" (Epilogue 4–7). The same concept may well apply to this chapter about *As You Like It* and overcoming adversity, other forms of which deserve mentioning.

The courage of Kirk Gibson and Orlando is hardly inconsequential: one conquers a physical debility, the other an emotional trauma. Adversity, however, can also take the form of societal prejudice—for example, racism—and those athletes who have stood up to discrimination in sports have not only demonstrated exceptional courage, but have advanced the cause of social justice through their strength.

Two African American athletes made especially important strides in the 1930s, both by helping to open up sports traditionally closed to people of color and by confronting Nazism abroad. One of them, Joe Louis, was the longest reigning world heavyweight boxing champion to date. He held the title from 1937 to 1949. One of his three losses, out of 70 fights during his career, was to Max Schmeling, in 1936. Louis should have beaten Schmeling, but Schmeling had trained assiduously for the match, and Louis underestimated him. Schmeling identified a weakness in Louis' form and managed to exploit it to capture the win.

Two years later, when the boxers met in a rematch, Schmeling had been embraced by the Nazis as proof that a black man couldn't prevail against an Aryan. Schmeling was accompanied to the U.S. by a Nazi publicist, and the Nazis vowed to use his prize money from the rematch to build tanks. In actuality, though, the fight lasted barely over two minutes, during which Louis pummeled Schmeling, whose trainer hastily surrendered the victory to Louis.

3. "The uses of adversity" 69

Boxer Joe Louis, left, and opponent Max Schmeling, 1938.

Franklin Delano Roosevelt, U.S. president at the time, had told Louis that his win over Schmeling would be symbolic. Louis delivered.

Louis was also a pioneer in integrating the sport of golf, which was traditionally closed to blacks. In 1952, he was the first African American to play in a PGA event. This grandson of former slaves, whose family was forced out of Alabama by the Ku Klux Klan and resettled in Detroit, rose up from racism and financial hardship during the Great Depression to become the first African American national hero in the United States.

An equally compelling athlete-hero, Jesse Owens, won four gold medals at the 1936 Summer Olympics in Berlin: for the 100-meter race, the 200-meter, the long jump, and the 4 × 100 meters. As a student at Ohio State University, he had already set three new world records during one 45-minute period in 1935: the long jump, the 220-yard sprint, and the 220-yard low hurdles. At the same time, he had also tied the world record for the 100-yard dash.

A legend has persisted that, at the Olympics, Hitler exited the stadium before shaking hands with Owens, although an eye-witness account suggests that Hitler did indeed shake Owens' hand and Owens himself repeatedly

Jesse Owens competing in the 1936 Berlin Olympics.

denied the rumor about being snubbed. In any case, Owens offered the Nazis inconvenient proof that black athletes could out-perform Aryans. Willy nilly, then, Owens became something of an anti–Nazi symbol during World War II.

But he was discriminated against in the very country that made him into that symbol. Ohio State University didn't so much as recognize Owens with a scholarship, so he had to work part-time to finance his education. He was forced to live off-campus with other African American athletes and, while traveling with the OSU team, was required, to eat at restaurants and stay at hotels designated as "blacks only." While steadfastly denying that Hitler snubbed him at the Berlin Olympics, he often pointed out that his own President, Franklin Delano Roosevelt, never acknowledged his Olympic medals with a telegram, an invitation to the White House, or congratulations of any sort. Owens attributed a large part of his athletic success to Charles Riley, his junior high school track coach in Cleveland. Because Owens had to work after school in a shoe repair shop, Riley allowed him to practice early in the morning, before school started. Like Old Adam's support of Orlando, the gesture of one caring person, who recognized Owens' potential and encouraged him to realize it, made a remarkable difference in the athlete's achievement.

Another athlete who broke the color barrier, Jackie Robinson was the first African American to play in Major League Baseball. His contract with the Brooklyn Dodgers in 1947 effectively brought an end to segregation among professional baseball teams. His 10-year career in the MLB was studded by recognition, including the National League Most Valuable Player in 1949, the first ever awarded to an African American. Robinson was inducted into the Baseball Hall of Fame in 1962, and in 1997, his uniform number, 42, was retired across all Major League Baseball teams.

During his lifetime, Robinson made considerable advances in civil rights through both his athletic achievement and his personal conduct. After having been drafted into the army in 1942 and stationed in a segregated cavalry at

The Brooklyn Dodgers' Jackie Robinson slides into second base in the 1953 World Series.

Fort Riley, Kansas, he applied to the Officer Candidate School with sufficient qualifications for admission. The acceptance process was delayed, however, because of his color. Here, Robinson and Joe Louis crossed paths: Louis, also assigned to Fort Riley at the time, successfully protested on Robinson's behalf, beginning a lasting friendship between the two men. In 1944, Robinson again faced racial discrimination in the army when he boarded a specifically integrated bus and was ordered by the driver to sit in the back because of his race. When Robinson stood his ground, the bus driver summoned the military police at the end of the trip. They took Robinson into custody, and, although Robinson was cleared of the charges he faced and was eventually honorably discharged from the army, he was prohibited from being deployed in combat because of the court martial.

Robinson again faced racial prejudice when he joined the Major League. Members of his own team threatened to sit out rather than play with him. But Dodgers manager Leo Durocher reserved some characteristically savory language to discourage such behavior. Other teams, particularly the St. Louis Cardinals, openly discriminated against Robinson by threatening not to play with him and, once they played with him, subjecting him to rough physical treatment. The combination of Robinson's popularity with black baseball fans, support among his positive teammates, and a Major League management intolerant of racial prejudice enabled Robinson to use his exceptional athletic skill for the good of both his team and the country's progress toward achieving civil rights. All along, Robinson's physical talents had spoken for him, but the resistance he encountered because of his color posed obstacles that took extraordinary courage to overcome.

Louis, Owens, and Robinson, of course, aren't alone in displaying such courage. Other African American athletes have hurdled or broken through the color barrier; so have those of other races. Yao Ming, All-Star NBA player for the Houston Rockets, is from China. Japanese Ichiro Suzuki, Major League Baseball player for the Seattle Mariners, holds numerous records, including the MLB record for most hits in a single season: 262. Giannis Antetokounmpo, whose parents immigrated from Nigeria to Greece before he was born, was a late-comer to basketball. He made up for lost time by becoming an All-Star player for the Milwaukee Bucks. Panamanian-American Mariano Rivera pitched for the New York Yankees from 1995 to 2013 and repeatedly won All-Star status. Roberto Clemente, right-fielder for the Pittsburgh Pirates, died at age 38 in a plane crash while en route to help earthquake victims in Nicaragua. He was the first Latin American and Caribbean Major League Baseball player to be inducted into the Baseball Hall of Fame (1973).

All such examples are to be both admired and emulated.[9] While some sports are now far more racially integrated than they were in the past, others have a long way to go before overcoming racial imbalance and offering access to people of color. Resistance to prejudice among both the establishment and those previously excluded will, like Duke Senior's positive outlook in his exile, remain essential to continued progress.

Discussion Questions for *As You Like It*

- How is the court of Duke Frederick characterized? Look in particular at 1.2, 1.3, and 3.1.
- Le Beau, one of several choice cameo roles in *As You Like It*, helps characterize the court. He appears only in 1.2, although he enters twice in that scene. What's his dramatic function?
- How does Touchstone contribute to characterizing the court in scenes throughout the play?
- Based on 2.1 and subsequent scenes with Duke Senior, how would his court be different from Duke Frederick's?
- What's the significance of Orlando's defeating Charles in a wrestling match? Why not a round of bowling, for example (a sport that Elizabethans actually played)?
- Old Adam is another gem of a minor role in *As You Like It*. How does knowing that Shakespeare likely played that role himself affect understanding?
- Shakespeare may also have played the cameo role with his name on it: William in 5.1. What's William's dramatic function, and why would knowing that Shakespeare took the role matter?
- The play's depiction of nature is complex. How so? What is nature's relationship to nurture, education?
- Touchstone's paradoxical statement that "the truest poetry is the most feigning" is a borrowed idea from Sir Philip Sidney's treatise in defense of poetry, "An Apology for Poetry." Some audience members would have recognized the source and seen that Touchstone is playing with the idea. What does the statement mean? How does it reflect the entire play?
- What does the Phebe/Silvius subplot add to *As You Like It*?
- A case has been made that Rosalind is a feminist, and the opposite case has been made. Start with a definition of feminism and make a case for each side of the question: is Rosalind a feminist? Look especially, but not exclusively, at 3.2 and 4.1.
- What's your opinion of Rosalind's threatening Orlando with cuckoldry if he breaks her trust? Does she seize too much power over Orlando?
- A dramatist takes a risk in having a character narrate a story onstage—as Oliver does his encounter with the lioness and Orlando's

bravery (4.3)—rather than show the story through onstage action. What devices does Shakespeare employ in Oliver's narration to keep the audience engaged in the story he tells, rather than shows?
- Audrey is yet another beautifully drawn minor character. Why is Touchstone so eager to marry her?
- While Oliver's moral conversion is somewhat explained in 4.3, Duke Frederick's comes out of the blue and off stage. Similarly, Celia and Oliver fall directly in love in 4.3 with a speed that Orlando and Rosalind/Ganymed make fun of in 5.2.25–41. Are these sudden moral and emotional changes believable? Do they have to be for the play to work? Could they be thematic?
- The Epilogue of *As You Like It* continues to play with gender identity, as Rosalind identifies herself as both a woman and a boy actor underneath a woman's façade. Does the Epilogue work with or against the larger play's comic resolution?

An Interview with Coach Bob McKillop

Bob McKillop is no ordinary college basketball coach. After being named MVP at Hofstra University and briefly going pro with the Philadelphia 76ers, he amassed winning records as coach at two high schools, where he also taught. He then became the men's coach at Davidson College in 1989. The longest-tenured coach in Davidson history, he holds the Southern Conference record of 230 wins and was named Southern Conference Coach of the year eight times and A-10 Coach of the Year in 2015. His most recent recognition is the Lapchick Character Award for 2017. McKillop is known broadly as keen-eyed recruiter and a cultivator of players' talents. More specifically, he is recognized for having recruited Stephen Curry when virtually no other school did, then nurturing Curry all the way to the NBA's Golden State Warriors. Coach McKillop talks about his views of coaching, Stephen Curry, and parallels between basketball and theatrical performance.

The way you talk about coaching sounds a lot to me like teaching.
Absolutely. I think our world is unfortunate that coaches today are nurtured as salesmen. I was nurtured as a teacher. I had to prepare a lesson plan. I had to be inspirational. I was vulnerable. I was in front of a class five times a day for 40 minutes teaching Afro-Asian Studies and European History. When you have to be on stage five times a day, 40 minutes—and in those days, you were teaching five days in a row, the same students—it forced a tremendous degree of creativity, created a lot of anxiety, and was an incredible

Davidson College men's basketball coach Bob McKillop directs his victorious team against the Charlotte 49ers, 2013 (courtesy David T. Foster III, *The Charlotte Observer*).

training ground. Teaching history, you have the great fortune of going over the boundaries and including every part of life—whether it's your family life, your spiritual life, your career, your life in the neighborhood, or your relationship with the other sex—it was a magnificent way to give lessons to young, impressionable students in their very formative years.

My impression of you—both from watching you and from students I've taught who have had you as a coach—is that you are very keen on supporting the academic program. Very keen on their being students as well as athletes. But I also suspect it's gotta be hard to share these guys that you would like probably to have all to yourself.

No, but see, I guess the difference between me and so many other coaches is I see myself as a professor on this campus rather than you as a coach on this campus. And I see the gym as my classroom. And if I have a lesson to teach, and I expect my players to be accountable to fulfill that lesson, I think they will be accountable the more they are held accountable. So in four classes every semester, they are held accountable by professors. So you guys are doing my work for me, and that's what I think is great teamwork. Now, we don't all operate on the same page, on the same wavelength, but I think there's an extraordinary relationship between the professors and many of the coaches here at Davidson College.

Have you ever sensed tension between your part of the athletic program and academics?

Not personally directed at me. Never, ever, from any of my players. We all understand the deal when we come here. Whether we're a professor, a student athlete, or a coach, we understand the deal. Sweep in front of your door, and the world will be a clean place.

Stephen Curry leaves [in 2009]. That next year, the expectations were extraordinary, and everyone's trying to be Stephen Curry. Everyone was feeling pressure and sort of going off on their own. Everyone was carving out a little piece of the pie for themselves instead of realizing it was one big pie. So one day, we're losing. It was January, and the players were in the arena warming up for practice. I go into the locker room, and I take everyone's clothes, books, and throw them on the floor in the middle of the locker. Call the players, and say, "Let's go back into the locker, gotta talk to you about a few things." They walk into the locker room, and their eyes just bulge, looking like, "What's this mess out here?" I say, "Sit in your locker, and clean up your stuff." And all of a sudden, the locker room's clean. And the message was: do your job. Play your role. Don't worry about anyone else. Don't worry about Stephen Curry, but clean in front of your own house and the world will be a clean place. It's a message I think is vital in our world today.

You've dropped a lot of hints about why you've stayed at Davidson for so long. You have a huge fan base, and that has to be part of it.

That's a big part.

It's also got to be the great kids who come to school here, and you must love the Davidson community. But what else might we not know about why you have dedicated—

Well, my family has loved it here. And I took my family from the most comfortable environment that you could want as a father, as a spouse. And first couple of years were really, really difficult, and they stuck with me, and they stayed with it. And for me to uproot them after they had invested themselves so willingly and so lovingly—I don't think that that was a smart thing to do. And I have so many of my coaching colleagues who have dysfunctional families and dysfunctional marriages because the demon of success and the demon of money and the demon of fame constantly tear you apart from what can be a magnificent experience.

Is there any particular objective as a Division I, A-10 coach, that you still want to pursue?

I think when you start creating statistical objectives—whether it's number of wins, getting to the Final Four, winning successive championships—you immediately limit yourself. I was asked a similar question after the Elite Eight run, and we had just lost to Kansas. And my response to that is the same response I have now. I'm in search of the "beautiful game." It was something I stole from the Brazilian soccer team. They talked about the "beautiful team," having the "beautiful season," playing the "beautiful game." And that's what I want. Somewhere out there is magnificence where players are in harmony with each other. And that harmony revolves into harmony in the town, and then harmony in the bigger community, and then harmony in the world.

You know, when I watch Stephen play with the Golden State Warriors, they sort of have this "beautiful game" mentality, and they play with great joy. And that's my aspiration, where we play with great joy. And the joy with which we play, that resonates with all those people who watch us—

Oh, it really does!

And we become a joyful community, and we become a shining star.

I have to ask you, do you get butterflies before a game?

That's a great question. There's a wonderful song by Barbra Streisand that goes something like, "I don't know what I'm thinking, standing in a hallway," as she's about ready to go onstage. Before I go out, I have tremendous butterflies. I think through every scenario that could happen, and I try to have an answer for it, and my mind becomes so cluttered. I'm not functional. So I take a deep breath, and I start thinking about what I'm actually doing. And before I go out, I think of certain faces that I know I'm gonna see as I walk out. And I try to see myself making eye contact with those faces as I walk out.

Living in the moment is the hardest thing for a basketball coach. Because he's so worried about a mistake, he's so worried about a referee, so worried about a mis-shot, so worried about not making the right decision that his mind becomes cluttered, and he's not free. So I try to walk through that whole scenario and see myself free. And when I make eye contact with that fan, and I smile—and I constantly have to do that during the game—and I am not always successful, but I find myself in those moments to be living in the moment. And that's what a coach has to do. He has to live in the moment, and that's incredibly challenging, no matter how much experience you have.

That's really interesting.

Do you think that basketball is, relative to other sports, more improvisational? That the responses to what happens are more spontaneous?

Much more so than baseball, and also for soccer and football. In soccer not as many of the same experiences get repeated over and over again, because there's only a limited number of scorers, and there's only a limited number of actions, whereas in basketball, there's a constant ebb and flow. And there's constant action and reaction. Football, they blow the whistle, they stop, they huddle up, they talk to each other, they come out. And it's generally choreographed to the T. There's so much more opportunity for improv, for spontaneity, in basketball because it's five guys in a very small space. And I think the space element is really important. That space forces reaction, response, improv, spontaneity, at a much higher intensity than it would in a soccer field or a baseball field or a football field.

I can see that.

The basketball court is the size of a stage. What's so beautiful about the Broadway stage parallel, which I use all the time, is that someone over here could be saying something, and someone over here has to be able to respond to that and be in a cohesive pattern.

I'm fascinated by the coaches on the sidelines who are constantly talking to the players. I know there's a lot of variation there, and that not all coaches do that, and some are much more expressive than others and show their emotions a lot more than others. But what is the purpose of that? Because from the bleachers, it doesn't look to us as if they can really hear you. Do you think those guys are actually hearing you, or are they just so cued to your voice that they're listening for it, and they're gonna pick up on it, and what you're saying is actually gonna affect them?

I don't think my words are as important as my animation or my emotion. There's two expressions I use: "butter" and "milkshakes." Someone's shooting a shot right in front of our bench, and before he even shoots it, I'll go "butter" in his ear. And it immediately resonates with him that it's going in. 'Cause we'll do that in practice—go, "Butter! Butter! Milkshakes! Milkshakes!" And they hear that word and see the picture of the ball going through the net.

It's called visualization, right?

Correct. So, especially when a guy shoots in front of our bench, our players, teammates will do the same thing.

Let's talk about referees. Sometimes you get a ref who's just really annoying and who—from my point of view—seems to be biased.

Correct.

So you think sometimes that's the case?

I think so, yeah. I think certain referees are influenced by what they read. It's much like someone in the audience before a Broadway show, and they read the reviews. And they walk in, and they have this expectation, "Well, this particular part of the play is not gonna be very good. But this is gonna be the great part of the play." And all of a sudden, it's a substitute actor or actress in that play that they think is gonna be great, and they're let down tremendously, and they don't know how to react to it. And that's what happens when a referee reads who's supposed to win the game, and all of a sudden, well jeez, the team that's not supposed to win is making jump shots, and they don't know how to react to it.

So you think they come in with a sort of preconception?
They will never state that. They will deny it till the day they die.

And they probably think they're objective, right?
Yeah. And they're influenced by the fans. They're influenced by the emotion. You watch a referee—their calls are called "mechanics"—if it's a great call for the home team, they will really make the mechanic almost like, "Cheer for me." They're calling the fans down to cheer for them.

So their sense of how much influence they have can be pretty high.
In the immediacy of making a call, when they're not sure if it was the right call, they do what is called "selling the call." When there are questionable calls, watch how ostentatious the referee is in his delivery of the mechanic.

So that too is theatrical.
Absolutely. Referees know exactly who is at the game. They know if their supervisor is there, they know if a celebrity is there, they know if a distinguished guest is there. And they also know the history of the coach. They know the players.

And some of them probably have some history with coaches.
Oh, absolutely, yeah.

What are your strategies for yourself when a game didn't go the way you wanted it to, when a season is disappointing?
There's a poignant moment in the movie *Schindler's List* when Oskar Schindler—the war has just ended—and he's in a factory in old Czechoslovakia, and all the prisoners are freed, and he's walking out, and they made him a gold ring. And he's walking along the tracks, and he breaks down crying and says, "I could've done more." And it was such a poignant moment for me because I think that's sometimes what life is. "I could've done more." And I leave a game, and I'll walk across from there to here, and if it's a loss, what could I have done differently? I could've done more. At the end of a season, I'm constantly analyzing and reevaluating. I could've done more, I could've done more. That's me.

It sounds like you're guilt-tripping yourself. You're taking the responsibility on yourself.

I'm taking responsibility. Maybe if we worked a little bit more on this, maybe if I explained that a little better, maybe if I didn't react that emotionally, maybe if I emphasized this a little bit more. And yes, it's a guilt trip, but it's an introspection that is very, very energizing and inspiring because it then galvanizes you as you move into the next phase, which is the next season. And now you don't want that to happen again, and you do everything within your power to make sure you could do more.

So for you it's a motivator.

Yeah, yeah. It energizes me.

Can you talk a little bit about the crowd? The effect that an audience has on the players? I mean, the people in the crowd do so much—you know, like the way they hold their hands up for some free throws, or the swim team comes in and strips down to their Speedos. And we fancy that we're having this huge effect on the players, but …

It's a dynamic that is worth 10, 12 points a game.

Really?

Absolutely.

That's amazing that you can sift it down to that.

I do want to ask you about Steph Curry. I'd be interested in hearing you talk about his special gifts.

Stephen has—still has—a capacity to play in the moment. He does not let a mistake transcend the moment. He stays there. He does not get distracted. He has an incredible ability to slow down and understand where he is. I'm convinced that is the result of being nurtured by Mom and Dad, as a son of a professional athlete [Dell Curry, NBA player from 1986 to 2002] and a highly skilled volleyball player. Sonya was very good in volleyball at Virginia Tech. And I'm convinced that he sat in front of the TV, watching games when he was two, three, four, five years old. He went to games with Dell and Sonya, and he was immersed in the vision. That is, I think, one of his greatest capacities: his vision. He sees things.

An article in ESPN Magazine *focused on the basketball hoop at Dell's childhood home in Grottoes, Virginia. The sisters locked Dell out of the house, and all he could do was stay out there and shoot hoops.*

Yep!

But that, I thought, was—whether or not it's true—really revealing. Like Dell, Stephen pursued rote practice on that same hoop, which was also characteristic of Bill Bradley, the great—

Who was my childhood hero.

And I see some parallels between Bill Bradley and Steph. Do you?
I think the difference between Steph and Bill Bradley—and it could be the generation—Bill didn't look like he had joy. He looked like a mechanic doing his job. Very functional, very exact, very scientific. Stephen has joy. But they have the same approach to seeing the game. Steph knows where the ball is gonna be rather than where the ball is.

That's what John McPhee said about Bradley [in A Sense of Where You Are*].*
Exactly, exactly.

That he would throw the ball to where—theoretically, if the guy kept going where he was headed—he was gonna catch it.
And Bradley would catch the ball too. He would know where the ball was gonna be.

Yeah, he was a tremendous passer and catcher.
Extraordinary. But oh, I love Bill Bradley.

Something else that I think is in the ESPN *article is that Steph—when he started with the Warriors—met up with Cam Newton [quarterback for the Carolina Panthers]. And the joy that Cam Newton was taking in his game, and the obliviousness to what other people thought about him, that he was just gonna play his game and be himself and not let anybody else bother him, that had a big effect on Stephen, who may well have been given to that joy anyway, from way before, but maybe recovered some of it for himself when he saw it in Newton.*
Well, maybe he could also see that it could happen on a national stage. On a regional college stage, that was something that would be easy to do. Maybe Newton was the validation for Steph that it could happen on a professional team.

But Stephen has this remarkable capacity to see things before they happen. You may remember the game in his junior year, we played Loyola at Baltimore, and their coach made a determination, he was gonna make his name by holding Stephen scoreless. Stephen was the leading scorer in the country. And they played a defense called a "triangle and two." Three defenders play in a triangle zone, and two defenders play man-to-man on the two best players on the other team. So Loyola played this defense, but the two defenders both played Stephen. So there was a triangle zone, and two guys on Stephen, and we played four against three.

Stephen comes to the bench at the 16-minute mark—four minutes into the game—during a timeout, and says, "Coach, I'm just gonna stand in the corner with these two guys on me, and we'll just play four on three." Now, we wound up winning by 30 points, but Steph went scoreless. That's how team-oriented he was.

I've seen that kind of deference to team on the part of other really great Davidson College players since then. It has to be something you're nurturing in them, that you're cultivating in them.

I tell them, when the banner hangs in the rafters, every one of them is a piece of the banner. We have the canoe theory. Everyone is in a canoe, and everyone has a paddle. And I'm in the front of the canoe, and I'm looking out for rocks and currents. But if you've got the paddle, and it's just laying there in the canoe, it's slowing our boat down. If you're not paddling, we're not going as fast as we can. If you pull your paddle out of the water, we're not going as fast as we can. If you decide you don't like your seat—you don't like the view you have of the front—and you decide to change your seat, you're gonna tip the canoe over. The boat goes forward if all our paddles are in the water—

Together. That's a great metaphor. You've been quoted, I think, as saying that Stephen's not finished, that he's gonna get better and better. And I wonder if you have an area in mind where you think that maybe, spectacular as he is, he might even improve.

It's really not so much a technical area as it's an emotional area. He went through it last year. In the Championship against Cleveland, the Warriors were up three games to one. And the real story was not that they were up three to one, but Stephen was not playing very well. He wound up taking his mouthpiece out and throwing it. That's what he has to get better at. When he's riding at the highest level, the demons are even more intense than ever. And it's not just the physical demons of the basketball techniques. It's the emotional demons.

As soon as you say it, it makes so much sense. It's hard for those of us who see how accomplished he is, and how much he has going for him, to appreciate that his challenges are greater the greater he becomes.

And he's feeling tremendous pressure.

He's gotta be. And he always looks so relaxed!

But he lost his joy last year. And that was my message to him. You lost your joy. You don't throw your mouthpiece. You lost your joy.

You've had such a close bonding relationship with Stephen as coach and player, and now you're friends. I wonder what observations you have about him as a person.

He is someone who will never, ever say no to a request. He has this remarkable ability to try to be everything he can be in a genuine way.

My children are very humored by this story. I went to the playoffs last year, and they have a lounge for family after the game. So I'm in the lounge, and just joking with Steph, and he says, "Coach, I'd like you to meet somebody."

And he brings this gentleman over, and he says, "This is Drake." So I said, "Oh, hello, mis—," I didn't say "Mr. Drake," but I was all set to say, "Hello, Mr. Drake." Cause I didn't know who Drake was.

And he was charming as can be. You see a guy like Drake—now that I know him, or know of him, and how famous he is—and the way he acts around Steph, and they're just very normal, happy, joyful—not pompous, no arrogance. And that's to me the greatest gift Stephen has. He has balance in his life: freedom and responsibility, discipline and love, confidence and humility. Those are sometimes so difficult to balance in our lives. And he is incredible, how he has that balance in his life.

You watch the way he plays, he plays with great freedom, but he has responsibility. You watch the way he lives his life. He's disciplined. He really, really works at his conditioning and stamina, but yet he loves fun. And you listen to him, he's got great confidence when he speaks, but there's humility when he speaks. It's so hard to have those in concert together, and he does. Love and discipline is such a hard combination.

It is a hard combination, and it's part of teaching too. You want to encourage—
Your students. Yeah, absolutely!

And support, and even love, and yet tell them—you gotta deliver the bad news sometimes.
Correct. "Doesn't mean I love ya less."

"I'm telling you this because I want you to be as good as you want to be."
Correct. And in many cases, they don't know how good they wanna be, and they don't know how good they *can* be.

And somebody else can see that.
And drive them to get there. That's what coaches have to do. That's what professors, teachers have to do, leaders have to do. Don't you think so?

4
"Even play of battle"
Henry V, Agincourt and Super Bowl III

Cultural Tensions

"We're gonna win the game. I guarantee it," retorted New York Jets quarterback Joe Namath when a Baltimore Colts fan heckled him about the upcoming face-off between their teams. The game in question was 1969's Super Bowl III, historic as the first loss ever of a National Football League (NFL) team, the Colts, to an American Football League (AFL) team, the Jets, who were presumed far inferior. Through leading his team to victory, Namath made good on the boast that had seemed all but impossible to realize, paving the way to the previously unthinkable merger of the two leagues in 1970.

In October of 1415, another historic contest occurred in northern France that in many ways resembles Super Bowl III. On the field of Agincourt, British forces managed to claim France as their own through the military leadership and inspiration of their king, Henry V. Because the British, confronting even worse odds than the New York Jets, were outnumbered five to one, they viewed their unanticipated, spectacular victory as a miracle. After the battle, Henry declares that the defeat of the French by the diminished and bedraggled English army, in "even play of battle," manifests the "arm" of "God" (4.8.109, 106).

Nearly a century and a half later, the British triumph was still a story worth dramatizing, and that's what Shakespeare did with it in 1599. *Henry V*, one of the first plays staged at Shakespeare's Globe Theater in London, glorified the on-going sixteenth-century imperialistic ambitions of Queen Elizabeth I and her Tudor dynasty by praising her predecessor's conquest at Agincourt. Or at least it seemed to. For a subversive streak runs throughout the play, covertly undermining its overt nationalistic fervor. Through myriad subtleties, Shakespeare evokes an audience's skepticism toward Henry's

4. "Even play of battle" 85

The New York Jets' Joe Namath is interviewed by Kyle Rote about Super Bowl III, 1969.

character and the justness of his conquest of France, as well as the conquests of his own Tudor monarch, and indirectly calls attention to the more questionable Machiavellian practices of both rulers. In an age without individual citizens' freedom of speech, when even the slightest detection of criticism or opposition to the monarchy was punishable by loss of limb or life, raising doubts about royalty had to be managed craftily. By contrast, Joe Namath, as a late twentieth-century American, could afford to be blunt in forecasting the Jets' victory.

When Shakespeare's Henry V determines in act 1 to invade foreign shores, his brass, both admirably self-assured and shockingly arrogant, thus savors of not only of Elizabeth I's, but also of Joe Namath's. "We'll bend it to our awe," Henry boasts about France, "Or break it all to pieces" (1.2.224–25). His subsequent promise regarding the heir apparent of France, often referred to as the Dolphin (an Anglicized version of the French *Dauphin*), is equally boastful. In return for the Dolphin's ridicule, Henry vows to humiliate him in France: "I will rise there with so full a glory / That I will dazzle all the eyes of France, / Yea, strike the Dolphin blind to look on us" (1.2.278–80).

What has raised King Henry's hackles is the Dolphin's impertinent gift of tennis balls, meant to taunt Henry about his youthful "wilder days" (1.2.258, 267). Before *Henry V* opens, his escapades as the madcap Prince Hal have been amply portrayed in *Henry IV,* parts 1 and 2. Avoiding court, Prince Hal has spent his evenings drinking at the Boar's Head Inn in the Eastcheap section of London and his days plotting pranks with his low-life companions, principally Sir John Falstaff, a dissolute knight. In this, too, Henry V resembles "Broadway" Joe Namath, so named by his teammate Sherman Plunkett when he appeared on the cover of *Sports Illustrated* in 1965.[1] Dressed out in his number 12 jersey and full pads, he stands against a background of Broadway lights symbolizing his racy social life. In broad terms, the story of Joe Namath, known as "Joe Willie" to his friends, lies in how he blended his badboy image with athletic prowess to disarm his opposition, to establish the legitimacy of the AFL, and to become a potent cultural icon. Similarly, in Shakespeare's hands, King Henry's story traces his careful management of his unbridled past behavior in claiming victory over France and thus establishing his dominion.[2]

That story begins when the audience first meets Prince Hal in act 1 of *Henry IV*, part 1. Here he explains that, although he appears to be wasting his days in the company of thieves and slackers, he's merely biding his time and using his acquaintances, unbeknownst to them, for his own purposes (1.2.195–217). In unsentimental terms that raise questions about his general trustworthiness, Hal predicts that, at the right moment, he'll stage a "reformation" of his waywardness, publicly reject his present companions, and appear all the more virtuous for having overcome their bad influence upon him (lines 213–17). Throughout the two parts of *Henry IV*, Prince Hal keeps his promise in a series of steps that, upon his father's death, culminate in his coronation (*2 Henry IV*, 5.5). Outside London's Westminster Abbey, the new king turns his back on Falstaff, rebuking his irresponsible, parasitical ways: "I know thee not, old man, fall to thy prayers" (47). As the next play, *Henry V*, opens, the Bishop of Ely marvels at the prince's recent moral transformation from a petty thief and prankster to a king.[3] The Archbishop of Canterbury shares Ely's wonder: "We are blessed in the change" (1.1.23, 37).

"Broadway" Joe Namath never pretended to undergo such a radical shift, but rather reveled in his celebrity, unapologetically selling his image to commercial advertisers (including an ad that featured his shapely, shaved legs in Hanes Beauty Mist panty hose), linking arms with a series of glamorous women, and investing in a night club on Manhattan's Upper East Side, called Bachelors III, that catered to a shady clientele. Yet Namath's provocative popularity only enhanced his athletic accomplishment, partly by diverting attention from his considerable prowess and leadership. As sports historian Ed Gruver remarks about Namath's 1960s image, "In an era of long hair and free speech, Namath's shaggy mane and swinging lifestyle brought him more notoriety than most athletes.... But he was more than Broadway Joe.... Namath was also proving himself to be an astute field general" (235). Gruver adds that teammate Don Maynard, who "saw Namath as a natural leader" remembers that, as the Super Bowl approached, "We sort of told Joe that it was up to him to take us all the way" (49). Sports writer Larry Schwartz's description of Namath speaks equally for Prince Hal: "He was a charismatic presence who became a larger-than-life figure."

When Henry's men desperately need his support before the Battle of Agincourt in act 4, he provides it with perhaps the most rousing pep talk ever made: the famed St. Crispin's Day speech is a stunning appropriation of his public image, promising kinship with his soldiers. "We few, we happy few, we band of brothers," he addresses his men, "For he to-day that sheds his blood with me / Shall be my brother..." (4.3.60–62). Building up his bedraggled, demoralized army, he converts their woe at being outnumbered by the French into zeal to win the day. Similarly, Namath's boastful "guarantee" of the Jets' success galvanized his teammates by letting them believe they could win.

Ultimately, although Broadway Joe, Super Bowl III, *Henry V,* and Henry himself all avail themselves of many different readings, a theme binding them together is that of cultural tensions. More than Namath likely intended or was aware, he worked his own subversion, akin to Shakespeare's of Henry V, on American mainstream culture of the 1960s. The Colts' famed quarterback, Johnny Unitas, embodied that dominant culture with his crew cut and reserved personality, as his team, in modest, dark blue uniforms, also reflected the dominant NFL. Namath's flowing locks and Fu Manchu facial hair matched his tendency to speak what he thought and do what he wanted, including ordering champagne, which was off limits in the Jets' dressing room, to celebrate the Super Bowl win. The Jets' uniforms, in contrast to the more subdued Colts,' flashed showy green and white. As a result, social conservatives were quick to classify Namath as a "hippie," though, more accurately, he simply felt free to be himself. In any event, through his carefully tended persona, he came to represent a virtually new version of manhood sweeping across America.[4]

The Limits of Trust

King Henry's attention to his public image, which the two churchmen discuss even before he sets foot on stage, asserts itself when he enters in act

1, scene 2. He is seeking justification to invade and seize France, and the bishop and archbishop aim to supply it. They've already made their motives clear in the first scene: if they don't distract the king from a bill by which he proposes to tax the Church, they stand to lose a fortune (1.1.1–20). But if they can persuade Henry to attack France with their financial help—more backing, in fact, than the Church has ever afforded the crown—then they will forfeit less (1.1.75–81). In 1.2, they are prepared to tell Henry what he needs to hear, and, although Henry doesn't tip his hand, he may well be eager to embrace whatever reasoning they give him as sufficient. No doubt he sees the potential material returns on such a venture as they do—sizeable. Still, Henry is concerned to *seem*, if not actually *be*, entitled to France, and he warns his clerical advisers, "take heed how you impawn our person, / How you awake our sleeping sword of war—/ We charge you, in the name of God, take heed" (1.2.21–23).

The bishop and archbishop oblige Henry with three ways to rationalize the invasion. The first is demystifying the notoriously convoluted "law Salique," by which the French have long kept the English from inheriting rule through a woman. Canterbury discourses at length on why this law doesn't bar Henry from inheriting France, even though he makes his claim through his mother (1.2.33–95). For one thing, the Salic land isn't even in France, but in Germany, so Salic law wouldn't apply in France (1.2.40–64). For another thing, three French kings (Pepin, Hugh Capet, and Lewis the Tenth) have all held their titles through women, making the French hypocrites (64–95).

Henry V (Kenneth Branagh) listens as the Archbishop of Canterbury and the Bishop of Ely persuade him to invade France in the 1989 film *Henry V*.

When the archbishop's protracted, legalistic explanation doesn't prove as "clear as is the summer's sun," as he asserts, King Henry cuts to the judgment call about France: "May I with right and conscience make this claim?" (1.2.86, 96). Canterbury advances his second rationalization: the Bible. Specifically, the book of Numbers entitles a female monarch to inherit if a male is unavailable (1.2.98–100). The archbishop, seconded by Ely, bolsters this argument by appealing to the king's pride in his "mighty ancestors" who, in 1346, had earlier conquered the French at the Battle of Crécy (1.2.100–21). He also bribes Henry with the "mighty sum" he intends to contribute, in the name of the Church, to the cause of an invasion (1.2.133).

Canterbury's third rationalization addresses Henry's qualms about leaving northern England unprotected from the Scots, who are likely to invade England if he removes his military presence from the border. By now, everyone in the conference—bishop, archbishop, Exeter, and Westermerland—is in on influencing the king, who keeps his agenda concealed. Is he learning, as a new monarch, to work with advisors? Or, more shrewdly, is he presenting obstacles for his advisors to overcome so that they, rather than he, seem responsible for a controversial decision? With the ornate comparison between a bee hive and Henry's army, Canterbury tells the king that he can take just one fourth of his soldiers into France, leaving the other three quarters at the Scottish border (1.2.183–220). Although the time will come when the English in France will miss the soldiers left behind (4.3), Henry is, at this point, "well resolv'd" to proceed with the invasion (1.2.222). The clerics have saved their wealth, and Henry has his go-ahead. These tangled negotiations by which the Salic law is overturned and French dynastic claims are debunked resemble the Jets' successful challenge of the Colts' supreme reign and the complex process of merging the NFL and the AFL.

No doubt another, unspoken motive lies behind Henry's decision. Before dying, Henry IV, who had spent his reign dealing with civil unrest, advised his son to "busy giddy minds / With foreign quarrels" such as that in France (*2 Henry IV*, 4.5.213–14). The strategy works, as the Chorus in *Henry V* informs the audience at the opening of act 2: "Now all the youth of England are on fire" (2.chorus.1). Henry V will need this national fervor while, in acts 2 and 3, he addresses numerous challenges to his prospects of defeating the French.

The Chorus (who is actually just one man) previews such elements of the plot while also encouraging audience members to use their imagination in helping to construct the dramatic scene from a distant time and a place as far away as France. As the Chorus reveals in his prologue to act 2, chief among Henry's obstacles is his ability to trust his subjects, or even his friends, whether rogues like Pistol, Bardolph, and Nym, or nobles like Cambridge, Scroop, and Grey. About personal relationships Henry learns the hard lesson that, because he is king, even someone as close to him as his "bedfellow"

Lord Scroop might betray him for financial or political reward (2.2.8).[5] Such difficult issues of trust attend any leader of an organization, including a quarterback like Joe Namath, who must be able to trust his teammates while also earning their trust.

As sympathetic as Henry's vulnerability to betrayal may seem to the audience, Shakespeare complicates his character with questions about his own loyalties. His dramatic mode for doing so is to sandwich 2.2, in which Henry surprises the treasonous noblemen, between two other scenes involving his Eastcheap friends, so that the three scenes comment upon one another. In 2.1, we learn that Falstaff, who has entertained audiences in the two parts of *Henry IV* through his irrepressible ego and disorderly conduct, is now on his deathbed.[6] The cause, says Hostess Quickly, is that "The king has kill'd his heart" by rejecting Falstaff at the coronation, as he'd been planning to do all along (2.1.88). Still loyal to the king in their own way, Falstaff's friends Pistol and Nym defend his actions. "The King is a good king," Nym concludes in his idiosyncratic, obscure vernacular, "but it must be as it may; he passes some humors and careers" (2.1.125–26). Nym suggests that, to be a "good king," Henry will necessarily have to make painful personal choices.

The view of Henry's behavior with the disloyal noblemen in the next scene is equally double-sided. As a "good king," he needs to halt sedition and preserve order. But his trickery in exposing the three nobles' treachery is discomforting. In particular, when he maneuvers them into scripting their own punishment through condemning a man who "rail'd against" him the day before, Henry transfers responsibility for enacting justice from himself to them (2.2.41). Between this instance and his holding the clergy in 1.2 responsible for justifying war against France, a characterization is emerging: this king takes pains to avoid a negative public image by deflecting responsibility onto others. His avoidance, moreover, is impossible either to applaud or condemn. Rather, it involves a complex mixture of motive and tone.

On the one hand, Henry's personal removal, whether from punishing his betrayers or from his Eastcheap drinking companions, is wise. His old friends' abiding adoration for him doesn't extend to pulling their weight in the war on France, which should be Henry's chief concern as a politician and military leader. "Let us to France, like horse-leeches, my boys," Pistol urges Nym, Bardolph, and the unnamed Boy as they depart for the war, "To suck, to suck, the very blood to suck!" (2.3.55–56). This egotistical parasitism may reflect Henry's own attitude toward winning France, but for Henry to say so himself would undermine the higher notions of entitlement he has advanced in act 1. Indeed, distancing himself from Pistol's cynical outlook and illicit behavior is exactly what Niccolò Machiavelli would advise him to do in *The Prince*, possibly the most important political commentary in Shakespeare's time (although Machiavelli died in 1527).

Above all, writes Machiavelli (in a chapter suggestively entitled "How Princes Should Keep Their Promises"), a ruler should groom his public image so as never to seem anything but "all mercy, all faith, all integrity, all humanity, all religion" (66). *The Prince* advises a separation between the private man, who should embody the above qualities when he can, and the public leader, who should readily abandon those qualities when the need arises, though without appearing to (66–67). Such a division of selves works politically because, says Machiavelli, "Everybody sees what you appear to be; few perceive what you are," and those few tend not to ask questions (67). Machiavelli stresses that, of all the virtues a ruler should seem to have, none is more important than religion (66).

Thus, to live up to the Chorus' praise of him as the "mirror of all Christian kings," Henry V avoids personal retribution against the noblemen who betrayed him (2.chorus.6). "Touching our person," he says to them, "seek we no revenge" (2.2.174). Rather, he subjects the nobles to the country's impersonal "laws" (2.2.176). Henry's success at projecting the clean image Machiavelli recommends can be gauged by Cambridge's comment early in 2.2: "There's not, I think, a subject / That sits in heart-grief and uneasiness / Under the sweet shade of your government" (2.2.26–28). Cambridge's sincerity is, of course, dubious: he is attempting to curry the king's favor and conceal his corruption. The audience also realizes, however, the irony of his comment, having just heard in the previous scene that Falstaff is dying of a broken heart. Henry may be posing as a compassionate ruler every bit as much as Cambridge is pretending to be a loyal subject.

The king's emotional detachment from his subjects, as politically savvy as it may be, finally carries a high personal price: that of forfeiting true personal relationships. To put Henry's dilemma another way, the very kingship that threatens his trust in others also compromises their trust in him. Pistol's jaded observation that "oaths are straws, men's faiths are wafer-cakes" may reflect the king's behavior more than oppose it (2.3.51).

Public Image, Private Self

The pros and cons of Henry's use of his public image to win in battle arise immediately in act 3. His brilliant speech to his troops at the opening of 3.1—"Once more unto the breach, dear friends, once more"—urges the illusion of friendship with the warrior king as a reason for entering into the thick of the fighting at Harfleur ("Harflew" in some editions) (3.1.1). Inspiring? To some, but not all. As we might expect, Henry's best rhetoric doesn't have its intended effect on Pistol and Nym in the next scene, where the innocent and clear-sighted Boy describes their cowardice and greed (3.2.28–53). Yet in the same scene, officers from all over the British Isles—Fluellen from Wales, Macmorris from Ireland, and Jamy from Scotland—join in their support of Henry V. Their unity in diversity exemplifies the kind of solidarity an athletic team like the New York Jets must achieve in order to prevail. Although Henry's officers argue among themselves—Fluellen expressing the strongest opinions of them all about adhering to the old-fashioned "Roman disciplines" of war—they demonstrate the king's ability to unite his disparate forces (3.2.73).[7]

As the siege of Harfleur climaxes in 3.3, Henry again exploits Machiavelli's strategy of passing off responsibility for an unpleasant outcome. He threatens the town with unimaginable atrocities, including rape and child slaughter, unless the governor surrenders to the British, and he declares the French, not he himself, will be responsible if such cruelty comes to pass (3.3.10–14). "What is't to me, when you yourselves are cause," he bullies them, "If your pure maidens fall into the hand / Of hot and forcing violation?" (3.3.19–21). In the 1989 film version of the play with Kenneth Branagh in the title role, the king lets a faintly perceptible sigh of relief escape his lips when the governor surrenders, begging for "mercy" (3.3.47–50). Here Branagh's performance determines a simplified view of King Henry V that the playscript itself complicates. The audience has no way of knowing what the king might have been willing to do in order to win, and the dark undertones in the following scene, where Princess Katherine makes light of her imminent danger in his path, suspends the answer to that question.

The playful English lesson between the Princess and Dame Alice, her lady in waiting, belies the sinister suggestions just beneath the surface. Although the Princess seems eager to embrace the language of her soon-to-be conqueror, she nevertheless reminds the audience that he is, in fact, her conqueror. "Il faut que j'apprenne à parler," she says, which translates, "I *must* learn to speak" (3.4.4–5). That she will have no other choice than to abandon her own language is underscored by the way the English lesson anatomizes her body, correlating it to a map of France. As Henry V gradually occupies her country, town by town, he is also advancing to overtake her; as she learns the English for each bodily part in 3.4, she surrenders herself, bit by bit. Her girlish attraction to an approaching suitor, then, is offset by Henry's frightening aggression, glimpsed outside the gates of Harfleur in 3.3.

In Branagh's film version, the Princess' father passes by her chamber just as she and Alice are making lightest of her English lesson. The French king shoots a somber glance at her, indicating her misplaced frivolity. The next scene, 3.5, reveals him dealing with the serious, imminent threat of being overtaken by foreign troops, in contrast to Katherine's whimsical game. We also better understand the Princess' apparent openness to English domination when the Dolphin reveals that

4. "Even play of battle"

> Our madams mock at us, and plainly say
> Our mettle is bred out, and they will give
> Their bodies to the lust of English youth
> To new-store France with bastard warriors [3.5.28–31].

Much as Joe Namath's athletic celebrity led to his status as a social icon and an alluring playboy, Henry's military prowess, confidence, and, above all, success are both attractive—even erotic—and dangerous.

Joe Namath (with Ann-Margret) displays his bad boy image as a biker in the film *C. C. & Company*, 1970.

Such traits help us track the double-sided nature of his character that continues to surface throughout the play. More than any other of Shakespeare's ten chronicle history plays about specific kingships, *Henry V* concerns the nature—the personality, we might almost say—of its protagonist. If character takes its life-likeness from contradiction and complexity, King Henry presents abundant realism. In parallel, during the era of Super Bowl III, much of the Jets' relatively brief history and cultural significance was bound up in Joe Namath's person, given to swings between independence and conformity, wildness and discipline.

As generations of literary critics have wrestled to pin down Henry's elusively human qualities, they have come to understand him as psychologically vital, most especially in his ability to project, at one and the same time, both heroism and heartlessness, compassion and ruthlessness, piety and moral neutrality, if not outright immorality. The best known critical essay on Henry's perplexing character remains "Rabbits, Ducks, and *Henry V*," by Norman Rabkin. Rabkin uses the image of the rabbit-duck, from gestalt psychology, to illustrate the audience's sense that the king is also two different creatures in one.[8] That sense is suggested by early nineteenth-century critic William Hazlitt's description of Henry V as a "very amiable monster" (170), a term that mirrors Larry Schwartz's for Joe Namath, "lovable rogue."

The audience's ambivalence toward Henry's character constantly threatens to undermine the play's seemingly glowing view of a national hero, as well as its nationalism. Much the same can be said of athletic stars gone awry, for whom Machiavelli's advice to project a spotless image is as applicable as for royalty. By virtue of their celebrity, such figures as Kobe Bryant, Lance Armstrong, and baseball's Pete Rose find themselves, rightly or wrongly, in the position of role models, especially for youth. Thus, allegations of rape, doping, or gambling (not to mention lying about any such missteps) may readily tarnish their fans' idealized views of them. Similarly, Namath's club, Bachelors III, attracted a crowd so worrisome to NFL commissioner Pete Rozelle that he pressured Broadway Joe to divest himself of the enterprise for his reputation's sake.

One King, Two Perspectives

Repeatedly, these opposing perspectives on Henry hinge on the moral decisions he faces while making his way to the climactic encounter at Agincourt. So, for example, when his old crony Bardolph is caught for stealing a cross of small value—a "pax of little price"—from a French church, Henry not only condemns him to death under the strict military protocol he has established for his men, but he also pretends not even to know Bardolph

(3.6.45, 98–113). This mixture of reasoned discipline and emotional callousness confuses audiences and later takes various other forms, as when, in the thick of the Battle of Agincourt, the king orders the slaughter of the French prisoners in 4.6 (lines 35–38).

Here Shakespeare muddies the plot and therefore the morality of Henry's snap decision in the heat of the moment. Is he retaliating only in response to the sound of the French alarum, which signals a new attack? If so, his command is excessively cruel, as even the Elizabethan historian Raphael Holinshed, who is sympathetic to the English king, remarks (Bullough 397).[9] Or is Henry avenging the admittedly horrific French killing of the English boys who were guarding the troops' luggage, as Fluellen suggests when he accuses the French, rather than the English, of violating the "law of arms" (4.7.1–2)? If so, Henry's retaliation seems justified, as Captain Gower attests—indeed, urged by the mere fact that the innocent Boy who once accompanied Pistol, Bardolph, and Nym has sacrificed his life (4.7.7–10).[10] Such an unspoken detail is the very opposite of the many long speeches in this play, some of them intended to persuade or cover up. In this case, as in many others, Shakespeare's most significant and controversial statements require the fewest, if any, words.

In depicting the eve of the Battle of Agincourt, Shakespeare modulates the audience's further responses to this monarch, often with supreme subtlety, though sometimes blatantly. In one clear case, he ridicules the fidgety and prickly French nobles in 3.7 for their arrogance and mercenary attitude. Through such excesses as the Dolphin's precious attention to his horse, Shakespeare exposes French affectation and coaches the audience to root for Henry's cause (3.7.11–66). Meanwhile, over in Henry's camp, the mentality is far from "confident and overlusty," as the Chorus labels the French (4.chorus.18). The British, tired and sick, know they are severely outnumbered and feel doomed.

In 4.1, desperate to bolster their morale and curious as to what his men might reveal to him if they didn't recognize him, the king wraps himself in the cloak of Sir Thomas Erpingham and moves among them. At first, his approval ranks high, as he hears Pistol extol him and then watches Fluellen faithfully carry out his duties as captain (4.1.44–48, 64–82). When the disguised king finds himself in the company of foot soldiers named John Bates, Alexander Court, and Michael Williams, however, he hears himself questioned and criticized, and his defensiveness amplifies his twofold characterization.

The intricate dialogue among Henry and the soldiers in 4.1.85–229 can be challenging to follow, but, as one of the keys to grappling with the play, it is worth some effort. It centers on the recurring issue of the king's responsibility and whether he can be trusted to accept it. In pretending to be a common man among his soldiers, Henry not only seeks to reassure them and learn from them, but he also wants their acceptance and appreciation. In his vulnerable state, he seems to crave being "but a man," rather than other men's champion (4.1.101–02). Perhaps he misses those more carefree, youthful days when he cavorted with commoners, but, in a less appealing light, he also hesitates to be held accountable for the current situation, which he himself created in 1.2 when he declared war on France. If he were a mere man, subject to mistakes and fears like anyone else, then, although he might not be able to escape blame for the consequences of his decisions, those decisions would at least be of less consequence than declaring war. At the same time, though, being only a man would require him to relinquish royal standing and prerogative, which, as a king who relishes wielding his power, he is loath to give up. In conversation with the foot soldiers, Henry's tug and pull between retaining power and accepting the responsibility that goes with it produces the drama.

One particular soldier, Michael Williams, quickly becomes Henry's nemesis. When Henry floats the assumption that his "cause" for invading France is "just" and his "quarrel" is "honorable," Williams instantly calls him on it: "That's more than we know" (4.1.127–29). Although Bates takes the position that the king's subjects shouldn't question the king's cause, Williams presses his point, noting "all those legs, and arms, and heads, chopp'd off in a battle," loyal subjects for whom the king will have a "heavy reckoning to make" if he exploits them merely for dynastic ambitions (4.1.130–46). The lengths to which Henry goes in justifying his position should be the first indication that, to invoke another Shakespeare play, he is protesting too much to be believed (*Hamlet* 3.2.229–30). As the archbishop's tortuous disquisition on Salic law in act 1 calls his honesty into question, so the effusiveness and questionable logic of Henry's rebuttal of Williams portray him as squirming in the face of responsibility.

Throughout this heated exchange, Williams assumes the voice of all those soldiers, citizens, and audience members required to follow the orders of a political leader who may not deserve their trust. The abbreviation for Williams in the playscript—*Will.*—may even tempt us to think of the character as a version of Shakespeare himself, an opposing viewpoint to King Henry's moral evasions. When the skirmish between Henry and Williams ends, the specific issue is the army's ability to "trust" the king on the matter of whether he will eventually ransom himself to the French, in which case, as Williams correctly observes, his already slain soldiers will never know they've died for nothing (4.1.190–202). Williams has by now deeply embarrassed Henry and exposed the king's fragile moral fiber to the audience.[11] In the follow-up encounter between the two (4.8), arranged in 4.1 when they exchange gloves whereby to recognize each other later, Henry will have the chance to recoup some respectability from his lowly foot soldier. For now, Williams' questioning of his righteousness throws Henry into something of an emotional tailspin, producing some of the play's most sonorous poetry in the subsequent speech on "ceremony" (4.1.230–84).

Henry's phrase for ceremony—"thrice-gorgeous"—could pertain to the speech as well, and the message, if not profound, is sound: sometimes, the line between royal and commoner may amount to little more than pomp and theatrical display (4.1.266). As beautiful as the verse and as true as the content, though, the speech amplifies the most unattractive attributes of the king, most of them by now highly visible. Most especially, he pities himself for possessing the power that is not only his privilege to use well, but that he could always give up if it's truly too much trouble. At the same time, this tense scene on the night before battle credits Henry's fear of letting down his men and his sense of being overwhelmed by responsibility for them. His prayer to the "God of battles" renders him most sympathetically human (4.1.289–305).

Victory

Where his military leadership is concerned, from this point on Henry embraces his responsibility, igniting his men with the St. Crispin's Day speech, refusing one last opportunity to ransom himself, despite his beleaguered state, and losing relatively few men once the day at Agincourt is done (4.3, 4.8). Historically, the English victory in a battle the audience must imagine, but is never shown, owes to two reasons: Henry's archers, strategically placed and protected in the forest and armed with the deadly long bow, and the sheer heaviness of the French armor (Saccio 83). Because it had been raining for days, the field of Agincourt was a muddy mess. When the French nobles rode out, decked in full regalia, their horses promptly sank in the ooze under their weight. The consequences of French vanity, hinted at when the Dolphin and others hasten to "arm" themselves the night before, finally unfolded in disaster (3.7.89, 154–55).[12] The soldiers Henry humbly describes as "warriors for the working day" prevail against the pretentious French, for whom, the Dolphin laments, "Reproach and everlasting shame / Sits mocking in our plumes" (4.5.4–5).

Joe Namath rose above his own, humbler circumstances, transcending doubt and criticism, to lead a team that had its initial reservations about him, his cockiness, and his enormous paycheck. The gangly kid from Beaver Falls, Pennsylvania, who became a star quarterback at the University of Alabama, began his professional career on a learning curve, gradually righting himself as his passing improved and as he brought his mental play in line with his physical game. Writes Ed Gruver, "At the start of the 1968 season, Namath was named offensive captain by the same teammates that had doubted him just years earlier. Having convinced them of his abilities as a passer, he was now being asked to make the transition from being a great quarterback to being a leader" (23). Members of opposing teams would make the mistake of underestimating him, as the French do Henry V, and for similar reasons. "The Colts and the public had been well aware that Namath was a dangerous passer," writes *Life* reporter Paul O'Neil, "but still considered him a sore-kneed sort of freak whose skills, poise and judgment would inevitably be damaged by the awful pressures of 'real' football" (27). Failing to size up Namath accurately, the Colts, concludes O'Neil, were his "dupes" (27).

During the Super Bowl game, the Jets prevailed in ways uncannily parallel to the British at Agincourt. The Colts, led by Unitas, were as given as the French forces to the assumption they'd win. But at half-time, the Colts had yet to score. "The talented and bruising Colts," as O'Neil describes the game, "threatened, constantly, to break it wide open but never did–as much because of their own ineptitudes as any Jet defensive brilliance" (24). In effect, they too sank in the mud under their own graceless weight.

But Namath, according to other sources, also deployed effective strategy against the Colts—in particular, calling at least fifty percent of the plays as audibles at the line of scrimmage and thus repeatedly escaping predictable defensive moves. Gruver reports that teammate Don Maynard believed, "Nobody could read defenses like Namath." Said Maynard, "We'd get in the huddle, and he'd call 'Play at the line.' That meant that we didn't have a set play, that he'd call it when we got up to the line" (qtd. in Gruver 235–36). O'Neil also cites as Namath's strengths the "instant understanding of the complex Baltimore defense, masterful and malicious use of his backs and truly startling exercises in whiplash passing" (28). In addition, sports writer Joe Garner cites Namath's surprising the Colts with more running and less passing than they expected, "keeping the Colts defense from establishing a rhythm" (53).

The Jets held the Colts to one touchdown, beating them, against seven-to-one betting odds, by a final score of 16–7. Namath himself completed seventeen of twenty-eight passes for a total of two hundred, six yards and was named Super Bowl MVP. Although Shakespeare tilts history in *Henry V* by attributing twenty-five casualties to the English, set against ten thousand to the French, the actual numbers of four to five hundred English losses versus seven thousand French deaths are still staggering (4.8.75–106). The play is also generally accurate in citing how very many of the French casualties were noblemen (4.8.87–90). Namath had reached the pinnacle of his career. His bad knees, from this point on, held him back. Henry was on a similar path. Although the triumph at Agincourt eventually proved decisive in the king's claiming France in 1420, through the Treaty of Troyes, Henry V's death, two years later, resulted in the reversal foretold in the Shakespearean sonnet that is the Chorus' Epilogue: England soon "lost France" (line 12). Both figures guided the merging of foes into a peaceful union, although the joining of the NFL and AFL has lasted longer than that between England and France.

No example of winning against literally incredible odds is more extraordinary than the emergence of Leicester City as England's Premier League football (soccer) champions in 2016. The team was so weak that it was teetering on the verge of being relegated to the second tier of competition. But a startling comeback in the 2015 season heralded its rising star. In the same year, the team received a new coach, Claudio Ranieri, who'd had, to that point, a checkered career: Leicester City was his 16th job, and he'd been fired from his 15th. Once the team had won their first nine games in the new season, Ranieri promised them pizza if they could keep an opponent from scoring. In the next game, having done so, the team enjoyed their first of many pizzas to come. As of the first of the new year, they were in first place, and they managed to stay ahead and achieve victory even after one of their stars was benched for a bad reaction to a referee's call.

At the beginning of Leicester City's winning season, bookies put their odds of winning at 5,000 to 1. Writing about the stunning upset for the *New York Times,* Sam Borden puts those odds into context: "By comparison, the so-called Miracle Mets of 1969 were a 100-to-1 choice, and Buster Douglas was just a 42-to-1 underdog when he upset Mike Tyson in 1990 to win the heavyweight championship.... The odds that Simon Cowell, ... of 'American Idol,' would become the next prime minister were only 500 to 1, ... while those that Hugh Hefner, who founded *Playboy* magazine, would reveal that he was a virgin were set at 1,000 to 1" (1). In other words, Leicester's triumph was, as Henry V views the English victory at Agincourt, on the order of a divine miracle.

Remaining Questions

Without dramatizing the calamitous events after 1420, Shakespeare concludes with a few scenes that persistently alternate the audience's view of Henry's character. Most telling may be the conclusion to the episode involving Michael Williams, in which Henry sends Fluellen, unawares, to take his blows from Williams for him when he asks Fluellen to wear Williams' glove in his cap (4.7.172–73, 4.8.8). It's a comic gag, worthy of Prince Hal. Fluellen, absurdly devoted to the king, is the king's fool. But the comedy is also dark. Henry betrays the blind trust Fluellen expresses when he says to the king, "I need not to be ashamed of your Majesty, praised be God, so long as your majesty is an honest man" (4.7.113–15).

So Henry abuses Fluellen's trust to evade his responsibility yet again. This episode is thick with the language of oath-keeping and the attendant irony of oath-breaking. When the king makes a point of grilling Fluellen as to whether Williams' challenger ought to honor his oath even if he outranks Williams, the Welshman affirms that someone should never use social standing, no matter how high, to compromise a promise (4.7.119–46). While Henry appears in this passage to promote the upholding of oaths, he is in fact setting up Fluellen and Williams for their confrontation in the next scene, a confrontation where he himself belongs, but from which he notably absents himself. When Williams finally meets the king and emphasizes that, in striking Fluellen, he has "been as good as my word," he calls attention to Henry's not having been so trustworthy (4.8.31–32).

Ignoring Fluellen's opinion that social standing shouldn't affect honesty and integrity, the king pulls rank. He accuses Williams of offending royalty and demands "satisfaction" (4.8.41–42, 49, 45). Risking more offense, Williams sets him straight:

> Your Majesty came not like yourself. You appear'd to me but as a common man; witness the night, your garments, your lowliness; and what your Highness suffer'd under that shape, I beseech you take it for your own fault and not mine; for had you been as I took you for, I made no offense; therefore I beseech your Highness pardon me [4.8.50–56].

Williams implies that the king must either surrender his royal power and become a commoner or accept responsibility for how he uses power—by now a familiar theme. Rather than suppress Williams' boldness or concede to his argument, Henry simply offers him money, another apparently high-handed move by which he avoids responsibility and attempts to buy him off (4.8.57–61).

Such discomfort with manipulation pervades the final wooing scene, as well, which also jostles the audience's sensibilities. Superficially, Shakespeare treats viewers to a romantic interlude between two young royals as attractive in 1599 as Prince William and Princess Kate were in 2011. King Harry of England plays the love struck warrior to the hilt, charming Princess Katherine with his earnestness and false modesty about his lack of speaking skills. (This is, after all, the same character who spontaneously composed the St. Crispin's Day speech in 4.3.)

Yet the pretense of wooing a woman who has already been conquered amounts only to so much veneer. As Henry has said of Katherine, "She is our capital demand" for negotiating peace (5.2.96). How could he possibly "love" her, as he continually protests, without even knowing her (e.g., 5.2.126–27)? How could she possibly love him, as he repeatedly begs her to, given the injuries he has visited on her, her father, and France (e.g., 5.2.166–68)?

Perhaps, then, the point of Henry's wooing is cosmetic—to cover up the unpleasant truth that Katherine isn't just already won, but possessed along with other spoils of war. Subtly, the scene's language indicates Henry's absolute power over a situation, involving both Katherine and France, in which he merely seems to be a suitor. Take, for instance, the line in which Henry refers to the French king's inevitable agreement to the marriage: "it will please him well, Kate; it shall please him, Kate" (5.2.248–49). Although contemporary American usage rarely observes the distinction between *will* and *shall*, Shakespeare's audience would have recognized the difference: *shall* implies coercion. From Henry's perspective, Katherine's father has no more control over whether to accept Henry's terms for a treaty than she does over her conqueror's calling her by his own preferred nickname, "Kate."

According to this darker reading, the play has come full circle on the political use of image and sanitized language to veil a distasteful truth—whether the justification for or the aftermath of military invasion. Although Shakespeare couldn't say so outright, his own monarch, Elizabeth I, was as given to Machiavellian practices like Henry V's. Hence the interest of Shakespeare's audience in a monarch, although long gone, who modeled their own. For all appearances, *Henry V* ends as patriotically as it began, the Chorus extolling its hero, who, at every opportunity, piously attributes his successes to God (e.g., 4.8.111–12, 122–23). Yet when, in the penultimate scene, the thieving, cynical, and jaded Pistol resolves to return home and, exhausted of all honor, become a "bawd" and a "cutpurse," the bitterness abides (5.1.85–86).

Much as Shakespeare's play captures Henry V at his zenith, so does Super Bowl III represent the height of Namath's career. The victories that made both figures larger than life when they triumphed gave them iconic public afterlives, although each suffered decline. Henry died young, before his son was old enough to rule, and Broadway Joe, disabled from play by his knees, involved himself in opening night clubs, selling shaving cream on TV, and appearing often on Johnny Carson's late night show. As a result, neither can be reduced to a stereotypical hero; both prove more compelling as men of mixed virtue.

Discussion Questions for *Henry V*

- Review the end of 1.2, where the Dolphin insults Henry V with the gift of tennis balls (ll. 245–97). Like so many other instances of male rivalry in the play, this one is grounded in proving masculinity. How are the French characterized? How are the English characterized by contrast? For more speculation on the gift of tennis balls *per se*, consult the essay by Rebecca Ann Bach, "Tennis Balls: Henry V and Testicular Masculinity, or, According to the OED, Shakespeare Doesn't Have Any Balls."

- The argument in 2.1 between Pistol and Nym is also based in male rivalry. How does it reflect the larger conflict between England and France?
- In 3.6, why does King Henry treat the French herald, Montjoy, with more humanity than he reveals for his old friend Bardolph, who is sent to his execution without any acknowledgement from Henry that he even knows him?
- Fluellen tends to become easily captivated by the images various men project, most especially Henry V. In 3.6, he mistakenly assumes that Pistol is a brave soldier. How does he get that impression? What's the significance of his mistaking Pistol for a brave warrior?
- In a similar vein, Fluellen's idolatry of Henry leads him to compare the king with Alexander the Great (whom he refers to as "Alexander the Pig," or "the Big") (4.7.13). Although he intends to illustrate through the comparison that the king is a "gallant king," he unwittingly and ironically undermines his argument (4.7.10). How?
- What is the Boy's role in the play, and why is his long prose monologue placed where it is in 3.1.28–53? He states at the end of his speech that he intends to leave the service of Pistol, Nym, and Bardolph in search of "better service"; where does he wind up serving instead (3.2.51–52)?
- How is the French nervousness on the eve of the Battle of Agincourt portrayed in 3.7? How is the English nervousness portrayed by contrast in 4.1?
- As the Battle of Agincourt approaches, Henry starts referring to his men with the word *brother*. In his famous St. Crispin's Day speech in 4.3, he elaborates:
    > We few, we happy few, we band of brothers;
    > For he to-day that sheds his blood with me
    > Shall be my brother; be he ne'er so vile,

    In other words, the soldiers who survive the battle, however low their rank through birth, will become "gentle"-men as a result of fighting successfully and bravely with Henry himself. In addition to being a way of rousing his men, however, the king's reference to the men as "brothers" here, as well as elsewhere, matches his recurring desire to be (4.1.101–02). Look for other instance in which the word *brother* assumes special significance as a way of Henry's fulfilling his wish to be one of the guys.
- Another word that saturates *Henry V* is *mock*. The Dolphin, says Henry, "mocks" him with the tennis balls, and he will avenge himself on the French, mock for mock (1.2.281–97). In what other contexts

and with what other meanings is the word used in the play? What over-arching concept might tie together the various uses of the word?
- Yet another word that recurs throughout the play is *reckoning*, used most often in the sense of an *accounting*. Williams speaks of the King's "reckoning"—his heavy responsibility—if his "cause be not good" for entering the war (4.1.134–35). King Henry prays later in the scene to the "God of battles" that his men will be relieved of their "sense of reckoning"—that is, their awareness of how small their numbers are as compared with the French. Where else does the word occur, and why does it keep coming up?
- The victory of England's Leicester City football (soccer) team, discussed in this chapter, has also been frequently compared with the so-called "Miracle on Ice," the triumph of the U.S. hockey team over the Soviets at the 1980 Olympics. The Soviet team's sense of invincibility is the analogy in Chapter 2 of this book (on *Richard II*) for the overconfidence of King Richard II, who is deposed by Henry V's father, Henry Bullingbrook, later Henry IV. But Leicester City's victory also illustrates how an underdog with almost no chance of winning can overcome the greatest of odds under the right circumstances. What circumstances in particular pertained to Leicester City's victory? (See the following interview with Kevin and Della O'Neill for some response to that question.) What other examples from sports history illustrate a similar story of overcoming extraordinary odds?

AN INTERVIEW WITH KEVIN AND DELLA O'NEILL, LEICESTER CITY SOCCER FANS

Kevin and Della O'Neill grew up in Leicester, England, dated in high school, and later married. Although they've lived in the United States for many years, they retain their distinct British accents and their love and support for Leicester's "football"—that is, soccer—team. The Leicester City team won the Premier League championship in 2016 against seemingly impossible odds. Leicester was also in the news not so long ago for the discovery of the corpse of King Richard III, who had been buried underneath a parking lot. In Shakespeare's play about Richard, he is portrayed as a hunchback whose physical deformity mirrors his moral deformity. The unearthed remains of the King, who lost his battle against the Earl of Richmond (later Henry VII) on Bosworth Field in 1485, confirm once and for all that he wasn't in fact a hunchback. But his bones show that he was severely beaten by his enemies.

Kevin and Della talk about how the discovery of Richard's remains coincided with Leicester's phenomenal win, about being life-long Leicester soccer fans, and about how they felt when Leicester took the League title.

You two are both from Leicester. Were you aware of the soccer team before they walked into greatness? Or were they just a nonentity and not worth worrying about?

KEVIN: Oh, no, I've been a Leicester fan for all my life. I've been to games since I was a little kid.

DELLA: I've been to some games. I'm not as avid a fan as you are. I mean, it was your thing that you just grew up with.

KEVIN: Yeah, lots of people I knew were Leicester fans. So it was a huge thing. Leicester's a city of, I don't know, 400,000 people, and they've got one soccer team. And they've got one rugby team, and they've got one cricket team. So they're the big sports. A lot of people follow the local sports. And there's nobody else to support. It's not like in London, where you've got lots of different teams. I'd say the vast majority of people who live in Leicester support Leicester city.

Della and Kevin O'Neill (courtesy Della O'Neill, 2016).

Have they ever had a good season before 2016—a season that pumped you up and made you look forward to the next season?
KEVIN: They did in the mid to late '90s. They had a really good team. I think they finished sixth in the league, and they won a trophy for two seasons, but it was the third-level trophy that you could win. There's various trophies. The Premier League championship is the best, and then below that there's an FA Cup [Football Association Challenge Cup], and below that is the League Cup, and they won the League Cup twice. So they had won some stuff, but the best they finished was 6th. And then they had a really good team, like the best team that anyone could remember that they've ever had. The team in the late '90s. The manager was Martin O'Neill, and he was Irish. Spelt the same as my name. So it was great.

The names are funny because now the coach is Craig Shakespeare. Did you get to see any of the 2016 season?
KEVIN: I did. I saw, I think, three games that season. I know that I saw Bournemouth at home—it was nil-nil. And then, I saw Norwich at home, and we won one-nil in the last minute. It was incredible. It was one of those games that was really frustrating. We missed about 20 shots. None of them went in. We just thought, "Oh, this is it." This was in February, so we were near top of the league. We'd been doing really well. But you thought, it's not going to happen. And then in the last minute, the ball came across. And everyone went just crazy. And I read in the newspaper afterwards that at Leicester University they've got a seismology department and they registered a small earthquake when the goal went in.

That's amazing.
KEVIN: Yeah. It was one of those where it just builds up, builds up, builds up, and suddenly the goal just goes in. I'll say for that game, and the Bournemouth game, tickets were really hard to get. We ended up getting tickets. But I was about as far from me to you away from the guy who has the big drum, all game, going, "boom, boom, boom, boom."

Aw, you got a headache.
KEVIN: I had to go down at halftime. I got a headache. And everyone in that area were all youngsters. And they were singing the whole time. It was good.

Where were you when they won the title?
KEVIN: I sat on my sofa watching the game. When they won the title, it wasn't a game that Leicester played. It was a game that Chelsea and Tottenham played.

How did that happen?

Kevin: Well, Tottenham had to win to still have a chance of catching Leicester. And Tottenham, with two-nil up at halftime, was cruising to win. And then Chelsea came back and scored one, and then scored another near the end of the game. And that made it 2-2. And then Leicester won. And it was a great shot. So that was it, we won the league. And I was there on my own, and I was in shock, really. And then on the TV they showed a clip and said, "We're going to go over now to Jamie Vardy's house." You know Jamie Vardy plays for Leicester.

The cameras are in Jamie Vardy's house. And all the Leicester players are there. When the final whistle went, all the players just went crazy. And it was a great shot because you don't normally see that. You don't normally see the camera right in with the players like that, in their house, while they're celebrating. And the players had agreed ahead of time that they were all going to get together, without anybody else—no friends, no spouses, anything. Just the players, to watch this game. Because they thought they could win it that night. And then they also allowed TV camera—I think it was just Leicester City media there. It was brilliant to watch it.

Della: Now there're T-shirts. So that spawned a whole thing of T-shirts of "Jamie Vardy's having a party."

Kevin: And that's what the fans sing to him now. That's his song. "Jamie Vardy's having a party." Because all the players have their own song.

How did you feel when you won?

Kevin: Shocked. Unbelievable. It's great. It was a fantastic season. It was just incredible to see your team do that. And it was, very …

Kevin and Della: Surreal.

Della: Because until it actually was official, you still couldn't quite believe it was going to happen. And then even when it *did* become official, it still didn't quite sink in, because how could it have happened?

Kevin: There's no salary cap in soccer. So what's happened over the past 20 years is that the big teams have just got bigger. And if there are any young kids with talent, the big teams buy them up, and they get to play in the reserves. Teams like Manchester United, Manchester City, Arsenal, Tottenham, Chelsea, these are the big clubs. They have all the money. They buy all the best players. If you're a team like Leicester or Stoke, you know, a provincial team, you've got absolutely no chance of winning the league. Their reserve teams are better than Leicester's first team, or Stoke's first team. You've just got no chance of, over 38 games, getting enough points to win. So that's why it was so incredible.

Even when Leicester was in the top four around Christmas time, everybody on TV was saying it was amazing what they had done, but it can't last.

They're going to get some injuries, they're going to get some suspensions, they're going to lose some key players. And then Leicester went top of the league, which was around February. Again, everybody on TV said, "Oh, this is amazing, the story continues, I can't believe it." They said, "What a great fairy-tale this is. But it can't last. There's no way Leicester can win the league." So you sort of believed yourself that even going into the last games, something was going to happen. You can't possibly win the league. And then it did happen. They won the league by ten points. That's more than three wins better than the next team.

DELLA: I've told Kevin he needs to get a tattoo of it, because it's a once in a lifetime thing. You need to have Leicester City, with the fox, and then you need to have "Champions," and put the year.

KEVIN: Oh, you reckon?

DELLA: Yes, I do. It'll probably never happen in our kids' lifetimes again.

KEVIN: I mean, I can't believe that it happened the first time. That Tottenham game, it was just mad. Amazing.

Besides Jamie Vardy, who are the team's heroes?

KEVIN: I think the best player of last season was Mahrez. Mahrez won Player of the Year, voted by fellow professionals. He and Vardy, who won a few awards that year, were considered the best players in the whole league.

DELLA: Didn't Vardy have a record of scoring in every game?

KEVIN: He broke a new record. I think it was nine games in a row that he scored.

DELLA: And only two years before he was playing—

KEVIN: He played at a level that I played at. Which is a long way from playing for Leicester City. So he played part time, not getting paid. And then he got paid a little bit of money. So he started out at a local team, playing for the Stocksbridge Park Steels.

Right. And it was more recreational than professional.

KEVIN: Yeah. And then he was then best player on that team. And then another team came along and took him. And then he was the best player on that team. And then another team came along, at a slightly higher level and took him, and he was the best player on that team. And eventually he gave up his job at a factory and got paid to be full time. But even at full time he was making a few hundred pounds a week. He wasn't making big money. And then he moved to a bigger club, but was still not getting paid a lot. And then Leicester City bought out his contract for a million pounds, which is the most ever paid for what's called a non-league soccer player, which means you're not a full professional. And then he came to Leicester. But even at Leicester the first couple seasons he didn't do a lot. He wasn't the player he is now.

And he was, I take it, crucial, to the—

KEVIN: Oh yeah. He scored something like 25 goals, I think. Mahrez scored 20 goals. They were crucial, those two. There was a player in midfield, N'Golo Kanté, who I thought was the best player of all of them. He moved to Chelsea last summer, at the end of the season. He's the only one that left. And he's now just been voted player of the season. Chelsea are just about to win the league this year. So I think he was a really key player last year for Leicester. Captain's Wes Morgan. He's critical. I think the goal keeper was really important—Kasper Schmeichel.

I'm probably not the only American to get lost in all the leagues. The Premier is the top. Then what is the Champions League?

KEVIN: You're going to have to listen carefully. It can be difficult to comprehend. You play in different competitions. The Champions League is a league of Europe's best teams. To qualify to play in it, you have to finish in the top four of the Premier League. That make sense?

Yes.

KEVIN: So at the end of the season, the teams that finish in the top four places in the English League get the opportunity to play in the Champions League the following season.

I see. So the Champions season is going on simultaneously with the Premier season, but they're teams who excelled in the previous season.

KEVIN: That's correct. And the Champions League is typically played midweek. They'll play Premier League either Saturday or Sunday, and then they'll play a Champions League game on a Tuesday or Wednesday.

So they're staggered.

KEVIN: Yes. Champions League is the best teams in Europe. How good your league is determines how many teams from your league play in the Champions League. So from England, four get to play in the Champions League. They take all the teams that won their leagues, or came second or third to play in the Champions the following season.

DELLA: How many different countries do that?

KEVIN: All across Europe, so over twenty countries.

What if you're in the Champions League, and you're also playing in the Premier League? Can you be playing two different leagues' seasons?

KEVIN: Absolutely. This year [2016–17], Leicester played the regular Premier League, and they've also played Champions League games throughout the season, as well. They've done great in the Champions League.

Oh, they have?

KEVIN: Oh, yeah. They just got knocked out in the quarterfinals, which is the last eight, of the Champions League. And they were the last English team left in it.

Can we talk about Ranieri [the coach during the team's Premier League winning season]? I've read a lot of controversy about whether he should have been fired, and how he was fired. What's your take?
    KEVIN: I think it was really sad to see him get fired because everyone loves Ranieri. There were so many good things about last season. Everything was perfect. And one of the things was that Ranieri was the coach. And he was such a nice guy. He never said anything bad about referees, he never criticized his players, everybody loves him. All the other coaches love him, the other teams love him. You'd see him in the local paper, he'd go out to local restaurants. We were at the Norwich game and he was in a restaurant that we were in. He'd just go out and hang out with people. And he got this team bonded together. I wouldn't say they were misfits, we had some good players, but he made them play way above their level. He did so great last year. And of course this year we were terrible at first.
    We've spent over a hundred million pounds on new players. And we're worse, none of these new players could get in the team. You'd think by spending all that money ... I mean we broke the transfer record three times in the summer, brought in all these extra players. They've not really improved the squad. We go through games where we don't even have a shot. We got beat easily. And eventually we got into the relegation zone. In the Premier League the bottom three get kicked out. You don't change something, you're probably gonna go out the league. So they decided to get rid of him. And I think it was really, really sad that it happened that way. But since Craig Shakespeare took over, we've been great. Now we're winning again. I think with Shakespeare they've won four games on the trot. They've won more than they've won the rest of the season. And now we're out of the relegation zone. And now we're out of the Champions League, but we played really well in the Champions League.

But what do you think happened with Ranieri? Why did he lose his touch?
    KEVIN: I don't know. I would love to know one day, the truth behind that. What did happen? Did Ranieri lose the plot? Was he just lucky the season before? People got fed up with his odd ways? I really don't know. But one day somebody will write a book and tell the full story about what happened.

Yeah, I think probably somebody'll write a book about the Leicester City team.
    KEVIN: I'm sure. Ranieri will come back to England, and he will be another coach in the Premier League. Absolutely. There are teams that want him. They want that bit of magic that he brought. So you know in the end, I

shouldn't feel too bad for him. But it was sad how it happened. The club got a lot of criticism.

I've read a lot of criticism about it.
  KEVIN: They treated him badly. And the press, they treated him wrong. And then they blamed the players, and said the players wouldn't play for Ranieri. I don't know.

Where did Shakespeare come from?
  KEVIN: He was the assistant coach. He's been at Leicester for a long time. He was assistant coach under Ranieri. He's never been a head coach until now. And there's a debate of whether he's going to get the job next season because he only has the job until the end of the season, which is four games away. So they may go for another big name foreign coach, or they may keep Shakespeare.

Which is a big name in another way. Speaking of Shakespeare, didn't you tell me that there was an urban legend in Leicester that the recovery of Richard III's remains was the catalyst for what happened with the Leicester City soccer team?
  KEVIN: Yeah, since they found Richard III, Leicester City's fortunes have definitely been on the up. And they won the League. That's what we say.

Do you think that soccer in England is an elitist sport? Or do you think it's more a working-class sport?
  KEVIN: Traditionally, soccer has been a working-class sport. There's still a lot of that. There are people whose lives revolve around soccer. The closest thing I've heard to the equivalency over here is when friends of ours who are from Philadelphia talk about the Eagles. They can't wait for the weekend. They live for it. The whole week is geared up to that Sunday when they play. And there's a lot of people in England still like that. They live and breathe their football teams, and it's their world.
  DELLA: It's very much a man's world. Here when you go to see the Panthers, it's families. It's not like that. At all.
  KEVIN: I think in the past, probably fifteen years, it has changed in that now, the amount of money in soccer is crazy. The ticket prices have gone through the roof. So it's priced a lot of people out. I mean, you gotta be seriously devoted to your team to buy a season ticket, or go to away games, or travel if they play games in Europe, things like that. It's a small fortune. So a lot of the working-class fans have been pushed out. It's moved into more of a middle-class sport, and there's a lot of corporate people at games now. Not so much at Leicester because Leicester's a provincial team. I've never been to Arsenal Stadium, but apparently it's like a morgue. It's silent, there's no atmosphere. All these people are corporate people. It's not like that at Leicester.

The place is rocking. The vast majority of working class people will follow soccer. It'll be their number one sport. You think?

DELLA: Oh, definitely.

I know that you attend some plays, and some Shakespeare plays, and I'm interested in your thoughts. Do you, as a spectator, have any of the same feelings when you're watching theater and sports, or do you see them as completely different forms of spectatorship?

KEVIN: I think sport is like theater really, isn't it? You know, it's entertainment, which is the same as theater. Thing is with going to Leicester City game, it's not guaranteed entertainment.

There's more left to chance in a game.

KEVIN: Yeah, definitely. But I think there are some incredible highs. It's like that game when they scored against Norwich. It's just amazing how you feel. It's different in a lot of ways. But I think it is drama, and it is theater, and it is entertainment.

Can you remember seeing a play that made you feel high in a way that's kind of like feeling high at a soccer game?

KEVIN: No, nowhere near. But I've never seen a play that made me depressed, either.... The other thing, if we're talking about being a Leicester City fan, you kinda got some collateral benefit. We went away on vacation. I always take my Leicester T-shirts and I throw them on, and people come up to you and go, "Oh, well done. Great. Congratulations." And these were fans from other teams that normally you'd see in another shirt. And you see people now wearing Leicester City shirts.

DELLA: And you never did before.

KEVIN: And when they won, my phone was just going mad. It seemed like everybody I knew, who knew I was a Leicester fan, gave me a call before the game, "I hope you do it." And the phone just lit up with texts from people I hadn't spoken to for years. "Congratulations, that's great, I'm so pleased." I think everybody wanted them to win.

DELLA: It was a thing when the Leicester fans weren't the only fans that wanted them to win. Really everybody wanted them to win the League.

They were rooting for the underdog.

KEVIN: They were. And Tottenham was the only other team that could catch them. So unless you were a Tottenham fan, every other set of fans rooted for Leicester.

Well that's the thing about sports—once your team is eliminated, and you have nothing to lose, you can afford to support another team.

DELLA: But people don't tend to do that in soccer. In England.

KEVIN: Not really. Not in this way. I've never seen anything like this. I remember my brother-in-law, he's got a house in Spain, and he said he went into his local bar in Spain—a lot of Brits live in this place in Spain—wearing his Leicester City shirt. He said they all stood up and started applauding him. 'Cause he's a fan, so he's a part of it. You get a part of the glory for being a fan.

DELLA: Especially if you've been a forever fan, and people know you've been a forever fan. Rather than jumping on the bandwagon at the eleventh hour.

Kevin O'Neill outside the Leicester City King Power soccer stadium (courtesy Della O'Neill, 2016).

KEVIN: The crazy thing is that you thought this was absolutely impossible. Not just for Leicester City, but for any team outside of those top five big teams, you would say it's impossible. It can't happen. And the way they won it. They just went at teams. It was like they didn't care. They just went out and just went straight at teams, right from the kick-off. And they'd score one, two, three goals. It was just amazing. Teams couldn't stop them. They just got all this team energy built up. When they get their tails up, and they go at teams, they're unstoppable.

DELLA: You definitely need to get your tattoo, dear. You're so passionate about it. Really, really need to do that.

KEVIN: The whole thing is incredible. Never forget it.

5

"I am the man!"
Twelfth Night and Women of Prowess

Women in Men's Roles

In the second scene of *Twelfth Night*, Viola resolves to disguise herself as a male for vague motives (1.2.56). Her first impulse is to seek out the object of Duke Orsino's affection, the Countess Olivia. "O that I serv'd that lady," she tells the unnamed sea captain, "And might not be delivered to the world / Till I had made mine own occasion mellow / What my estate is!" (1.2.41–44). Here she may be divulging at least one important objective of her disguise—self-protection. She's been thrust onto the shores of Illyria during a storm that she believes has killed her twin brother; grief-stricken, scared, and vulnerable as a young woman in a foreign land, she understandably craves safety. Her disguise—curiously, not that of a "eunuch," as she first proposes, but of a pre-pubescent boy—will become a cocoon within which she can mature until she can be reborn—"delivered"—as a woman in her new surroundings (1.2.56).

Although Viola's comic line "I am the man!" expresses bewilderment, her male disguise as "Cesario" also temporarily gives her far more freedom and security in a man's world than if she were a lost girl (2.2.25).[1] In 2.4, she's able to speak with Orsino as if she's a man, simultaneously educating him about women and learning first-hand about men. Olivia, Viola's female counterpart, achieves comparable social freedom not only through her noble rank, but also because, after having lost her own brother, she is the sole heir to her father's estate. To be young, single, and in charge of great wealth was rare for an Elizabethan woman, and enviable—comparable to being a man. She doesn't have to marry Orsino in order to thrive; she can afford to marry for love or not at all. Still, she, like Viola, finds the world outside the walls of her house intimidating, so much so that she shuns all would-be suitors and shrouds herself in mourning, represented by her black veil.

Beginning in the 1930s, American women athletes, trying to establish themselves in a realm dominated in every way by men, faced challenges similar to those of Shakespeare's women as they navigate a patriarchal society in search of their identities. Women transitioning from lady-like amateurs to true sports professionals adopted male forms, attitudes, and appearances as they perceived necessary. In some cases, imitating the masculine version of a sport helped women overcome sexism and prove their ability to compete at a serious level. In other cases, women who adopted male traits encountered backlash: they were mocked as inferior athletes and vilified as lesbians. The actual sexual identity of a woman aside, characterizing her as a lesbian in a culture that discouraged same-sex attraction was (and still can be) a means of oppressing her. As a result, women athletes who shunned the public label of homosexual felt impelled to prove their femininity through subscribing to various conventions—in particular, heterosexual marriage.

A pivotal figure in such regards was the "Texas Tomboy," Babe Didrikson Zaharias, "the most multi-talented athlete of the twentieth century, male or female," writes historian Susan E. Cayleff (28). Although best known as a prodigious golfer—winning 13 tournaments and helping to found the Ladies Professional Golf Association (LPGA)—Babe also played championship basketball, won two gold medals and one silver for track and field in the 1932 Los Angeles Olympics, and excelled at numerous other sports. In addition, she performed in vaudeville acts and was an accomplished seamstress. She knew, moreover, how to promote herself, often bragging about and inflating her achievements, then stunning her public by living up to her boasts.

Alternately proud of and defensive about her androgynous appearance, Babe was a lightning rod for her society's insecurities about gender identity. Much as Viola assumes a male persona, Babe deliberately emulated male athletes, writing in her autobiography, *This Life I've Led*, "I always liked to play golf with men and boys.... I was told that it would be better competition for me, and that I'd learn more by trying to hit the ball the way the men did" (91). Nor did she feel her gender disqualified her from defeating men. "Before I was even into my teens, I knew exactly what I wanted to be when I grew up," she writes. "My goal was to be the greatest athlete that ever lived" (27).

Babe's self-confidence and superior athleticism, however, brought her criticism. Women warned their daughters against becoming mannish like her, and men ridiculed her as a freak. Paul Gallico, a writer Babe beat sorely at golf, avenged himself in two pieces for *Vanity Fair*. The first, in 1932, referred to her as "the strange ... girl-boy child" who could fit right in a men's locker room (qtd. in Van Natta 140). The second, in 1933, presented her as the transparently fictionalized character, "Honey," whose bad looks and failure to attract men sexually drive her to wreak revenge through sports on the entire male gender (Van Natta 143). Biographer Don Van Natta explains that "More

Babe Didrikson Zaharias displays her champion stroke in the late 1930s.

than one sportswriter wondered whether Babe was actually a man masquerading as a woman and demanded that she should undergo a 'gender test'" (144). No wonder, then, that Babe settled on golf—at the time, an acceptable woman's sport, which, as Cayleff writes, she "revolutionized" (30)—and made a public show of marrying former wrestler and sports promoter George Zaharias.[2]

Babe's choice of golf, traditionally a sport of the privileged classes, also entangled her in snobbery toward her working class origins. Other female pioneers followed, fighting sexism, classism, racism, and homophobia, in addition simply to pursuing their sports. Nancy López began displaying the qualities of a golfing prodigy at age nine, but her Mexican-American, working class family was excluded from the local country club in New Mexico, so her father regularly drove her 200 miles to play in Albuquerque. "No LPGA player has had a debut like López," writes Mercedes Marrero. After winning nine tournaments in her rookie year, López went on to set record after record and win tournament after tournament, serving as an example to girls, women, people of Latina heritage, and those of modest economic means. Triple-gold-medalist Wilma Rudolph overcame polio, for which she wore a brace until age nine, to become the world's fastest woman at the 1960 Rome Olympics. One of 22 children in her African American family and admired for her loveliness, she dispelled negative stereotypes of gender, race, and socio-economic status for generations to come.

Tennis star Billie Jean King helped to form the Women's Tennis Association in the early 1970s and worked to bring parity to women's prize money, which lagged far behind men's. Her famed match in 1973 with vocal sexist Bobby Riggs, whom she trounced, altered the public's perception and reception of women's professional athletes immeasurably, and her subsequent announcement of her bisexuality blazed another trail over the ragged terrain of discrimination.³

However monumental her contributions to the advancement of women's sports, King has sometimes downplayed her characterization as a political activist. "We were fighting for our own cause," she's stated about her colleagues'

Billie Jean King in action, c. 1973.

efforts on behalf of women tennis pros, "for fairness, recognition, and the right to control our destinies, not for some greater principles of women's rights within society" (qtd. in Spencer 399). But more recently, on the occasion of Title IX's 40th anniversary, King has acknowledged that her match with Riggs was about the sweeping matter of "social change."

Professional racing driver Danica Patrick, formerly with IndyCar and later with NASCAR, firmly brushes off the feminist label. "I actually feel very different than maybe the stereotypical breakthrough people do—'I'm doing it for women,' and stuff like that," she's told journalist Peter Boyer. "I'm much more for people in general just being successful at whatever it is that they want to do." Patrick's position may constitute what is now called "postfeminist" or "third-wave feminist" thinking—a disinclination to view women's equality as politically charged. Or she may be taking for granted the inroads that older women have paved for her, as well as the debt she herself may owe to younger women who dream of venturing into an overwhelmingly male-dominated arena.[4] Neither do *Twelfth Night*'s Viola and Olivia actively crusade for women's rights, but, like King, Patrick, and others, by situating themselves in traditionally male circumstances, they exhibit and exert more influence than they may anticipate or understand.

Suspended Identity

Much as Patrick's status as either a kind of feminist or an anti-feminist remains unclear, so Viola's efforts to obscure her identity blur gendered categories, at least temporarily. One complication is that, in Shakespeare's theater, Viola's and Olivia's roles would have been acted by boys, not women, so that, when Viola dons the disguise of Cesario, she/he is actually returning to her/his original gender, raising questions as to what, exactly, gender is: a costumed theatrical performance? a set of physical traits underneath the costume? force of habit? something else?[5]

In the midst of such confusion, though, *Twelfth Night* tends inexorably toward both the characters' self-discovery and their revelation to others of who they are. Multiple factors work to wear down and strip away barriers behind which characters attempt to hide. One such factor is what might be called "nature." Eventually, a character's genuine inner nature—whether selfishness, goodness, or gender—asserts itself, as when Orsino perceives Cesario's feminine appearance and voice:

> Diana's lip
> Is not more smooth and rubious; thy small pipe
> Is as the maiden's organ, shrill and sound,
> And all is semblative a woman's part [1.4.31–34].

Various characters, especially Feste, help nature along. As 1.5 opens, Feste is in trouble for a long absence from his mistress Olivia's house (lines 3–4). To reclaim her favor, he involves her in a jest, adeptly turning the tables on her by proving her a fool (1.5.57–72). In addition to saving his own skin, though, Feste makes fun of Olivia's morbid grief, described in the play's first scene in the unsavory terms of curing dead meat (1.1.27–31). If, as Olivia believes, her brother's soul is in heaven, then, argues Feste, she has no cause to mourn him (1.5.69–71). Olivia herself notices the healing effect of Feste's mockery—"doth he not mend?" she asks, referring to both his making amends and improving her spirits (1.5.73–74). Feste seems to understand that Olivia's grief is blocking her healthy social interaction.

Surely Olivia's social withdrawal owes partly to her lack of interest in Orsino, who himself hides behind clichéd images and expressions of love. From the start, Orsino admires his self-presentation as an unrequited lover: "Away before me to sweet beds of flow'rs, / Love-thoughts lie rich when canopied with bow'rs" (1.1.39–40). But when Orsino sends Viola / Cesario to woo for him, Olivia encounters quite another creature, one who refuses to budge when she arrives at Olivia's gate (1.5.116–18). Paradoxically, Viola seeks to prove her love to Orsino by vigorously courting another woman for him. Her persistence and impertinence pique Olivia's curiosity. Malvolio reports that the "[shrewish] boy" is "fortified against any denial" to be admitted to Olivia's house; "he'll speak with you, will you or no" (1.5.145, 160, 153–54).

Once Viola/Cesario gains access, her match of wits with Olivia is among the finest exchanges in Shakespeare's canon (1.5.166). Both women want the same outcome: to penetrate the façade of the other without losing a smidgeon of her own. By the scene's conclusion, each has gained some access to the other, but not without a struggle. Viola/Cesario enters armored in her male disguise and wielding a memorized speech composed of Orsino's love clichés. Olivia protects herself with her veil and her lady Maria's presence (1.5.164–65). Each works to get around, behind, and through the other's padding.

For starters, Olivia rejects the canned speech that Viola/Cesario "took great pains to study" because, being studied, it "is the more like to be feign'd" (1.5.194, 196). At the same time, Olivia appears intrigued by the boy's precocious vocabulary, including words like *comptible* and *sinister usage*, and with his nature and purpose (1.5.175–76). "What are you? What would you?" she asks him (1.5.212–13). When Maria fails to usher Viola/Cesario out, the page keeps trying to wear down Olivia's resistance, finally asking her outright, "Good madam, let me see your face" (1.5.230). Here is the scene's first climax. Olivia raises her veil in line 234, eliminating a barrier to her self, yet maintaining distance from Viola/Cesario by mockingly pretending to unveil a painting: "Look you, sir, such a one I was this present. Is't not well done?" (1.5.234–35). Quick-witted Viola/Cesario undercuts her coyness. "Excellently done, if God did all," she responds, implying that Olivia's beauty might actually owe to make-up, referred to at the time as "painting" (1.5.236).

Having surrendered some of her defenses, Olivia is now more motivated than ever to crack Cesario's shell. She continues to spurn the page's clichés in regard to Orsino's love—"adorations, fertile tears, / ... groans that thunder love, ... sighs of fire" and the like (1.5.255–56). Olivia wants to hear from Cesario, not Orsino. When Olivia asks Cesario how he would woo her, the disguised Viola finally speaks from the heart, precipitating the scene's second climax:

> Make me a willow cabin at your gate,
> And call upon my soul within the house;
> Write loyal cantons of contemned love,
> And sing them loud even in the dead of night;
> Hallow your name to the reverberate hills,
> And make the babbling gossip of the air
> Cry out, "Olivia!" O, you should not rest
> Between the elements of air and earth
> But you should pity me! [1.5.268–76].

Viola/Cesario has abandoned unoriginal love language and adopted her own voice. Her imagery, noticeably non-courtly, evokes nature and the freedom of the outdoors. Instead of referring to Olivia as a generic "lady," she calls her by name. The result of such genuineness is plain: Olivia is smitten. "You might do much," she immediately responds (1.5.276).[6]

The match concluded, Olivia throws herself into love, ordering an unsuspecting Malvolio to follow Cesario with a ring she knows the page didn't leave behind, but that Cesario will understand as a test of his affection (1.5.289–306). As the plot thickens, so does love's madness.

Crazy, Foolish Love

According to the play's seemingly unconventional stance, as characters give up control, let down their guard, and open themselves to love, their behavior becomes increasingly, though beneficially, foolish. Unbounded, whole-hearted love has its peculiar wisdom. Olivia succumbs to it, acknowledging she's as "mad" as Malvolio, who falls prey to it (3.4.14). No character embodies it more obviously than the play's other sea captain, Antonio.

Antonio's thorough "devotion" to Viola's twin, Sebastian, is inexplicable, except insofar as he saved Sebastian's life during the shipwreck that Viola also survived (e.g., 3.4.359–63). If the strength of his passion isn't crazy enough, it is also unconditional and unlimited. He subjects himself to danger by following Sebastian into town, gives Sebastian his entire "purse" in case

Sebastian frivolously fancies "some toy," and substitutes himself for Viola/Cesario, who he thinks is Sebastian, when he believes his friend is in mortal danger (2.1.45–48, 3.3.38–46, 3.4.312–14). His extravagant expressions of love for Sebastian contrast with Orsino's half-hearted, hackneyed phrases. Antonio's is the language of religious devotion. "If you will not murther me for my love, let me be your servant," he begs Sebastian (2.1.35–36). When he defends the youth he takes to be Sebastian, his line has Christian overtones. "If this young gentleman / Have done offense," he announces, "I take the fault on me" (3.4.312–13).

Such boundless "dedication," as Antonio calls it, traces to St. Paul's concept of wise folly in the New Testament (5.1.82). What prompted Christ to sacrifice his life for undeserving sinners? How crazy does someone have to be to die willingly in order to "redeem" someone else (5.1.79)? Antonio's self-sacrificial love for Sebastian reflects Christ's for humanity: it is without reason, without "restraint," and yet, paradoxically, wise in its folly (5.1.81). Appropriately, it thrives in Illyria, a name that echoes not just *Elysium*, as Viola notes, but also *delirium* (1.2.3–4).[7]

It raises questions, to be sure, some pertaining to Antonio's shady, possibly criminal entanglement with Orsino, which Antonio says entailed no bloodshed and which Orsino's officer just as assuredly asserts it did (3.3.26–37, 5.1.60–63). Antonio also berates Viola/Cesario for "deny[ing]" him by withholding his money in 3.4—an ambiguous choice of words, since it conjures the denial of Christ by a disciple (lines 340–47). Yet Antonio here appears all too human, more self-interested than generous, while Viola's willingness to share money from her small "having" exceeds what most people would do for a stranger (3.4.345). Even so, when Viola/Cesario offers merely to "lend" Antonio "half her coffer," the disparity between his having *given* Sebastian his *entire purse* in 3.3 and her limited generosity is stark (3.4.345–47).

As flawed as Antonio may be, his magnanimity nevertheless provides a standard against which other characters come up short. Malvolio's "sick … self-love" is its antithesis (1.5.90). He'll fall for the forged letter in 2.5 because, as Maria notes, he's "so cramm'd (as he thinks) with excellencies, … it is his grounds of faith that all that look on him love him" (2.3.150–52). As if fulfilling Maria's prophecy, Malvolio wastes no time "crush[ing]" the letter's misleading riddles into confirmation of Olivia's desire for him (2.5.140).

A spoil-sport, whose name literally means "ill-wisher," Malvolio craves Olivia's favor for the wrong reason—to rise socially above others in the household. He competes with Feste for Olivia's attention, resents Sir Toby's inherited privilege, and threatens to tattle on Maria for failing to keep order in the household (1.5.75–89, 2.3.121–24). In the "letter scene," his worldly ambition manifests in his fantasies of becoming "Count Malvolio," humbling Sir Toby, and fingering a "rich jewel" around his neck, rather than the chain that identifies him as a servant (2.5.35, 61–80, 59–60). His comeuppance at the revelers' hands renders him the fool who trips himself up on his own pride, versus the truly humble man who, like Antonio, risks danger for the sake of another. Malvolio is the "wise" man, "folly-fall'n," whom Viola contrasts with the wise fool (3.1.68).[8]

Viola herself, while swaddled in protective clothing, reveals a milder form of Malvolio's self-interest. Her instant realization of why Malvolio has followed her in 2.2 confirms a perceptiveness and resourcefulness vastly superior to Malvolio's, but she's too clever by half: she deftly displaces her own responsibility for her actions. In her famed soliloquy, after Malvolio departs, she discerns that the ring Olivia has sent after her connotes Olivia's affection (2.2.17–25). But she blames her "Disguise" as the "wickedness" that has brought her to this pass, rather than acknowledge her agency to call off her masquerade and spare Olivia further embarrassment (2.2.27). She knows that revealing herself would arouse Orsino's anger and forever squelch her romantic fantasies. When she determines she'd better leave the "knot" she's created to "time," she fudges, privileging her own well-being over Olivia's (2.2.40–41).

Yet two scenes later, in conversation with Orsino, she hints to the audience that hiding her love is wearing her down (2.4). Alluding to herself through her story about her "sister," she confesses that, because her sister "never told her love," "concealment, like a worm i' th' bud / [Fed] on her damask cheek" (2.4.110–12). "[S]he pin'd in thought" while her youth wasted away (2.4.112).

Viola's impulse to closet her identity and emotions coincides with many a contemporary instance of "concealment" for fear of rejection. Athletes are hardly the only susceptible population, but because their livelihood often depends upon their brand, their public following, and their ability to endorse products, they have special incentive to seal off their private lives. Writes sports historian Susan Cahn about the double-bind for 20th-century women athletes, "Femininity presupposed lesser athletic ability, and athletic success in turn signaled masculine power and failed femininity" (213). Babe Zaharias is but one salient example of this double-bind. Another is Billie Jean King, whose bisexuality was forced into the open by a palimony suit in 1981, although she didn't officially come out until 1998.

At the same time Viola's disguise threatens to smother her, it also grants her opportunity both to hear Orsino talk frankly, man-to-"man," and to speak to him about women without fear. This chance to learn and teach in mixed company, rare in Shakespeare's time, has no doubt also arisen for women who have taken positive athletic cues from men's sports and, in turn, developed new ways of thinking about and pursuing sports from a woman's perspective. Specifically, Viola/Cesario doesn't let Orsino get away with outrageous stereotypes of women. In response to his comments that "no woman's sides / Can bide the beating of so strong a passion / As love doth give my heart" and that women "lack retention"—a sure-fire laugh in the theater—Viola/Cesario assures him that "men may say more, swear more," but their vows often boil down to mere "shows," not substance (2.4.93–96, 116–18).

Viola/Cesario also impresses upon Orsino's healthy ego the possibility that Olivia may never return his affections. When he declares, "I cannot be so answer'd," she realistically advises, "Sooth, but you must" (2.4.87–88). Her counsel, of course, applies to herself, as well. Caught in a bind of her own making, she yearns to expose her love and yet dreads the consequences. As she continues on her course, her disguise becomes ever more problematic and less tenable. Pursued by an enamored Olivia (3.1), duped into a duel with the (actually harmless) Sir Andrew Aguecheek (3.4), and mistaken for her twin Sebastian (3.4), she accelerates conflict that makes her disguise increasingly fragile.

Revelations in the Romantic Plot

To paraphrase Robert Frost, something there is in *Twelfth Night* that doesn't love a wall. That something is love. As both Antonio's example and Viola's predicament indicate, intimacy is possible only where barriers between people dissolve. Olivia is another case in point, and Sebastian needs little provocation to follow suit. When Olivia mistakes him for Cesario, he happily agrees to be "rul'd" by her, then follows her to the altar (4.1.64, 4.3). How can the audience believe she really loves Sebastian if she just met him and can't distinguish him from Viola/Cesario? Likewise, how can Sebastian marry a woman he's never seen before? The irrationality of their passion is the point. Gradually, love's madness prevails.

The connection between pure, unconditional love and emotional transparency is implicit in the play's title, which refers to the Christian feast of Epiphany, occurring on January 6, the twelfth day of Christmas. The holiday marks the manifestation of the infant Christ to the Magi—in other words, the revelation on earth of God's love, as incarnated in Christ. As scholar Anne Barton notes, what was originally a holy feast had by Shakespeare's time degenerated into a secular "annual orgy": "the celebration of a world turned ritualistically upside down" that "the Church found itself struggling to suppress" (438). *Twelfth Night* fuses the sacred and the profane associations of Epiphany, playing on the notion of (lower-case) *epiphany*, meaning any manifestation of divinity in the human realm. The love that the play's characters eventually express, whether romantic, sexual, fraternal, or friendly, is a worldly reflection of divine love, figured forth in Christ's birth. Though impure because it is of this world, it nevertheless points beyond itself, mirroring an ideal.

Fittingly, the revelation of Viola's identity occurs moments after her open expression of unconditional love for Orsino, though it can easily be missed in the confusion of 5.1. Enraged to think that Olivia prefers Cesario to himself, Orsino threatens to avenge himself on Olivia by killing Cesario, whom they both adore. "I'll sacrifice the lamb that I do love," he tells Olivia, "To spite a raven's heart within a dove" (5.1.130–31). The reference to the sacrificial lamb recalls Antonio's irrational, self-sacrificial love, which Viola/Cesario now offers to Orsino. "And I most jocund, apt, and willingly," she responds, "To do you rest, a thousand deaths would die" (5.1.132–33). Viola/Cesario rewards Orsino's hostility with undeserved "willing love," which Antonio earlier showered upon Sebastian (3.3.11).

Orsino seems too agitated to appreciate Viola/Cesario's devotion at the moment, and his anger builds as he discovers that his page has apparently married the woman he's been pursuing (5.1.143–45). But Viola/Cesario's full disclosure of her love amounts to the exposure of her identity and thus leads naturally to the public revelation of who she really is. Sebastian's entrance, which brings out the truth, is staged as a miracle, a virtual double resurrection. Orsino can't believe his eyes and ears, and Olivia gasps, "Most wonderful!" (5.1.216–17, 225).[9] As Viola once projected, time has worked out her dilemma, though not without her free choice to make her feelings known.

The main, romantic plot seems harmoniously resolved, though the easy and convenient switching off of marriage partners may prove difficult for modern audiences. But it is profoundly complicated by additional revelations, arising from a subplot so significant that it might be considered a second main plot. These discoveries, related to the revelers' treatment of Malvolio from 2.3 on, both reflect those in the romantic plot and darken the play's overall tone—how much so is a key critical question about *Twelfth Night*.

Complications in the Subplot

Whether audience members view Malvolio's punishment as just or cruel affects their understanding of the entire play. Whatever the answer to that ultimate question, most audiences can probably agree on two points: first, Shakespeare's handling of the question is ambiguous; second, the revelers' behavior becomes increasingly violent and hurtful, whether or not it eventually goes too far. The action and dialogue of the subplot are, on the surface, some of the most delightfully funny in Shakespeare's works. Yet just beneath them lie discomforting implications. An audience laughing at the humor Sir Toby extracts from Sir Andrew, for instance, might keep in mind that Andrew is Toby's "manikin," a puppet to whom he's feeding false hopes of marrying Olivia while parasitically draining him financially (3.2.53–55).

Questions about the nature of the revelers' trick on Malvolio emerge in 2.3, when Maria, Sir Toby Belch, and Sir Andrew Aguecheek first plot against Malvolio in reaction to his intolerance for drunken revelry. Maria, the plot's mastermind, refers to it in terms of three distinct and contradictory motives: "revenge," "[s]port royal," and "physic" (2.3.153, 172, 173). "Revenge" and "physic" are opposed: the first is about satisfying oneself at another's expense, and the second, referring to a medical cure, is intended to help someone else. "Sport" may lie somewhere in between, implying that the joke on Malvolio will entertain the others, possibly, though not necessarily, through cruelty. At this point, the audience, likely on the revelers' side, may believe that no retaliation to Malvolio's obnoxiousness is too harsh.

In the "letter scene" (2.5), where Maria's plotting comes to fruition, the ambiguity stemming from "revenge," "sport," and "physic" abides. Malvolio's pomposity can be described only as hilarious. "Contemplation makes a rare turkey-cock of him," Fabian aptly summarizes (2.5.30–31). The revelers' physical proximity to Malvolio, sometimes close enough for him to catch them if he weren't so self-involved, amplifies the humor, as does their offense at the insults he feels free to utter about Toby and Andrew. Maria's reference to the letter plot as "jesting" at the opening of this scene primes the audience to savor Malvolio's well-earned humbling by falling for the forged letter (2.5.20).

At the same time, the revelers' responses to Malvolio's vanity and sense of superiority are repeatedly tinged with physical violence. Sir Andrew's "'Slight, I could so beat the rogue" and "Pistol him, pistol him!" together with Sir Toby's "Shall this fellow live?" and "does not Toby take you a blow o' the lips then?" make the letter trick less about "physic"—teaching Malvolio a lesson—and more about "revenge"—acting on self-centered motives (2.5.33, 37, 62, 67–68). Toby and Andrew's impulsiveness seems capable at any moment of ruining the trick, causing bodily harm to someone, or both. It may explain Maria's departure during the trick itself and Feste's total absence from 2.5: both clever characters, seeing the possibility of getting caught because of Toby and Andrew's recklessness, prudently avoid the risk.

The revelers' main motive is to dupe Malvolio into wearing yellow stockings and cross-garters, a combination Olivia "abhors" and "detests," and to appear to her "smil[ing]"—all affectations that will make the joyless Malvolio seem ridiculous, again, to the audience's gratification (2.5.199–201). When Malvolio enters in 3.4 following all of the letter's instructions and hailing Olivia with "Sweet lady, ho, ho," he fulfills Maria's prophecy by becoming "a notable contempt" (3.4.17, 2.5.203–04). Taking Olivia's affection for granted, he woos her with painful awkwardness. Concerned about his mental health, she asks him if he should "go to bed" (3.4.29). When he misconstrues her

5. "I am the man!" 125

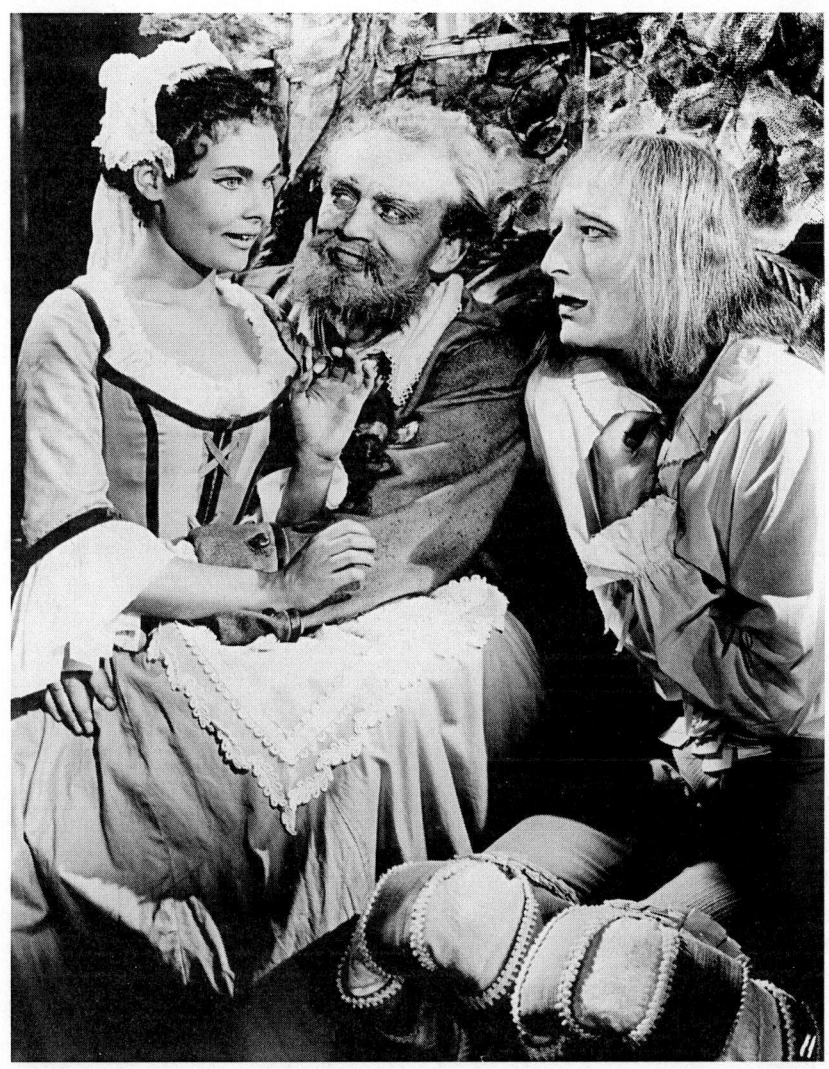

A young Judi Dench as Maria sits on the lap of Sir Toby (Joss Ackland) as Sir Andrew (John Neville) looks on in a production of *Twelfth Night* at the Old Vic in London, 1958.

meaning as sexual, he makes a total, unwitting fool of himself: "To bed? Ay, sweet heart, and I'll come to thee" (3.4.30–31).

So far, the plot to bring down Malvolio has remained relatively light and virtually harmless. Malvolio's out-of-character silliness is an antidote to his customary humorlessness and, although at his expense, is a welcomed variation on the positive madness that captivates the characters in the main plot.

As 3.4 progresses, however, the joke on Malvolio turns gradually darker. The revelers' treatment of him as demonically possessed is funny so long as Malvolio continues to obey the forged letter by being "opposite with a kinsman, surly with servants," as when he stomps off stage arrogantly proclaiming to Maria, Fabian, and Toby, "I am not of your element" (2.5.149-50, 3.4.124). But when Toby proposes to put Malvolio "in a dark room and bound," he robs Malvolio of the freedom to act foolishly and enacts not just his humbling, but his humiliation (3.4.135-36). Imprisoning Malvolio "for our pleasure and his penance," Sir Toby crosses the line between "physic," or even "sport," and "revenge" (3.4.135-41).

This long scene, 3.4, also portrays the revelers as losing control through over-extending their amusement. Sir Andrew's taunting letter to Cesario, which parallels Maria's forged letter in 2.5, is a gem of laughable absurdity, and the confrontation between him and Cesario that Toby and Fabian painstakingly arrange is a marvelous bit of stage business that audiences love (3.4.143-83, 218 ff.). But from another perspective, Sir Toby and Fabian are turning against one of their league, even if not maliciously, and in heedlessly provoking Andrew and Cesario into a duel that neither wants, they invite Antonio to draw his weapon in defense of the person he takes to be Sebastian (3.4.311). Although no physical violence results immediately in 3.4, Antonio is arrested and, eventually, Andrew and Toby provoke Sebastian to violence (5.1.175-82).

Toby's and Andrew's injuries result from an imprudence that marks the "prison scene," 4.2., both literally and figuratively the play's darkest passage. The scene divides into two parts, marked by the departure of Toby and Maria in line 20; the second is the more disturbing. Absent now are Fabian, arguably the least vicious of the revelers, and Andrew, the least acute. Keen-witted Feste takes their place, though with ample caution, needlessly disguising himself in the robe and beard of Sir Topas the curate although Malvolio can't see him in the dark (4.2.1-3, 64-65). As Maria and Toby listen on, Feste pretends he's arrived to exorcise the devil causing Malvolio's lunacy. From the revelers' and the audience's point of view, a great deal of the dialogue is funny. Feste speaks playful nonsense, denying the room's darkness while confirming it with such contradictions as "transparent as barricadoes" and "lustrous as ebony" (4.2.36-39). By teasing Malviolio about his rejection of Pythagorean reincarnation, Feste truly is, in a sense, trying to help Malvolio appreciate his gross intolerance of others' viewpoints, a kind of undesirable madness (4.2.50-60).

The lesson, however, is lost on Malvolio, whether because of his own limitations or because of his severe treatment at Feste's hands. Malvolio's experience in the prison is many people's worst nightmare: that others will think we're mad when we know we're sane. In the scene's second portion, Feste exploits that fear.

At the departure of Toby and Maria, the trick on Malvolio sours. Toby calls it off, not out of compassion for Malvolio, but rather for "convenien[ce]"; he doesn't want to get in further trouble with Olivia (4.2.66–71). But rather than follow Toby's request, Feste lingers to needle Malvolio further. Feste's song—"Hey, Robin"—cloaks meanness with a thin veil of innocence by hinting that Olivia—"My lady"—"is unkind" because "She loves another" (4.2.75, 79). Feste also cruelly pretends not to hear Malvolio's increasingly panicked cries for help—"Fool, fool, fool, I say" (4.2.102). Traces of light humor linger even in this second part of the scene, as when Feste, posing alternately as Sir Topas and himself, advises Malvolio to "leave thy vain bibble babble," the alliteration so silly as to dispel the tension (4.2.96–97). Before Feste finally comforts Malvolio by fetching him "ink, paper, and light," though, he plies his victim with the most biting question of all (4.2.109–10). "But tell me true," he prods Malvolio, "are you not mad indeed, or do you but counterfeit?" (4.2.113–14).

The degree to which the "prison scene" proves toxic depends partly on choices of staging. So, for example, if viewers can see Malvolio's face registering distress, they will likely sympathize with him more than if his face isn't visible. One more objective measure of this scene's malevolence may be the language that repeatedly describes Malvolio's suffering. In 4.2, he refers to himself as "notoriously abus'd," a phrase he echoes in 5.1, when he cites the "notorious wrong" done to him (4.2.87–88, 5.1.329). That Olivia corroborates his sentiment, referring to him as "notoriously abus'd," lends credence to his perception (5.1.379). The announcement of Maria's marriage to Sir Toby nearly completes his deflation: Maria is now his social superior, not his subordinate (5.1.362–64). To whatever extent, Malvolio's ordeal has unavoidably altered the otherwise festive conclusion of this romantic comedy.

The notion of *festive* is especially relevant to the unsettling element of "revenge" in the play's last act. Stepping forward to "confess," Fabian tries to salvage some "[sport]" and "laughter" from the trick on Malvolio, to smooth over hurt feelings on "both sides," and to sustain the "[wonder]" of the twins' reunion (5.1.355–68). But Feste spares no rancor while rubbing in Malvolio's humiliation. In his final speech, he impersonates Malvolio's pride during the "letter scene," desperation in the "prison scene," and criticism of Feste, way back in 1.5, as a "barren rascal" (5.1.291–300, 370–77).

When Feste concludes, "And thus the whirligig of time brings in his revenges," he's telling Malvolio that his imprisonment has been pay-back for his reproach in 1.5 of Feste's foolery (5.1.376–77, 1.5.73–89). Feste has a long memory, linking him to the concept not just of *festive*, but also of *fester*. He's managed to reinforce, rather than cure, Malvolio's most self-defeating tendencies, prompting Malvolio's pitiful exit, his self-exclusion from the new social order, and his ineffectual vow, "I'll be reveng'd on the whole pack of you" (5.1.378).[10]

Unresolved Matters

Twelfth Night joins a variety of other artistic visions projecting equal footing, at least temporarily, for women in a men's world. Some of these visions involve sports in particular. For example, George Cukor's 1952 film *Pat and Mike* portrays Katharine Hepburn as Patricia Pemberton, an independent, strong-willed golf and tennis player who jumps off a train to avoid marrying the wrong man and disarms two thugs attacking Spencer Tracy's character, Mike. (Incidentally, the movie showcases Babe Zaharias and other athletic celebrities of the day.) Performing in front of a "fella" makes Pat flub up, but she finds self-confidence around Mike, who assures her, "I like everything five-O, five-O" between the sexes, although, he also says, "I like a he to be a he and a she to be a she."

More recently, *A League of Their Own* has fictionalized the historical establishment of the All-American Girls Professional Baseball League during World War II, when male athletes were serving in the armed forces. Although sometimes given to sentimentality, the movie, featuring Geena Davis and Madonna, portrays realistic frustrations that continue to assail today's female athletes—society's feeling threatened by capable women and fearing women's "masculinization," the sense that women athletes have to be pretty to succeed, the predominately male-managed women's athletic associations, and the common recognition that men's sports draw more fans than do women's sports. "Why did it have to end?" sings Madonna at the film's close in reference to the league's disbanding in 1954. Answer: the men returned from war, resumed playing, and displaced women's baseball.[11]

Geena Davis' character, Dottie, also enacts the still familiar narrative of the multi-talented woman who gives up her professional career for marriage, rather than surpass either the athletic or managerial performance of many a man. As Susan Cahn characterizes this common, 20th-century story, "the 'masculine-athlete-reveals-true-feminine-self' and the 'tomboy-turned-woman' narrative suggested that the women's athletic identity was by nature temporary … headlines like 'Babe Didrikson Takes Off Her Mask' implied that women athletes assumed a façade, an illegitimate representation of masculinity soon shed for a truer, more rewarding feminine persona" (217). Now, in the 21st century and 40 years after the enactment of Title IX, many elements of this narrative, and issues related to it, await further resolution.[12]

Twelfth Night stands apart in this regard, largely owing to the effect of what remains unresolved about its plot and its comic nature. Although Viola's identity and love for Orsino have been revealed and resolved in act 5, she is the sole cross-dressed Shakespearean heroine who doesn't reappear in her women's clothes before the play ends. The whys and wherefores of this loose end apply to many other elements left dangling as Feste closes the play with his melancholy refrain, "it raineth every day" (5.1.392). Will Malvolio be "entreat[ed] ... to a peace," as Orsino commands (5.1.380)? What of Antonio's fate? As the play closes, he's still enchained, his open, unconditional love for Sebastian as powerful as ever, yet metaphorically as bound as his body.

Among the intriguing matters that *Twelfth Night* leaves open-ended is what constitutes a person's gender. Although Viola, who's being played by a boy actor, succeeds at convincing some characters that she's a woman and others that she's a man based solely on her clothes, in the play's last scene, she is resolutely female. She refuses to "embrace" her brother, Sebastian, until she has changed her garb to match her woman's identity (5.1.249–56). In her insistence that her external appearance match her internal sense of self, Viola resembles modern day transsexuals, who undergo extensive physiological transformation so that their outward appearance and sexual characteristics will align with the gender they are inwardly convinced is theirs.

Confusion over how gender is defined is also a part of today's sports scene, as some women with outstanding athletic records, suspected of being male, are subjected to testing for DNA and testosterone levels. In an extensive report for the *New York Times*, "The Humiliating Practice of Sex-Testing Female Athletes," Ruth Padawer reveals the prevalence of such testing, which often occurs without the knowledge of the athletes, who are told they're being subjected to a routine examination. Many of these athletes, who have identified as female all their lives, are found to be "intersex"—that is, "competitors whose chromosomes, hormones, genitalia, reproductive organs or secondary sex characteristics don't develop or align in the typical way" (3). Some members of this group are found to have undescended testicles; some produce testosterone at a level more common to men. But some female-identified athletes with high testosterone levels aren't biologically capable of processing the testosterone, so that claims to their unfair advantage among other women competitors by virtue of testosterone are invalid.

From their viewpoint, these "intersex" athletes competing in women's sports are being unjustly singled out for merely presumed advantages that, they reason, are no more beneficial or unfair to others than are a host of other biological traits—like height and lung capacity—or environmental privileges—like wealth that affords good nutrition and training. When these self-identified women are suddenly judged by strangers to be men, not only is their competitive edge likely to be misconstrued, but their very selfhood is jeopardized. Whatever scientists or governing athletic bodies (like the International Association of Athletics Federations) determine their gender to be, they are certain that they're women. Dutee Chand, an Indian Olympian runner whose gender has been challenged, has said, "I was born a woman, reared up as a woman, I identify as a woman and I believe I should be allowed to compete with other women" (qtd. in Padawer 11). For Chand as for Viola, gender may be understood as, at least partly, if not wholly, what an individual person says it is for herself or himself.

That *Twelfth Night* is the only of Shakespeare's plays that has come down to us with an alternative title—*or What You Will*—is to the point. Emphasizing the audience's choices once the "play is done," it transfers its unresolved issues to the audience's world, the world we have power to alter, if we "will" (5.1.407). *Twelfth Night* invites us to fashion a world in which Antonio's love is liberated, Malvolio is included in the cosmic dance, and Viola fully realizes herself. By extension, it opens onto a world where Brandi Chastain can indulge in a universal gesture of triumph without raising an eyebrow and where women athletes can be both themselves—different from men—and equal.

Discussion Questions for *Twelfth Night*

- Social class, its privileges, and its liabilities figure prominently in *Twelfth Night*. Where does class benefit a character? Where does it put a character at a disadvantage?
- How is Antonio especially hampered by his class?
- Maria is of a lower class than Sir Toby and Sir Andrew and yet prevails over Malvolio. How and why? Why does Sir Toby marry her?
- Some of the characters in *Twelfth Night* are quite obviously named to suggest types. Sir Andrew Aguecheek's name implies he's scrawny and sickly: an "ague" is a cold. Sir Toby Belch is named after the effects of drinking. Are the stereotypes these names conjure misleading? In other words, are characters with names like "Malvolio" more complex than their names suggest?
- In the same vein, the frequent, though often unfair, stereotype of the athlete is of a thug or bully who gets away with bad behavior because of his athletic ability. Does Sir Toby fit that stereotype? Do other characters in a play full of "sport" and game mirror other athlete-stereotypes?
- In the interview with actor Graham Smith that follows this chapter, Smith refers to *Twelfth Night* as a lot of "fun" for actors. He seems to find the play's tone relatively light, as do many actors, directors, and audiences. What features and passages of the play back him up?
- Where is the comedy darker in tone?
- Does the play ever abandon comic humor completely? What is the ultimate tone of this tonally mixed play?
- How does *Twelfth Night* define gender? What makes a man male and a woman female?

- Does the play endorse and/or question Antonio's unconditional love of Sebastian? What's the evidence on both sides?
- How is the rearrangement of couples at the end prepared for, if at all? Does the unlikelihood that Olivia and Sebastian would get together in real life—versus within a fantastical play—mar or undermine the play?
- How would *Twelfth Night* be different without Fabian? Is he a necessary character?
- *Twelfth Night* is full of letters—so full that their recurrence virtually constitutes a theme. How many letters appear in all? What is the significance of each and the significance of the entire group? Why is so much of the communication in the play conducted in letters?
- *Twelfth Night* alone among Shakespeare's plays carries a subtitle: *What You Will*. What's its significance?

An Interview with Shakespearean Actor Graham Smith

Graham Smith has been an actor virtually all of his life. When he was a child, he traveled with his parents and four siblings both in the U.S. and abroad to perform magic shows. He turned professional after graduating from college and has made over 40 appearances in Shakespeare's plays. He has acted four times in *King Lear,* three times in the title role and once as the Fool. He has twice portrayed Lord Capulet in *Romeo and Juliet* and has acted six times in *A Midsummer Night's Dream*. His other roles include Stephano and Gonzalo in *The Tempest*; Shylock and Gratiano in *The Merchant of Venice*; Oliver, Jaques, and both Dukes in *As You Like It*; and Malcolm and Lennox in *Macbeth*. In the following interview, Smith uses anecdotes from performances to illustrate key points about Shakespearean acting, reflects on what makes Shakespearean acting an exceptional experience, offers advice to aspiring actors of Shakespeare, and suggests parallels between acting and athletics.

Can we start by talking about your career specifically as a Shakespearean actor?
   Well, it's rowdy in the morning. And by that I mean we do a lot of school performances. Those are rowdy.

Interesting.
   Actually, they used to be, fifteen or twenty years ago, because they brought in public schools. Now, because there are more limited resources, there's a lot more culling—the kids that want to come or that are motivated

or read it or are from advanced classes. But sometimes in High Point [North Carolina] we'd get a thousand kids straight out of public school, and you had to play ahead of them all the time. In the morning, the stronger, authoritative kind of scenes work better. Family scenes work better. The more poetic stuff, where people are not as active, but—

Graham Smith as King Lear, 2011. Photograph by Mark Garvin (courtesy People's Light).

Intimate?
Unless it's intimate between young lovers. You go to what's there, what's gonna play. But those are sometimes really rowdy.

I remember one time performing *Hamlet* in a school, the guy playing Osric came on with the swords for Hamlet and Laertes' fight, and as he was walking on, the swords—he had a big pillow, the two épées were on the pillow—they started to slide off. So he was trying to keep the pillow underneath the épées as they were moving. He kept getting lower and lower, and eventually got right to the proscenium and fell off stage.

Oh my gosh! I bet the kids burst out—
Oh, I mean, for a minute, just busted them. We were saying, "No, this is much better than anything we've heard, we're gonna stay in this moment." And then, when Osric came out for his curtain call, they *exploded*.

Osric never had it so good!
No, never!

And that speaks to an analogy between sports and Shakespeare. In sports, you have rehearsal after rehearsal after rehearsal, and yet there's a lot of improvised action. You rehearse in order to deal with improvisation as skillfully as you can. We have a little less improvisation these days than in original Shakespeare theater, but there's still room for that kind of improvisation that you just talked about—rolling with the audience and with the moment and converting a mistake into a great moment in theater.

You rehearse to learn how the play works. In the best of all worlds, you're rehearsing your performance. That was a big lesson for me, when I realized you should rehearse the play, and not to make your performance good. But giving that up and going, "I'm just going to rehearse to find out what the play is, so that I'm ready to perform and to play when it happens."

That's a big distinction. And I think football teams, when they rehearse, or when they practice, they're not always going all out. They rehearse to learn and to build trust and to build an instinct for playing with others, and once that happens—when a new actor or athlete is inserted into a big machine, the timing is off because the new players don't have that trust or those instincts. They don't have a feel for it yet.

What was your first Shakespeare role?
It was at Davidson College, and I played Puck in *A Midsummer Night's Dream*. And I remember the review because Dick Banks, who was the reviewer from *The Charlotte Observer*, said, "Graham Smith displayed a cleverly-worked-out, jumping-jack characterization of Puck, but his words were often incomprehensible." And I thought, "Hey pretty good! Fifty percent! I got half of it!"

Actually, the part that got me was *displayed*. Even then, I went, "Oh." I don't know whether he meant that or not. I took that as a real hit, although people seemed to enjoy it. I'm still a little embarrassed about it. But that's me.

What was your most recent Shakespeare role?

I guess *Lear*. For the last five years, I haven't done any Shakespeare. I'm getting ready to do *R and J* next spring. I hear I'm gonna be the Friar. I've done the Friar, and I've done Capulet twice. I like Capulet.

It is maybe the least recognized great role in Shakespeare.

It's got tremendous range. And—ah, man! And some of the earlier stuff, the little scenes, they're so mysterious. And there's such room for personalizing stuff. And then you've got the flex of that scene—

Yeah, 3.5, where Capulet explodes and abuses Juliet.

Oh my God!

Oh, he's so awful.

The athleticism of doing a scene like that, and having to play small and large at the same time—I mean, head to toe—and vulnerable, and at the height of your anger ... that total involvement and total transparency is what's thrilling about it. Because you can't really quite manage all of it. You have to be willing to play it, and be played by it, at the same time. And you can't plan that. You have to rehearse it well enough that your ideas about it go away.

Yeah, it struck me—I've directed it a couple of times with students—and it struck me as I've gotten more familiar with it that Juliet and Capulet are fueling each other. The more he tries to get her to be grateful to him, the more upset she becomes. And the less power he has over her to make her happy because of what he's done for her, the angrier he gets. And if you just work with that dynamic between the two of them, then you've pretty much got that scene.

And you've been in Twelfth Night?

In *Twelfth Night*, I've always been part of the same platoon. I've played Aguecheek, Malvolio, and Toby Belch. The best scene to me in all of Shakespeare is 2.5—the letter scene in which the revelers trick Malvolio. The most fun to be in.

It is so fun!

Because it's got such great terrain. And you can take time with it, and 'cause you get to be drunk and sentimental and angry and carouse. And because it's subversive. It's great fun. I haven't played Maria yet—who knows? I was amazed that they offered me—that was at People's Light—Toby Belch because I'm going, "That's the role I wanna play." And the director said, "Would you be interested in Toby?" And I said, "Yes!"

Usually he's more corpulent.

Well, my view of him was essentially about his wasted talent—or how he's dissipated in wasted talent. But in all those characters there's a lot of room. Maybe you lose something by not being corpulent, but it actually affords you a different possibility, 'cause there's something stock about the big guy who you think, "OK, that's going to be funny." I think it afforded me a chance to make him a little—for lack of a better word—a little bit more tragic. And also funny because drunks are funny onstage, if they're not too mean.

I had a great time in that because the director came up and said, "We want to use a wheelbarrow in this production. Do you have any ideas about it?" And I went, "Let me think on it." And it became gold! It became gold! We were trying to figure out how to use it in every scene. So, at the end of the first scene Toby has with Maria and Aguecheek, Fabian comes onstage, and they're gonna go out for a night of carousing. And so at the end of that scene, I went, [mimes whistling]—and, I couldn't do that, actually. The guy playing Fabian can whistle, but he's right offstage—

So he did it for you?

And then Fabian came on with the wheelbarrow—and it had hay on it, but the hay was a false top, and I think there was a chest in it. And you opened up the top of the wheelbarrow—the chest—and it was filled with liquor bottles. So that was the beginning of our foray into the evening. And then the next morning, Toby comes back in, trying to sneak past Olivia. And I was trying to do the wheelbarrow myself because I lost all my compatriots, and there were empty bottles in it. So I'm trying to sneak it past, and then in the course of that scene, I sat on the edge of it and lay back for a second and fell asleep in it and then had to be carted off.

And then the next time, I guess maybe it was 2.5, Fabian came in with the wheelbarrow—this was another night of drinking—and Aguecheek and I were both in the wheelbarrow. But we're passed out, and I'm lying down in it. And my legs are out, and Aguecheek is propped up in it. So it looks like he's being wheeled in. But it's my legs draped over the front, and he says something, and I pop up so it reveals that there are two of us there. That stuff is just gold!

That's ingenious! People ask me all the time, "What's your favorite Shakespeare play?" and it's like choosing your favorite child. But I'm gonna ask you that vexing question. Is there a particular play or a role in a play that has been especially fulfilling to you?

Well, I would say *Twelfth Night* has provided the most fun. I think it's a play you just want to be in because it engenders an affinity amongst all the players.

Other plays are meaningful, depending on the production, but the fun is actually in getting steeped in the language and hearing it over the monitor or playing it. That's a different thing. You're grateful to be a part of it, rather than just having a great time with it. And I would say that *Lear* is that for me, that's the one that has the greatest amount of respect. There's a moment in *Lear*—"Pray you undo this button"—and someone undoes it, and Lear says, "Thank you, sir." That's one of my favorite moments in all of Shakespeare.

He's learned humility at that point.

Just a little thing like that. And it's *everything*. That's astounding.

I agree. I was in Stratford in 1981 for the World Shakespeare Conference, and I was in a workshop with John Barton and Patrick Stewart. They did that little section in Lear *where Edmund orders the captain to kill Cordelia [5.3.26–39]. And they took that one passage and showed how the language characterized the captain, Edmund, and the relationship between them. And I remember thinking, "Oh my Lord." There was so much there!*

Once in grad school, somebody came and worked with us on sonnets. And he would start and work—like, the first syllable was "Oh"—so he worked on that for a while. Whoever he was working on would go "Oh," until he finally got it. And he worked for probably for 30 or 40 minutes on that one line. And he'd go, "OK, you got the 'Oh,' now try to go on to 'that I.' Oh, you got 'that I,' but you lost the 'Oh.'" And he wouldn't watch, he would just listen—and I went, "OK, I'll just listen." And I hear it. I hear the difference. This is impossible! How do you get that present on every vowel? What does that require? How do you get to that? It requires that you live life that way virtually all the time, so that it's second nature to always be—

Tuned in.

And released. I don't know if you can do that all the time. I think people like Meryl Streep can live that way. But she's a *creature*. She's not human. She lives like a seamless artist. There's no difference between her art and her being, and that's why she's able to do that. And that's what Shakespeare asks of you.

Can you remember a moment in performance that was, for you as an actor, the equivalent of what a great moment in a sports event would be? Like a three-pointer in basketball from way far away, or catching a long-distance pass in football game, something like that? It could also be a moment of discovery, where you sort of surprised yourself, and you channeled the play in a way that you had never experienced.

Rather than a moment of celebration, those are moments where you feel like you are in the eye of the storm because you're so in the moment of discovery that it's not even about you. You are simply in it. The moment is the discovery, not "I discovered something." That's something afterwards, and that gives you—

But there's gotta be a lift there. There's gotta be a euphoria.

But it's a different kind of euphoria. Those guys like Joe Montana, or Tom Brady, or Peyton Manning (sometimes) that are able to come into a crowd of 60, 70 thousand people in a big moment in a game, and the game is slowed down for them. That's where those guys are creatures. It's a scramble, but they're seeing all these different things happening at the same time. But it's in slow motion for those guys. The reason they're able to be successful again and again is because they're *actually* present. They're not present in an idea about what they think they're supposed to execute. They're actually living *fully* in the space of a few seconds, and operating on all cylinders. And they're taking in everything, they're giving, they're adjusting at a rate where life around them is going a billion miles an hour.

I've had some of those moments, and they're beyond you. They're religious moments on some level because you go, "I'm not capable of this. I was allowed to be in it by circumstance—or maybe preparation, all those things might have helped me get there—but allowed to distill everything down into something that I didn't understand before." And even the articulation of it afterwards is wrong, or approximate, because it could only exist while that was happening. And that's the wonder of theater at large. But for some reason, if it happens in Shakespeare, it's all the truer. And I've had that…. That's happened a couple times in *Lear*. It's the kind of thing where you—without it even being at the forefront of your mind—you know that everything that you do is right.

Everything is falling into place.

It's actually not even you because in those moments, you're attentive to everything else. You're not attentive to you. That's what I mean, you're in the moment of discovery. If it's a discovery, you're actually struck.

It's what T.S. Eliot wanted of poets, right? Total cancellation of self.

But it also means everybody in the room is in the same moment, because it's not going to work if it's just you. And that's where, in those moments, it almost feels that you're naked before God, and it's OK. And a lot of times, before I do a play, that's what I'll hope for. And I'll go and stand in an audience, and look at each seat, and I put it in my head and into the possibilities of the universe that I can actually be transparent. And that would include all my inadequacies as an actor. My self is actually allowed to be there, not some idea about who I am. And when that happens, acting is easy because you've got nothing to hide. You're not trying to put anything past anybody. You're just engaged. And that's difficult, and that's one of those conundrums about doing anything, because I wanna be the guy doing it, and I wanna do well.

Right. There is some ego attached.
But that's the one thing that stands in your way. Wanting to be good. Any of those desires.

Writing presents so many analogies to that.
All art!

Getting out of the way of yourself.
I used to think that's theater, but that's gotta be all art. That's gotta be true of a fiddle player as well. Painter.

What advice you would give to an actor just beginning and had aspirations to play a Shakespeare role? I feel like you've been giving that advice, which is sort of that erasure of self...

I probably wouldn't give somebody advice who was doing their first Shakespeare. I'm not opposed to giving advice. I do that more than I should, actually. Abigail Adams, who's the artistic director at People's Light—where I just played Horace in *The Matchmaker*—has started pairing older actors with younger actors, so that they can coach. People don't do that in theater. They should, but they don't. So that I'd actually coach them in a rehearsal, then I'd listen to them, always keep tabs on their scenes during performances, so that I could give them old guy advice. So I'm not opposed to giving advice.

But there's already so much of an obstacle that people have in their heads about coming in and doing Shakespeare for the first time that the first lessons are probably to learn how to be yourself, and next you're gonna try to look for a way to bring the role to you. And once you've done it enough, how are you gonna open up to being played by the role? I'm not sure a new actor would understand what it means to be played by a role. I mean, people always say, "Use the language! Use the language!" which doesn't make any sense to me anymore. I think you have to let the language use you. I don't know if a younger actor would really get that yet, until they've done some more stuff.

Keep it simple, trust the language, all that stuff we say that gathers meaning as you do it, that gathers meaning over a lifetime. Well, actually, yeah, here's some nuts and bolts. Drive to the end of the line. No downward inflections. Explode out the end of the line. Or accelerate it. Find that little thing in the middle of the line that accelerates it. Look for that. Demand the next player's line.

You've gotta come in with enough energy and intention so that you can relax into performance. You can't come in and warm up to it. You've gotta be living life this big, so that you can come down to something nuanced and fully inhabited. But if you start off by trying to be simple, and trying to be real, any of those things, you'll never be played fully enough. You have a lot of chores, tasks, responsibilities in Shakespeare that are clear, and they're already defined. And you've got to perform all those. Those are merely the calisthenics of it. That's before you get to the life of it. My advice would be make choices that make the play bigger, or make the production bigger, not smaller. Learn how to be efficient! Efficiency is tremendously important.

In writing, too.
    Seek simplicity.

That sounds like Polonius!
    Yeah, it does! But that's the key to all of it—reduction. Once you line up on language, then you reduce, because everything else could fall away. Don't adorn your acting, but play fully on the language. That's more than sufficient.
    Oh, I was gonna say, before I forget: there's a lot of language in sports that's—

Theatrical.
    We use the same language. Some of the things that occurred to me are metaphors for acting too. When they talk about a runner going through the line in football. For some reason football kept coming back to me in Shakespeare more than basketball, probably because the scale is more like a Shakespearean play, and you've got platoons of people. Like the guys in *The Tempest*, that might be your receiver corps. Different kind of corps. But the runner comes to the line—a lot of times, they'll talk about how he's patient. He's not running all out all the time. He takes the ball, and he's following his blockers, or he's coming up to the line, and he waits to see how the play is gonna unfold before he picks his spot. So here's a guy, all of a sudden he's coming in slowly, with a restrained sort of power, and then waiting for the moment to explode. Exploding through the line. That's sort of like what we're supposed to do when we're acting Shakespeare and driving to the end of the line. Explode out the middle of the caesura, accelerate there. That's similar.

I wanted to ask you your thoughts on the analogy between the ensemble, or the repertory company, and the team. Just as on a sports team, you have people coming in and leaving, but there's a core there which would seem to me to engender trust and lead to more interesting, creative risk.
    Should. Doesn't necessarily, it can also lead to—

To atrophy.
    To atrophy, yeah. It's fun to get in somebody new. I really buy into the notion of company and working with the same people, and shorthand, and the shared history, and what becomes sort of an institutionalized aesthetic that hopefully is still evolving. There's a shared language. Everybody says the same things, but you actually know what it means because you've applied it many times. I know a lot of times at People's Light, who are concerned about the balance of, "Who are our core people and how many are outside people?"

Sometimes you can't worry about that, but sometimes—depending on the play again, too—it can only absorb so many new people and still be the same thing. And yet the new people sort of re-engage you in a different way. And then they're also finding out where they are by walking into a room and going, "Oh, this is how we rehearse. This is how we do things here."

People talk about the feeling of the locker room—the esprit de corps. In theater, you talk about the room, which is always the rehearsal room. "What's the feeling in the room?" Or "It's a good room."

It's about relationships.

And how we're exploring. "It's a good room"—that means you stay. You're learning things, having a good time learning and discovering with other people. And sometimes it's specifically the dressing room. "Oh, that's a fun dressing room."

And perhaps there's an analogy between a season and the run of a play. Because they talk about the beginning of the season. You know, you've got exhibition games.

In theater you've got previews.

Sort of like a preview. You're finding out what works and what doesn't work, not changing personnel.

And you're warming up to your audience, your fan base.

Well that's probably more true in theater. I mean, you're warming up, you're going to change things in theater, depending on how the audience reacts. In football, the metric is very defined. You either won, or you lost, or you're able to see what the numbers your offence and your defense yielded. And so the changes that you might make in theater are gonna be a little more psychic. Sometimes they're immediate, the construction of the moment or something. "We're losing them." That would be the language in a play. "We're losing them here. Why is that?" We need to be more generous, maybe, in our playing at the beginning, so there's more invitation. We're analyzing how the audience is coming to the play. Where are we meeting? Are we meeting halfway? And a football team's not doing that.

There's another thing. You talk about role players, on a basketball team in particular. They're not the stars, they're not the leads, they're the role players. And we have role players in the theater, or we have roles. That language is similar too.

So positions on a team would be comparable to theatrical roles.

You have Shakespeare types—you know, your fat comic guy and your offensive lineman.

In football, they talk about stepping up. When one guy goes down, everybody steps up on some level. And you can actually drop a pass in theater if somebody pitches you something. We talk oftentimes about what's being pitched. As a matter of fact, sometimes, especially when you're learning how to be in Shakespeare, you might have a ball—you're actually pitching the end of the line to somebody, and they're receiving it and then giving their line out and pitching it again. And then sometimes, that ball actually gets pitched to the audience. But if you pitch it short—if I pitch my intention short—and the ball drops, then you haven't done your job because the next person essentially has to go and pick it up and start the play over again. So we talk about dropped passes. We don't specifically use that term, but—

There's a similar phenomenon.

There's a similar responsibility. That's what I mean about demanding the next line. And if you don't, then the play does fall apart.

6
"Vaulting ambition"
Team versus Self and *Macbeth*

Addiction

On October 5, 2007, Olympic track and field champion Marion Jones stood on the steps of the District Courthouse in White Plains, New York, and wept as she publicly confessed to having lied to federal agents about taking performance-enhancing steroids. "You have the right to be angry with me," she told her audience. "I have let [my family] down, I have let my country down, and I have let myself down." Jones served six months in prison and performed 800 hours of community service as punishment. Two months after her confession, the International Olympic Committee (IOC) formally rescinded the three gold and two bronze medals awarded to Jones at the 2000 Sydney, Australia, Olympics. Even more disheartening, the IOC also recalled medals given to those U.S. athletes who had run relays with Jones. Although this decision was appealed by seven of Jones' teammates and overturned in 2010, it bears witness to how the choices of one potentially outstanding person can adversely affect an entire group.

To consider *Macbeth* in relation to a story like Jones' is to think about it as the story of a man whose promise of military and political greatness is ruined by a string of increasingly destructive, irreversible choices. They are selfish choices, intended to advance Macbeth and Lady Macbeth at Scotland's expense. They are also addictive: once Macbeth has murdered Duncan, he believes he must continue murdering anyone who might take the throne from him or his (as yet nonexistent) heirs. They involve temptation: the witches play on Macbeth's ambition from the start, then alternate with Lady Macbeth (who shares some traits with them) as forces playing upon Macbeth's will (1.3, 1.5). Macbeth's choices also gradually numb his conscience, which continues to function in his two soliloquies about the prospect of killing Duncan (1.7.1–28, 2.1.33–64). Finally, they cause his tragic fall from a high place.

Macbeth's off-stage beheading constitutes an unusually extreme humiliation on Shakespeare's part: Macbeth is denied the respect of other tragic heroes—among them, Romeo and Juliet, Hamlet, and King Lear—whose onstage deaths are preceded by memorable speeches and observed by sympathetic characters (5.9.19). The demeaning of Macbeth reflects the ultimate blackness of his character and his tragedy, a darkness balanced by the light of Malcolm's eventually victorious virtue. When Macduff interprets Macbeth's demise as a sign that "the time is free" and calls Macbeth Scotland's "usurper," he refers to a man who has stolen rule from the rightful heir, Malcolm, and has abused power over his subjects like a "tyrant" (5.9.21, 3.6.22, 25). Now, Scots have liberty to work together for the good of the nation.

Much as Macbeth initially demonstrates military and political leadership, individual athletes come forward as natural leaders, whose exceptional physical or motivational abilities stand to enhance a team's performance. Some of those promising figures, faced with the temptation to gain more for themselves than they otherwise would, succumb to choices that compromise their reputations, raise doubts about their athletic records, and, in the end, harm their teams, even their nations. Through considerable efforts in their own sphere, heroes like Marion Jones have risen to a kind of greatness—as Macbeth has to Thane of Glamis and of Cawdor—and, also like Macbeth, they've fallen from their heights through dishonorable behavior. How they respond to their past mistakes—whether they take responsibility for their actions and express true remorse—can be just as significant to their careers as the mistakes themselves.

In recent decades, the American public has generally viewed the increasing reliance on performance-enhancing drugs as especially shameful.[1] In addition to Jones, high-achieving athletes like baseball's Jose Canseco, Mark McGwire, and Barry Bonds, and cyclist Lance Armstrong have either confessed to or have been accused of steroid use. But doping is only one way for a single player to go awry. Pete Rose's gambling is another. This former Cincinnati Reds switch hitter and, later, manager, remains the all-time Major League leader in hits, games played, at bats, and outs; his numerous awards include Rookie of the Year, two Gold Gloves, MVP, three batting titles, and 17 all-star appearances, uniquely at five different positions. But in 1989, three years after his retirement from active playing, accusations of his betting on baseball led to his permanent ban from professional baseball and, therefore, from election to the Baseball Hall of Fame. Another, older baseball great, New York Yankees' Mickey Mantle, spent 42 years as an alcoholic before seeking treatment at the Betty Ford Center. Like Macbeth's growing dependency on violence to advance and protect himself, sports figures' various addictions, some originally directed toward managing the high expectations of athletic performance, can instead thwart performance.

What appears to be Macbeth's addiction to violence is actually an addiction to what he constantly, and sometimes ironically, calls "safety." The word refers to protecting the throne from others who might covet and compete for it as much as he did when he murdered Duncan. In 3.1, before he convinces the murderers to assassinate Banquo and Fleance, he muses to himself about being king that "To be thus is nothing." He longs "to be safely thus" (3.1.47–48). Because the Weïrd Sisters (a name derived from the Old English word *wyrd*, meaning "fate") have prophesied that Banquo's heirs will become kings, Macbeth can't relax—can't "safely" be king—until Banquo and Fleance are dead (1.3.67). In the next scene, Lady Macbeth echoes the sentiment. "'Tis safer to be that which we destroy," she says to herself, alluding to the fear of being found out for murder, "Than by destruction dwell in doubtful joy" (3.2.6–7). When Macbeth meets the murderers again in 3.4, the audience perceives the irony that he misses in his question to them: "But Banquo's safe?" (3.4.24).

Banquo, of course, isn't safe. He's dead. To have him dead reassures Macbeth, at least for the present, of *his own* safety, although Fleance, having escaped, is still a threat. A few scenes later, when Macbeth hears the news of Macduff's having "fled to England" and instantly resolves to "surprise" Macduff's "castle" and kill his family, his newfound ease at ordering multiple murders for self-protection is clear even to himself (4.1.142, 150). "From this moment" he announces, "The very firstlings of my heart shall be / The firstlings of my hand" (4.1.146–48). From here on out, he won't hesitate to kill.

Recalling many an athlete's motive for offering false testimony about doping, Macbeth's urgent need to feel secure gradually engulfs his sensitivity and remorse toward harming others. Macbeth and athletes like Jones learn too late about the self-defeating consequences of buying a little time with lies. As the witch Hecate tells the Weïrd Sisters, "you all know, security / Is mortals' chiefest enemy" (3.5.32–33). Someone who believes he's made "safe" by dishonest means is fooling himself.

Temptation

In dramatizing how Macbeth moves toward his addiction, Shakespeare portrays the universal complexities of temptation. One of the play's central questions involves tragic cause: what motivates Macbeth to murder Duncan? What roles do external forces—like the witches' prophecies and Lady Macbeth's taunting—play in relation to the hero's own agency, his will? Is Macbeth fated or does he choose freely? This question of cause proves as difficult to fathom in the play as it does in life. The degree to which an audience holds the tragic hero responsible for his choices determines how sympathetic that hero will appear.

6. "Vaulting ambition" 145

Whatever the external influences on Macbeth, he admits to being predisposed to murdering Duncan because of his "vaulting ambition," an internal character trait (1.7.27). Still, the witches exert undeniable power over him, playing upon his character. Before they encounter Macbeth and Banquo in 1.3, they drop several hints about the extent and nature of their control. In 1.3, the first witch, irritated with a "sailor's wife" who refuses to share her "chestnuts," fantasizes about how she'll take revenge by finding the husband's ship, at which point, she vows, "I'll do, I'll do, and I'll do"—words suggesting potency through action (1.3.4–10). Specifically, she'll curse the sailor with sleeplessness and cause him to become emaciated (1.3.18–25). Her extensive power, however, has limits: "Though his bark cannot be lost, / Yet it shall be tempest-toss'd" (1.3.24–25). At the moment Macbeth enters, all three sisters proclaim, "the charm's wound up," another phrase suggesting the witches' sway over Macbeth: the original meaning of "charm" is a spell or incantation exerting power, and "wound up" refers to its being "ready for action" (1.3.37, "Charm," n. to 1.3.37). Once they have Macbeth's attention, they influence him with their predictions that he'll become both Thane of Cawdor and Scotland's king (1.3.49–50). Three times he's referred to as being "rapt" in their presence, an indication of how compelling he finds them (1.3.57, 142, 1.5.6). He is, in effect, "charmed."

Macbeth's treason could be construed as fated through his inheriting the title "Thane of Cawdor" from a traitor. But a more obvious factor shaping Macbeth is his wife, who is introduced as she reads his letter to her aloud in 1.5. Shakespeare's dramatic strategy here is worth noting. For one thing, her lone appearance on stage enables the audience to learn something authentic about her before she goes to work on her husband in line 54—for example, her opinion that Macbeth's "nature" is "too full o' th' milk of human kindness" to allow him to advance himself by committing violence (1.5.16–17). For another thing, despite Macbeth's absence in this scene, she nonetheless has a dramatic interaction with him. As she intermittently responds to his letter, she indirectly indicates Macbeth's intentions and motives. What's more, the audience has already encountered Macbeth repeatedly—both indirectly (1.2) and directly (1.3, 1.4)—before being introduced to Lady Macbeth. As a result, the audience will have formed an attachment to Macbeth, most likely a sympathetic one, before they meet his wife and learn of her plans to urge him toward murder.

Chief among the questions about Macbeth's motives is why he has written to his wife about his encounter with the Weïrd Sisters. On some level, he may be *inviting* her to encourage his murder of Duncan. By referring to her in his letter as his "dearest partner of greatness," he may be tempting *her* to tempt *him* because, as he discloses two scenes earlier, he can neither succumb to nor resist the witches' temptation without assistance (1.5.11). As he observes to himself, "This supernatural soliciting / Cannot be ill; cannot be good" (1.3.130–31).

As the same private speech continues, he confesses to already having thoughts about murdering Duncan (1.3.134–37), thoughts that seem intensified once the king, in the next scene, names Malcolm as his successor (1.4.35–42). Feeling blocked from the position he believes is promised to him, Macbeth refers to his "black and deep desires" before he has written to his wife or seen her in 1.5 (1.4.51). Shakespeare's portrayal of Macbeth's temptation as a mixture of his own ambition and others' "soliciting" of him realistically mirrors how an athlete's hopes for himself and nudging from coaches and trainers can combine in the temptation to abuse performance-enhancing drugs. If Macbeth's letter is subtly soliciting Lady Macbeth's seduction of his darker side, the line between his agency and hers becomes even more blurred than it is already by her pointed provocations, many of which call his manhood into question.[2]

Gender

Issues of gender permeate the play, including Banquo's confusion over the witches' gender: "You should be women, / And yet your beards forbid me to interpret / That you are so" (1.3.45–47). A similar confusion of gendered traits attends Lady Macbeth, who, before urging her husband to kill Duncan, summons "spirits / That tend on mortal thoughts," to "unsex me here" (1.5.40–41). When she bids those spirits, "Come to my woman's breasts, / And take my milk for gall," she may not be praying to become more masculine, but rather, to exchange her humanity altogether for inhuman cruelty, without "compunctious visitings"—without, that is, the interference of humane remorse (1.5.47–48, 45). However we understand her command to the "murth'ring ministers," she and the witches tend to break down traditional categories of gender, thereby causing Shakespeare's original audience (and possibly his current audience) some discomfort (1.5.48).

At several points, Lady Macbeth's identity as a mother is mentioned, but only in passing, leaving open the question of whether she has indeed, as she says in 1.7, "given suck" to at least one child and "knows / How tender 'tis to love the babe that milks me" (1.7.54–55). Has she lost a child? Has she killed a child, as she seems prepared to do in 1.7 when urging Macbeth to follow through on murdering Duncan?:

> I would, while it was smiling in my face,
> Have pluck'd my nipple from his boneless gums,
> And dash'd the brains out, had I so sworn as you
> Have done to this [1.7.56–59].

Macbeth (Alec Baldwin) is seduced by Lady Macbeth (Angela Bassett) in a production at New York's Joseph Papp Public Theater, 1998.

Could she be compensating for the loss of a child by killing Duncan and instating Macbeth, as well as herself, in his place? That such questions about Lady Macbeth's relationship with children remain unresolved in the playscript hasn't stopped critics from contemplating them by virtue of their potential significance.[3] What seems clearer is that, when Lady Macbeth's viciousness prompts Macbeth to respond, "Bring forth men-children only!" he alludes to a fearlessness that more commonly characterizes military men in battle than domestic women (1.7.72). The "undaunted mettle" he attributes to her is precisely the trait she repeatedly ridicules him for lacking, thus goading him into action (1.7.73). "What?" she later attempts to shame him when he reels from seeing Banquo's ghost in 3.4, "quite unmann'd in folly?" (3.4.72).

Chief among the ironies of Lady Macbeth's belittling is that, in war, Macbeth is "Valor's minion" and "Bellona's bridegroom," virtually married to the (virginal) goddess of war by that name (1.2.19, 54). He is anything but unmanly. But as a civilized person, he distinguishes between violence licensed by war—in particular, protecting Scotland against rebellion by the Thane of Cawdor—and treasonous violence whose immorality encompasses the violation of a house guest by his "host" (1.7.14). In this regard he resembles an athlete who must differentiate between using force legitimately in the context of open competition and misusing power, at the cost of the entire team, for self-advancement or to thwart a competitor. Lady Macbeth's initial ability to overlook the distinction between sanctioned and unsanctioned violence also turns ironic, though, when she confesses that she couldn't kill Duncan herself because he "resembled" her father "as he slept" (2.2.12–13).

Ultimately, the deep-seated revulsion toward murder that she struggles so mightily to ignore in earlier scenes catches up with her, resulting in her mad sleep-walking and inability to "sweeten" the smell of her blood-stained "little hand" (5.1.50–51). Until such time as her guilt smothers her, however, she practices no little manipulation on Macbeth with insults to his masculinity. "When you durst do it," she says, in reference to his fading resolve to commit Duncan's murder, "then you were a man" (1.7.49).[4]

Lady Macbeth's needling resembles reports of Lance Armstrong's bullying fellow cyclists from admitting that they, along with him, had doped in numerous races they won. According to *New York Times* writer Juliet Macur, "Armstrong managed to keep the dark side of his athletic success quiet … by using guile and arm-twisting tactics that put fear in those who might cross him" (A14). Former Armstrong teammate Floyd Landis, who had lost his 2006 Tour de France title when he failed a drug test, spent years denying his, Armstrong's, and others' doping before finally confessing to Tour of California director Andrew Messick in 2010. In explaining to Messick why he had kept silent for so long, Landis said, "When you're in the mafia and you get caught and go to jail, you keep your mouth shut, and the organization takes care of your family. In cycling, you're expected to keep your mouth shut when you test positive, but you become an outcast. Everyone just turns their back on you" (qtd. in Macur A1). Ultimately, Macbeth, even more than his wife, enters into the culture of using threats to manipulate fellow abusers, like the murderers in act 3. But because such abuse of power stems from cowardice, it turns out to be anything but manly.

Agency

In the last analysis, determining exactly how much of Macbeth's decline owes to his own choices, versus forces acting upon him, is impossible. Yet some combination of the two is clearly at work, such that external influences conspire to tap into the darkest recesses of his psyche. Do the Weïrd Sisters seek him out as especially vulnerable for his ambition, his malleability, and

Macbeth (Raúl Juliá) is seduced by the Weïrd Sisters in a New York Shakespeare Festival production, 1990.

his capacity for evil? Here again, although one witch says of Macbeth that "Something wicked this way comes," the text doesn't provide a definitive answer (4.1.45). But, through Banquo, it glances at the possibility that any man, put in Macbeth's position, might fall prey to temptation.

To an extent, Banquo is Macbeth's foil: he helps foreground Macbeth's immorality because he, too, hears the witches' prophecy, but doesn't commit murder in order to fulfill it. At the same time, however, the prediction given to Banquo—that his offspring will be "kings"—is different from the prophecies imparted to Macbeth in that Banquo's involves less ego and suggests less urgency (1.3.67). It is thus less immediately seductive. Banquo, moreover, appears tempted in his own right when he recognizes that the prophecies of Macbeth's future have become realized (3.1.1–10). "May they not be my oracles as well," he wonders to himself about the witches, "And set me up in hope?" (3.1.9–10).[5] His failure to expose Macbeth's murders, of which he's clearly aware (3.1.1–3), also indicates his complicity in Macbeth's crimes and his own ambitions, as noted critic A. C. Bradley discusses (301–08). Banquo's passivity reflects Lance Armstrong's teammates' similar failure to act, as well as the firewall constructed by and around groups of professional athletes who either resist or fear turning in a fellow player.

Banquo doesn't survive long enough to demonstrate whether he might follow Macbeth's path. But several times after both characters have encountered the witches in 1.3, Macbeth signals to Banquo that he'd like the opportunity to discuss their experience—once at the end of 1.3 (lines 153–55); again in 2.1.21–24, where he misleadingly tells Banquo he doesn't think about the witches; and possibly a third time in 3.1.20–22, just before he plots with Banquo's murderers. A single instance of this sort might be brushed off as insignificant, but the repetition of Macbeth's stated desire to confer with Banquo about the witches poses the intriguing possibility that, had opportunity permitted, such a conversation might have countered the effects of the witches and of Lady Macbeth and deterred Macbeth from some or all of his destructive choices. One could object that, had Macbeth truly wanted Banquo's advice, he would have created the opportunity, as he does in connection with Lady Macbeth through his letter (1.5). Still, perhaps Macbeth's doom isn't fully sealed until he has Banquo killed. In myriad ways, then, the matter of Macbeth's motivation is left perplexingly, but engagingly, open-ended.

The same ambiguity hovers over many athletes who have used steroids and other performance-enhancing substances. Journalist Malcolm Gladwell reviews the 1998 court case of an East German swimmer, Christiane Knacke-Sommer, who alleged she was unknowingly administered anabolic steroids by her coaches prior to and during the 1980 Moscow Olympics, where she'd won the bronze medal for the 100-meter butterfly. Speaking of the coaches, who gave her little blue pills, Knacke-Sommer testified, "They told us they were vitamin tablets" (52). Referring to the coach who injected her, she added, "He said the shots were another kind of vitamin" (52). Knacke-Sommer's outcry during the trial that her coaches "destroyed my body and my mind!" makes clear her preference never to have taken the massive doses of steroids that her coaches had forced upon her, and her testimony leaves little room for doubt that, at age 15, she was subjected to steroids unawares (qtd. in Gladwell 52). Since her court case, however, many U.S. sports figures, including Marion Jones, have issued similar, though less convincing, disclaimers.

Jones' case in particular reflects Macbeth's story, although with something of a gender-reversal. C. J. Hunter, her husband during the 2000 Olympics and himself an Olympic shot putter, may have played the role of her Lady Macbeth. After having placed second in the 2000 U.S. Olympic trials, Hunter tested positive for banned substances and was thus disqualified from competing in Sydney, where Jones claimed the five medals she eventually had to return. Did Hunter encourage Jones' doping? Even after she admitted to lying to federal agents about being injected with "The Clear," she maintained that, at the time, she didn't know it was a designer steroid. She said her coaches had told her the injections were "supplements" like flax seed oil. Because Hunter had coached Jones at UNC–Chapel Hill, where she was a student-athlete, her testimony indirectly incriminated him. In 2009, after serving her six-month prison sentence, Jones persevered in this mode, stating in an interview with Oprah Winfrey, "Never knowingly did I take performance-enhancing drugs."

Oprah's response, "That is really hard to believe," raises doubts that Jones could have been as passively acted upon by others as she contends. One factor leading to Jones' conviction for perjury was Hunter's testimony that he had seen her inject herself in her stomach with "The Clear." If he was truthful, then, contrary to her version of the story, she actively and knowingly chose to enhance her performance. True enough, Hunter could have contradicted Jones on the matter of her awareness for his own self-interested reasons, including his bitterness over the couple's divorce in 2002, her statements that his own positive drug tests damaged her reputation, and her testimony implying that he forced steroids on her without her knowledge.[6] Where responsibility lies for her original entanglement with doping is as murky as the question of *Macbeth*'s tragic cause.

While other athletes have made claims similar to Jones' about being misled by trainers and coaches, still others have openly admitted to steroid use for motives including justifying high salaries and medicating injuries to continue participating in their respective sports.[7] In his book *My Prison Without Bars*, Pete Rose discusses his addiction to gambling as a way to avoid depression (e.g., 122). Baseball great Mickey Mantle says much the same thing about his drinking in "Time in a Bottle," a moving autobiographical piece published by

Marion Jones on *Good Morning America*, 2008.

Sports Illustrated in 1994. He used it as a shield against "loneliness and emptiness" on the road, as a way to cope with his father's illness, and as a means of escaping his feelings (69, 72, 76). "I've always tried to avoid anything emotional—anything controversial, anything serious—" he wrote, "and I did it through the use of alcohol" (76). Many addictions—whether to the results of steroids or to gambling, alcohol, or sex—have been viewed more as diseases than choices, thus mirroring all the more the confusion of tragic responsibility in *Macbeth*.

Equivocation

Not surprisingly, those sports figures who are most open about having made poor choices are also those who tend to be most apologetic, remorseful, and interested in making amends, rather than excuses. Mickey Mantle tops the list. In his essay "Time in a Bottle," he recounts the inestimable toll his drinking took on his career, his family, and his health. Near the end of his life, following a liver transplant that delayed his death by only months, Mantle recovered enough to hold a press conference at the hospital. Acknowledging that fans had viewed him as a role model, he said, "This is a role model: don't be like me." Mantle's brutal honesty about himself is rare by any standard, but especially for a figure who stands to lose so much esteem from his disappointed fans. Easier routes for him would have been ones many other celebrity athletes travel, those of rationalization, self-justification, or outright lying.[8]

These forms of dishonesty are often referred to in *Macbeth* as "equivocation." Tragedy commonly hinges on the hero's inability to perceive accurately, and *Macbeth* is no exception. The focus of this problem for Macbeth is the witches' prophecies, which in 1.3 and 4.1 are technically true, but misleading because they omit context or information crucial to understanding them. From the start, the witches are associated with such equivocation. "Fair is foul, and foul is fair," they chant together in the play's first scene (line 11). Like their ambiguous gender, remarked upon in 1.3, their confusing communications are categorized as unnatural, allied with the devil. "I ... begin / To doubt th' equivocation of the fiend / That lies like truth," says Macbeth when, late in the play, Birnan wood appears to be marching directly up the hill to Dunsinane, although the witches implied in 4.1 that such would never be the case (5.5.41–43, 4.1.90–94).

As Macbeth sinks deeper into sin and becomes more motivated to hide his crimes, he resorts to increasingly dishonest language that echoes the equivocation of the witches and the "fiend." This decline begins in 2.2, where, having completed Duncan's murder, he is still obviously capable of remorse. When he hears the knocking at his castle's door, he wishes it would "Wake Duncan" from death (2.2.70 s.d., 71). Soon after, however, when faced with detection of his guilt, he lies to Lennox and Macduff about why he killed the guards outside Duncan's door, whom he's falsely accusing of the murder, by saying that, in the heat of the moment, his passion got the better of his reason (2.3.108–18).

Over time, Macbeth's lies come to him as easily as killing. *Macbeth* traces the descent of a man whose conscience might have curtailed his evil acts into a state of spiritual paralysis, egomania, and, finally, despair, the unpardonable sin.[9] Eventually, he changes positions with Lady Macbeth, crisscrossing her in his habituation to evil and his ability to "Stop up ... remorse" (as Lady

Macbeth once called upon dark spirits to do for her) while she goes mad with guilt (1.5.44, 5.1). The couple end in the same place, she presumably killing herself out of despair, he too steeped in both blood and despair to feel anything (5.5.7–8, 3.4.135–37).

Ironically, the man who was once so concerned with his own "safety" becomes numb to such worry. "I have almost forgot the taste of fears," he says when he hears the scream that marks Lady Macbeth's suicide (5.5.9). When her death is confirmed, his line "She should have died hereafter" confirms his emotional bankruptcy (5.5.17). What difference does it make when someone dies if life is meaningless, only "a tale / Told by an idiot, full of sound and fury, / Signifying nothing" (5.5.26–28)?

Before they die, both characters' decaying spirituality is metaphorically represented by disease. Of Lady Macbeth's malady, a doctor tells Macbeth, "Therein the patient / Must minister to himself" (5.3.45–46). Only she can cure herself, in other words, through penitence, an outlook the doctor in her sleep-walking scene reinforces: "More needs she the divine than the physician" (5.1.74). Macbeth's moral disease is contagious, affecting the entirety of Scotland. Examples include 2.4, in which all of nature rebels in response to Macbeth's murder of Duncan, and Macbeth's later fantasy that the doctor might "cast / The water of my land" (a figurative reference to analyzing urine for disease) to find out why "the thanes fly" away from him (5.3.49–51). Like those who were intimidated by Lance Armstrong, the Gentlewoman who accompanies the doctor to watch and hear Lady Macbeth's sleep-walking episode in 5.1 is so stricken with fear of Macbeth's tyranny that she won't repeat what she's previously heard her mistress say in her sleep. Because she has "no witness to confirm my speech," she refers the doctor to his own observations (5.1.17–18). Scotland's widespread illness—often represented by sheer terror—reflects and originates in Macbeth's diseased behavior.

The antidote to such disease on an individual level is confession and contrition, as opposed to equivocation. Macbeth elects instead a fight to the death, misunderstanding the witches' prophecy that "none of woman born / Shall harm" him until he meets Macduff in battle (4.1.80–81). But his failure to escape a man "from his mother's womb / Untimely ripp'd" points beyond itself to a larger failure of understanding (5.8.15–16).[10] Macbeth's tyranny and lies are subject to the judgment of a higher power, working through Malcolm and Macduff and, in a sense, even the Weïrd Sisters. Equivocate though he might to his subjects, Macbeth can't evade the truth that he suspects all along. "It will have blood, they say," he acknowledges after he's been visited by Banquo's ghost, "blood will have blood" (3.4.121). Whether he openly admits to his crimes, they will be found out and punished.

Shakespeare conveys this most serious of ideas in the least likely place—through the Porter's comic monologue in 2.3. One of the most coveted bit parts in all of Shakespeare's plays, the Porter, feeling the effects of heavy drinking, opens the castle gate to Macduff and Lennox and regales them with a round of lewd jokes about the effects of alcohol on the libido (2.3.20 s.d., 24–36). On his way to answer their knock, the Porter casts himself in the role of the proverbial devil who guards hell's gate and imagines he's answering the knock of an "equivocator" who's been condemned to his realm (2.3.1–21). In addition to alluding to recent history, in which Jesuits sought to avoid self-incrimination through ambiguous testimony ("equivocation"), the passage also speaks broadly to the futility of evading blame.[11] The Porter's reference to an "equivocator" who "could swear in both the scales against either scale," comes just after Macbeth has murdered Duncan and just before Macbeth's first outright lie (2.3.8–9). It thus not only implicates Macbeth for "committ[ing] treason enough for God's sake," but also foretells his exposure (2.3.9–10). Neither the "equivocator" in question—nor Macbeth—"could ... equivocate to heaven" (2.3.10–11).

The Thane of Cawdor doesn't try to, and his example yields a crucial contrast to Macbeth's. Although a proven traitor like Macbeth, he's finally a truer foil for Macbeth than is Banquo because he's gone to his death fully "confess'd" of "his treasons" (1.4.5). Cawdor earns dignity and respect in his last hour, answering his trespass with his life as if it were "a careless trifle" (1.4.11). By contrast, Macbeth's enduring denial and shame warrant Macduff's naming him "hell-hound" (5.8.3).

The religious framework invoked by *Macbeth*'s examination of morality may seem alien to the world of today's sports. But the correspondence between how Macbeth conceals his crimes and an array of sports figures who are either known or, like Jones, suspected equivocators is undeniable. Mark McGwire, insisting that his steroid use was meant to manage injury, maintains that, even without the drugs, he would have broken the record for single-season home-run hits in 1998. Public allegations of doping that persistently clung to Lance Armstrong, named the winner of the Tour de France seven consecutive times, finally prevailed when the cyclist announced he was tired of the back-and-forth with his accusers. Throughout the ordeal, his response to accusations was equivocal at best, at worst untruthful. Editorialist Peter St. Onge asserted in the *Charlotte Observer* that, when Armstrong gave up, he as much as admitted guilt. "That's the thing about cheaters—" St. Onge wrote, "getting the win ... is more important than actually winning" (14A).[12]

In what's perhaps the most offensive breach of trust in recent memory, Penn State football coach Joe Paterno covered up what he knew about assistant coach Jerry Sandusky's repeated sexual molestation of boys on the university's premises.[13] In editorialist Maureen Dowd's view, Paterno is the "tragic figure in the case"—on the order of Macbeth—who sold his soul for a flourishing and lucrative athletic program that was lining his own, individual pockets as well as Penn State's. Paterno, known for quoting Shakespeare "in his Brooklyn accent," convinced Graham Spanier, President of Penn State, and other university officials to forbid Sandusky from bringing boys to campus rather than report him to authorities. It was a bargain that, in effect, turned a blind eye to Sandusky's abuse. Paterno's addiction to what Dowd calls "the brand and their cash cow" was also a temptation to abuse power every bit as compelling as Macbeth's—so compelling that Paterno "put his own reputation above the welfare of children." Spanier and his cohort colluded in the bargain.[14]

The protectionism evident in the Penn State case is an extreme version of schools' widespread tendency to shield athletes from charges of sexual misconduct. One famous case involved the Steubenville, Ohio, high school football team, members of whom were charged with raping a 16-year-old woman from West Virginia after she had passed out from drinking alcohol. Steubenville residents, extremely attached to their team, rallied around the young men and sought to vilify the young woman, who had clearly been incapable of giving consent to sexual activity, rather than hold the players responsible. Ariel Levy, who has written about the case at length, describes Steubenville as living through the success of the football team. The town may be severely economically depressed, she writes, "But in football Steubenville is triumphant" (40).

While not all athletic teams are subject to the same insulation from responsibility, they receive a disproportionate number of complaints of sexual assault in comparison with the overall male population in high schools, colleges, and universities. Much as Macbeth is for a time immune from acknowledging his crimes because of his royal power to enact retribution, so are male athletes sometimes protected from their female accusers because of the perceived stature of their athletic prowess and accomplishments. In 3.6 of *Macbeth*, a muted conversation between Lennox and another Lord reveals that, to date, no one has dared confront Macbeth for being a "tyrant" (3.6.22, 25). They speculate about the trouble Macduff has brought upon himself for not answering Macbeth's summons and fleeing to England instead (lines 40–43). In comparison, women who have been sexually abused by men of unusual power—whether athletic, political, or economic in origin—often shrink from complaining or, once they have complained, find themselves overwhelmed and even attacked by prestigious men and their network of supporters.

An athlete doesn't have to be an addict in order to prove toxic to his team. Terrell Owens, a wide receiver who has played for San Francisco, Philadelphia, Dallas, Buffalo, and Cincinnati, is now over 40 and, despite being in excellent shape and ready to play football again, couldn't find a team to take him while he was still capable of playing. When he left the Bengals after a year with a torn ACL, he wasn't invited to return. "It's not his knee that's the problem," said an anonymous higher-up with a major NFL team, "it's his attitude" (qtd. in Hass). Owens committed too many affronts to players on his own and other teams to be given another chance, including disrespectfully celebrating touchdowns atop the Dallas star logo in 2000. From an early age, Owens' grandmother, who raised him, taught him never to apologize. "If there's one word Owens can't abide, it's regret," writes reporter Nancy Hass. In one last career move, Owens played for the Allen Wranglers of the Indoor Football League, from which he was released in 2012. This last affiliation represented a definite come-down.

The history of Pete Rose's confessing to his gambling could constitute a play unto itself. His reason for coming clean in 2004, after 14 years of denial,

Cincinnati Reds switch hitter Pete Rose at bat, 1967.

seemed to many of his critics suspiciously like a last-ditch effort to be voted into the Baseball Hall of Fame. The confession—which included his ongoing self-justification for betting on his own team (the Cincinnati Reds) only to win, never to lose—wasn't just tardy, but also too convenient. What's more, Rose conducted the confession in a book from which he stood to profit handsomely. Said sports reporter Hal McCoy, "He writes a book that will make him a lot of money. That's Pete, vintage Pete" (qtd. in Dodd).[15] A Baptist minister put Rose's case in religious terms savoring of those in *Macbeth*. "His [prolonged] lying ... suggests that his admission of wrongdoing lacks a purity of character," said the Rev. Robert Parham. "Divine justice should not be confused with cheap earthly grace" (qtd. in Dodd).

Redemption

Although Macbeth avoids confession and conversion, the spiritual disease with which he's infected Scotland avails itself of another cure: the dedication of other political leaders to the nation's welfare. England's King Edward represents the polar opposite of self-centered Macbeth. Known as Edward the Confessor for his legendary healing of citizens suffering from "the evil"— scrofula, a form of tuberculosis—he has provided Malcolm with asylum from Scotland and with troops to advance against Macbeth (4.3.146). Malcolm describes Edward in saintly terms that contrast with those clinging to the witches: "He hath a heavenly gift of prophecy, / And sundry blessings hang about his throne / That speak him full of grace" (4.3.157–59).[16]

Malcolm too is a spiritual-political healer. The very purpose of 4.3 is to clarify his, as well as Macduff's, concern for Scotland's future above all competing personal concerns, whether self or family. Although one contemporary director of Shakespeare's plays has referred to the "England scene" as the "most boring scene in all of Shakespeare" (and therefore a major challenge in performance), it is not only a crucial scene, but, once its subtleties are brought to light, a far more interesting one than it may at first appear.

During the earlier part of the scene, Malcolm tests Macduff on the matter of his commitment to the country, as, to a degree, Macduff is also testing Malcolm. The most difficult aspect of the testing for a reader to understand involves Malcolm's *falsely* describing himself as more riddled with "vice" than Macbeth, including with "voluptuousness," "avarice," and tyranny (4.3.51, 61, 78, 91–100). Because Malcolm wants to ensure that Macduff's loyalty is to neither of them individually, but to Scotland collectively, Malcolm falsely accuses himself in hopes he'll make Macduff reject him on grounds that he's too corrupt to lead his people. If Macduff finds Malcolm's (false) self-description too objectionable to accept, he'll have passed Malcolm's test.

After a point, Macduff does just that. At first, Macduff accepts Malcolm's self-described appetite for women, and, then, more reluctantly, Malcolm's professed greed (4.3.66–76, 84–90). But when Macduff hears Malcolm attest that he lacks a long list of "king-becoming graces"—"justice, verity, temp-'rance, stableness" and the like—he reaches his breaking point, crying, "O Scotland, Scotland!" (4.3.91–92, 100). When Macduff declares Malcolm unfit not only to "govern," but to "live," he has passed Malcolm's test (4.3.102–03). Satisfied that Macduff is pure of heart, Malcolm explains that he made up the "taints and blames" he "laid upon" himself (4.3.124). Malcolm is now convinced that Macduff cares more about Scotland than himself, and he's demonstrated his own similar loyalties to Macduff.

Another important aspect of Malcolm's testing in 4.3 concerns Macduff's explanation of why he left his "precious" wife and children in Scotland, alone, imperiled, and without a farewell (4.3.26–28). Of all the questions *Macbeth* raises, this one is perhaps the most perplexing. In the preceding scene, Macbeth's hired murderers have slain Macduff's family, unbeknownst to Malcolm and Macduff at the start of 4.3, and Lady Macduff's confusion about why her husband has deserted them speaks for the audience, as well. Despite her son's innocent defense of his father and the loyalty to her husband she exhibits in her own dying words, she goes to her death supposing his abrupt departure was cruelly self-serving, the act of a "traitor" (4.2.81–83, 44–45).

The playscript doesn't provide clear evidence that Macduff's flight to England was either thoroughly considered or justified. As 4.3 unfolds, his motives for leaving as he did appear to be his commitment to Scotland above all else and perhaps also his fear of jeopardizing his loved ones with information about his whereabouts. But, as Malcolm implies early in the scene, Macduff doesn't seem to have appreciated how vulnerable he made his family simply by vacating his home, where they remained defenseless (lines 26–28). (Rosse's hasty departure in 4.2—which appears motivated merely to avoid crying like a woman—raises a similar question (lines 28–30).) When Macduff learns of his family's slaughter in the latter part of the "England scene," his shock seems almost unbelievable (4.3.201–19). How could he have failed to see it coming? The audience, of course, has the privileged knowledge of what has happened at Macduff's castle in 4.2 and yet might still balk at Macduff's naïveté.

Nevertheless, Macduff's dedication to Scotland, even at the cost of sacrificing his family, seems enough to exonerate him, at least in Malcolm's eyes. Macduff's choice of his country over his private concerns opposes Macbeth's and aligns him with Malcolm, who tells him, "What I am truly / Is thine and my poor country's to command" (4.3.131–32).

Macduff's self-sacrifice is also bound up in the play's larger exploration of manliness, which, in the end, isn't defined as the courage to commit murder, as Lady Macbeth tries to convince her husband in the play's opening acts. How it's defined instead seems variable, even open to contradiction. On one hand, it's precisely the willingness to sacrifice oneself and one's private good for the country's welfare that we observe in Macduff. We see it again as such in young Siward, who, in Rosse's estimation, becomes a "man" at the very moment he gives his life defending Scotland (5.9.5–9). On the other hand, the concept of manliness entails feeling deeply, even if emotion threatens to interfere with serving the nation effectively. When Lady Macduff declares that her husband "wants the natural touch," she criticizes what she perceives as his lack of feeling—an inhumanity eventually shared by the Macbeths (4.2.9).

In 4.3, Malcolm himself seems to equivocate on these conflicting notions of feeling and manliness. At first he encourages Macduff to give full vent to his "grief" when he learns of his family's murder, although in the next breath he discourages Macduff from feeling his loss and urges him instead to "Dispute it like a man" (4.3.208–10, 220). At this point, Macduff grants himself the right to "feel it as a man" (4.3.221).[17] In this instance as well as others, having strong feelings and curbing those feelings aren't necessarily so much at odds as they are inter-dependent. What's more, "man" in Macduff's line may more accurately connote "human" than the specific gender. In a line that reads almost as an aside, Macduff observes about Macbeth, "He has no children," suggesting that Macbeth can't imagine the grief that the loss of a child could cause a parent (4.3.216). The same line could also glance at Malcolm, who would perhaps be more sympathetic to Macduff's loss if he had children, and the line calls attention to Macbeth's motive for killing all of Macduff's family. By the scene's end, Malcolm and Macduff seem to agree that the manly way for Macduff to feel his grief is to channel it into revenge upon Macbeth. When Macduff vows to cease crying and start fighting, Malcolm approves his choice: "This tune goes manly" (4.3.235).

Malcolm's care and caution in organizing his move against Macbeth's tyranny recalls what one of Lance Armstrong's teammates has said about why he waited such a long time before testifying to the rampant doping within the sport. In 2010, Jonathan Vaughters, who had remained silent for years, finally urged other cyclists to follow Floyd Landis in confessing to drug use if they were asked. Said Vaughters about delaying such testimony, "I waited and waited. It took a whole lot of patience and, frankly, it hurt me a lot over the years to hear people say I was weak for not speaking up. But I was waiting for an opening, and that opening was Floyd" (qtd. in Macur A14).

Much as a nation requires selfless cooperation among its members to thrive, so athletics depends upon players working together as a team. While sports history yields a good number of athletes who have persisted in denying they've chosen self over team, the stories of those who have changed can inspire and uplift. A sober Mickey Mantle announced his intentions to become "a good father and a good grandfather," to perform service work, and to start a foundation in memory of his deceased son (77). Marion Jones may never admit to knowingly taking steroids. But, determined to continue playing sports, she joined a WNBA team, the Tulsa Shock, for which she began training in 2009, just months after the birth of her daughter (and from which she was released in 2011) (*Marion Jones*). What's more, while completing her sentence of 800 hours of community service, she found she loved working with teenagers too much to quit. She's continuing her work with Take a Break, a community-outreach program aimed at helping young people make good

Cyclist Lance Armstrong in competition, c. 2005.

choices. "Doing this is absolutely a part of a healing process," Jones has said. "There are days when I wake up and the first thing I think about is... Why? Why did you...? And then I pull myself up and come to an event or go and speak" (qtd. in Thompson).

While Jones' detractors may never feel she deserves credit for "healing" after severely harming her fellow Olympians, her tone markedly differs from Rose's about a past that hurt his team. "I'm sure that I'm supposed to act all sorry or sad or guilty now that I've accepted that I've done something wrong," Rose writes in his book. "But you see, I'm just not built that way" (qtd. in Dodd). Neither, over time, is Macbeth. Across the landscape of errant athletes who have partly or fully admitted to wrongdoing and those who haven't, a little apology goes a long way.

New York Yankees switch hitter Mickey Mantle at bat, 1962.

Discussion Questions for *Macbeth*

- Is Macbeth singled out by the witches as a man who is tempted to evil unusually easily? Or is he a representative human being? In other words, does the play suggest that, under similar circumstances, any member of the audience might do exactly as he does?
- What are the implications of each of the two options above?
- How responsible is Macbeth for his own fall, and how much can be attributed to external forces like the witches and Lady Macbeth? Where does the most convincing evidence emerge?

6. "Vaulting ambition" 163

- Lady Macbeth is one of the most coveted roles in the theater. Why should she be?
- As Chapter 6 indicates, Macbeth and Lady Macbeth "crisscross" morally during the play. Where do they meet in the middle before Lady Macbeth is crippled by guilt and Macbeth is inured to it? Is it the same place where Macbeth reaches the moral point of no return?
- As Chapter 6 also states, Shakespeare wrote *Macbeth* in part to compliment the recently crowned James I, who was thought to descend from Banquo's bloodline. James I was also the author of *Daemonologie* (1599), a book about witchcraft, in which the greater part of Shakespeare's audience would have believed. How does the play's meaning shift if the audience takes the witches as real?
- How does *Macbeth* explicitly and implicitly define good kingship? How might that definition apply to leaders and players on sports teams?
- The causes and morality of Macduff's choices in act 4 are debated at length in Chapter 6. Ultimately, does the play resolve all of the difficult questions arising from Macduff's actions? Some? None?
- On the face of things, Macduff deserts Scotland in order to rescue Scotland. Does sports history yield comparable examples of athletes who may appear to betray a team (or some other group or single person) in the process or in hopes salvaging the team?
- What items does a list of the play's stage properties include? Examples would be the letter from Macbeth that Lady Macbeth reads aloud in 1.5 and the witches' cauldron. What does each physical object suggest metaphorically?
- How do Macbeth's soliloquies in 1.7.1–28 and 2.1.33–64 show his progression toward evil?
- Sometimes a character will begin speaking in rhyme, as happens in Macbeth's speech at the end of 5.4—lines 46–51. What effect might these couplets have in theatrical performance?
- Should an actual, physical dagger appear to Macbeth in 2.1.33? Or should the audience have cause to wonder about Macbeth's state of mind because they can't see a dagger?
- In the same vein is a question about the appearance of Banquo's ghost in 3.4, where a stage direction explicitly calls for it to appear (3.4.36). But the scene can be (and has been) staged without the ghost's entrance, partly because Macbeth's responses to the apparition indicate what it is and partly because an audience today will tend to know the play well enough to understand that Macbeth is seeing Banquo's ghost. What difference does this staging choice make?

- Sports history yields countless examples of athletes who have made personal choices that have compromised or hurt their teams. What are some other stories of athletes who seem to have owned up to their mistakes and turned their lives around, even inspiring others to take similar action?

INSIDE SHAKESPEARE: *MACBETH* AND THE QUESTION OF EMPHASIS

One of the determinations a Shakespearean actor must make is which word or words to emphasize in speaking a line in order to convey the line's meaning to the audience. Sometimes, but not always, an emphasized word coincides with a stressed syllable in Shakespeare's blank verse—defined as unrhymed iambic pentameter. Deciding where the emphasis falls often involves trying out different possibilities side-by-side and choosing the one that finally seems to express the literal meaning of the line most clearly and accurately.

Decisions about emphasis usually involve deliberation and resist shortcuts. But shortcuts—or something akin to efficiency—are the very objective of guides that seek to help ambitious actors get started with Shakespeare's scripts. All such guides attempt simple, straightforward explanations of blank verse, and they offer tips for determining emphasis in a line. In *How to Speak Shakespeare,* for instance, Cal Pritner and Louis Colaianni suggest that aspiring Shakespearean actors

> Learn to stress both verbs and nouns, almost always putting slightly more stress on the verb than on the noun. This is a guide to communication. This relative emphasis helps the audience "get" the ideas you're expressing. Occasionally there will be exceptions; but this system of emphasis is dependable in helping the audience understand meaning.
> Remember, stress the *verbs* most, and stress the *nouns* almost as much!

In general, Pritner and Colaianni's advice is sound: if good writers know to pay most attention to strong verbs and nouns, then actors, for whom writers of drama write, would do well to follow suit. But exceptions to this rule are more than "occasional," and following this guideline as a rule can lead to an actor's missing important cues.

Consider, for example, Romeo's response to Juliet's wishing him "good night" in the balcony scene:

> O, wilt thou leave me so unsatisfied? [2.2.125].

Certainly the verb *leave* receives emphasis, but *unsatisfied*, an adjective, warrants even more. *Unsatisfied*, after all, gives the punch to the punch line.

This is but one of thousands of instances in which a word other than a noun or a verb is emphasized most, and as a relatively obvious instance, it is easier to catch than many others that might go unnoticed by a reader or an actor doggedly following a rule.

On occasion, a choice presents itself that can completely alter a line's meaning by shifting emphasis from one word to another. Macbeth's line on learning of Lady Macbeth's death is such an instance: "She should have died hereafter" (5.5.17). In the theater today, the actor playing Macbeth usually emphasizes *should*, implying that Lady Macbeth died at the wrong time, at a juncture when her death barely receives notice because of their chaotic circumstances. Better she should have died, as Macbeth's next line suggests, when "There would have been a time for such a word"—that is, when word of her death would have received more notice (5.5.18).

In an alternative reading, *should* is an auxiliary verb (or helping verb) and is not the word emphasized; *hereafter* is. In that case, the line is far more cynical, indicating that Lady Macbeth was going to die sometime, so why not today? What difference does the timing of death make if it's inevitable? That reading, opposed to the other one, is in keeping with the nihilism of the ensuing speech, "To-morrow, and to-morrow, and to-morrow…" (5.5.19-28). This second reading is the one assumed in Chapter 6 to be preferable in the discussion of the line. But if this second reading is less favored in the contemporary theater, one likely reason is that the use of *should* as an auxiliary verb has become archaic; today, we'd say *would* instead of *should* to mean "she was going to die sooner or later anyway." So what might have been the original meaning of the line is more difficult for a modern audience to discern.

Turning to editors does little to resolve the issue. Some come down decidedly in favor of the second reading (e.g., *The Riverside* editors). A few single out the first reading (e.g., *The Norton* editors). Many turn the choice between the two options over to the actor. Kenneth Muir, having remarked upon the line's ambiguity in the older Arden edition, oddly concludes that "Perhaps 'should' is used indifferently to denote either what will be or what ought to be" (5.5.17 n.). However indifferent an editor may be to the meaning of *should*, an actor must choose, and where the actor's emphasis falls—whether on *should* or *hereafter*—will communicate his meaning. This choice is particularly crucial, extending as it does not just to what the line says literally, but to the character's frame of mind and even his moral state as he says it. Either he still reserves some capacity to treat his wife with humanity or he's chillingly apathetic toward her passing. He cannot be both.

This discussion of emphasis is excerpted from a longer article, "Emphasis Added: Reading Shakespeare's Language Clearly," from Early Modern Culture *12 (2017).*

7
"Sea change"
The Tempest, Andre Agassi and Second Chances

Prisoners

As *The Tempest* opens, Prospero, once Duke of Milan, has lived for 12 years in a "cell" on an island inhabited only by his daughter, Miranda, a slave named Caliban, and Ariel, an airy spirit invisible to everyone but Prospero (1.2.20). Prospero explains in 1.2 that he was exiled from Milan by his brother, Antonio, and arrived on the island with the assistance of a faithful lord, Gonzalo (lines 66–168). Using his magical art and Ariel's help, Prospero summons a tempest in the first scene so as to shipwreck those who ousted him and to reinstate himself as rightful duke.

In his autobiography, *Open*, tennis star Andre Agassi describes his childhood home in Las Vegas as his "prison," his "cell," because his father bought a house with a yard big enough for a tennis court, where he confined Andre to endless hours of practice (33). Agassi's father began training him in the cradle. When he was four, his father lined up pros like Jimmy Connors to hit balls with him. When he was seven, his father made a machine called "the dragon" to hurl tennis balls almost too fast and furiously for him to return. He was expected to hit 2,500 of these balls a day. His father's relentless pushing and criticism took their toll. As an adult, Agassi could either remain stifled or free himself from his father's expectations and identify his own.

Prospero and Agassi have not only survived personal trials, but, through their long suffering, both arguably arrive at a better, more fulfilling, more enlightened place. *The Tempest* is profoundly concerned with the "sea change" that many characters undergo as a result of an ordeal—a thorough transformation, as Ariel's song to Ferdinand describes it, from something flawed or ordinary into a treasure, "something rich and strange" (1.2.401–02). Accordingly,

A conventionally royal Prospero (Raymond Massey) and Ariel (Roddy McDowall) in a Stratford, Connecticut, production of *The Tempest*, 1955.

both Prospero and Agassi eventually receive a kind of grace, a precious second chance. But before that, both cooperate unwittingly in creating their own troubles.

While Prospero didn't hate ruling Milan as much as Agassi says he hated tennis, he preferred the private pursuit of the "liberal arts" over public governing and thus, "transported / And rapt in secret studies," he "cast" his government on his brother, Antonio (1.2.73, 76–77, 75). Antonio, attests Prospero, was in the grip of "ambition" (1.2.105). But Prospero also acknowledges that, by "neglecting worldly ends," he "Awak'd an evil nature" in his brother, who came to think of himself as "indeed the Duke" (1.2.89, 93, 103). Prospero allowed himself to be distracted by contemplation and learning while Antonio and Alonso, King of Naples, plotted his exile (1.2.66–132).

Fittingly, in a work as pervaded by paradox as *The Tempest,* Prospero's misfortune leads to remedy and restoration. As he narrates his lengthy backstory to Miranda in 1.2, Prospero says the winds that once blew them to shore, like his enemies, "Did us but loving wrong": the difficulty he and Miranda have endured has also improved them (1.2.151). Again paradoxically, the very books that once stole Prospero's attention from ruling become his means of recovering his dukedom because they're the source of his magic. Yet he realizes throughout the play that regaining his rule will mean relinquishing his "book" and the magic it affords him (5.1.56–57).

Agassi, too, played a role in his own downfall. His hatred of tennis from an early age is perhaps the most startling revelation in *Open,* since he'd always seemed to convince the media of his devotion to the game. Yet rather than play for himself, he lived for public approval, beginning with his father's, which he never received. As Agassi tells his story, the more he played, the harder he drove himself, until one day he recognized, "I've internalized my father" (38). No longer did he need his father's bullying to make himself feel inadequate; he'd turned into his own worst enemy. Mirroring Prospero's paradoxical relationship with both magic and political rule, the key to Agassi's transformation was finding an approach to tennis that empowered and nurtured, rather than drained and frustrated, him. "The same court on which you suffer your bloodiest defeat," he writes, "can become the scene of your sweetest triumph" (333). Prospero and Agassi each returns to his "court" after acquiring hard-won self-knowledge.

Teeterers

Prospero's and Agassi's struggles, then, owe to internal demons that must be controlled before each can regain his lost stature. In both cases, the most obvious of those demons is perfectionism. In Prospero's case, his yen for contemplative solitude may well give rise to his perfectionist tendencies, since his book learning is abstract and idealistic, rather than based in the imperfect world of real, lived experience. Constantly wrestling with outsized expectations of themselves and others, these two figures set themselves up for both exceptional achievement and recurring disappointment. Given to erratic highs and lows, they alternately inspire admiration and evoke skepticism or outright repulsion. Prospero and Agassi constantly walk a line between faith and despair, pride and humility. Teeterers both, they act out inner conflicts that make them intriguingly dynamic one moment, brash and immature the next.

Agassi's ups and downs couldn't be any clearer in his record. In 1995, he was ranked the number one player in the world, and in 1996, he won an Olympic gold medal. By 1997, he had sunk to number 141. That same year, he began the rigorous training for a turnaround; by 1999, he rose again to number one. In 2003, when he captured number one yet again, he became the oldest male player in the history of world rankings to reach that position, as well as the oldest player in 31 years to win a major tournament, the Australian Open. Throughout his career, winning streaks gave way to abysmal losses, and bouts of losing yielded to spectacular wins.

Agassi's lowest point, 1997, was personal, as well as professional. His short-lived marriage to celebrity Brooke Shields, about which he'd always had doubts, ended. Around the same time, he started using crystal meth, which even then he realized was a way of avoiding the tennis game he loathed. "I get an undeniable satisfaction from harming myself," he writes about those days, "and shortening my career" (248). Eventually, he failed a drug test, but, through an equivocal letter, he managed to convince the Association of Tennis Professionals (ATP) that he'd accidentally drunk from a soda that one of his employees had spiked with meth (253–54, 269). Although he'd quit using drugs by the time the ATP accepted his falsified explanation, he kept battling the "loss of control" he feared and sometimes gave into—as, for example, when he occasionally used enough profanity on the court to be disqualified from play (181).

By his own account, Agassi's need for control was rooted in "perfectionism," a problem his coach told him could "end my career prematurely" (186). At one point, his anxiety about falling short focused on his famous hair. Pictures of him from the early '90s show him in a headband, a spray of highlighted hair escaping above it and, below, longer strands trailing down his back and shoulders. "Women love me for it," he writes, "men hate me for it" (198). When he started to lose it, he patched it with a hairpiece that interfered with his tennis game, a ploy he preferred over appearing in public with balding spots. Eventually, Brooke Shields convinced him to shave his head, promising he'd feel "liberated" (197). He took her advice, making his first move toward self-acceptance. But pride in his image, bred of his desire to be perfect, continued to hound him.

Prospero's great challenge is to hold such pride in check. He explains to Miranda in 1.2 that his scheme for retrieving his dukedom "doth depend upon / A most auspicious star" whose influence he must take advantage of while it lasts (1.2.181–82). He suggests that his own power, his magic or "art," is justified by serving—or perhaps collaborating with—a higher power than himself. Just a few lines earlier, he also tells Miranda that, 12 years earlier, they arrived safely on the island "By Providence divine," another acknowledgment of a force exceeding his own (1.2.159). Such instances of Prospero's humility are juxtaposed against his sense of superiority regarding his own abilities and the control he exerts through his magic. Rebuffing Miranda's pleas to "have pity" on Ferdinand, for example, he seems demanding and dismissive of his daughter: "What, I say, / My foot my tutor?" (1.2.475, 469–70).

Prospero is even more domineering and gruff with Ariel, whose precise relationship to his master is difficult to pin down. Whether he's an extension or projection of Prospero's creative faculties or a being completely independent of Prospero, they're clearly mutually dependent through a creative process in which Prospero envisions a plan that Ariel executes for him, down to every

Andre Agassi sporting his famous hair at the U.S. Open, 1994.

detailed command.[1] When Ariel expresses his desire to be freed from servitude, Prospero reminds him of how he rescued Ariel from far more restrictive circumstances (1.2.250-93). Sycorax, Caliban's mother, had punished Ariel by imprisoning him in a "cloven pine," where he remained in "torment" when she died (1.2.270-91). Prospero, then, feels entitled to Ariel's service in return. Even if he's right, calling Ariel such names as "malignant thing" and "Dull thing" seems arrogant, counter-productive (1.2.257, 285).

Prospero flirts constantly with such overreaching, although his testiness during the day or so that elapses in *The Tempest* is, apparently, more pronounced than usual because of the pressure he's under to complete his plan successfully. Miranda apologizes to Ferdinand for Prospero's uncustomary "anger" (4.1.144-45). In addition, some of Prospero's crabbiness is, by his own admission, an act. Although Prospero has hoped that Miranda and Ferdinand will fall in love at first sight, promising to free Ariel for making it happen, he fears the lovers' youthful innocence (1.2.441-43). So he tests them by seeming to disapprove of Ferdinand and to doubt Miranda's choice. "[T]his swift business / I must uneasy make," he explains to the audience, "lest too light winning / Make the prize light" (1.2.451-53). In other instances, however, Prospero's inflexibility and impatience lack clear justification, as when he berates Ariel. Teetering between humility and superiority, he fluctuates between exercising his powers responsibly and grasping for control he doesn't really possess. To receive his second chance at ruling and merely belonging to civil society, he must come to terms with this tension.

Monsters

Nowhere is Prospero's tendency toward pride more evident than in his relationship with Caliban, for whom Prospero reserves his harshest treatment. His disrespectful language for Caliban—"slave!" and "Thou earth, thou!"— is accompanied by "cramps" and "pinch[es] more stinging / Than bees," physical punishments for Caliban's slightest rebellion (1.2.313-14, 325, 329-30). Caliban, by his own account, was once the object of Prospero's affection and teaching, but now dreads Prospero's wrath and curses himself for ever offering the newcomers hospitality (1.2.331-39). From Caliban's perspective—and quite possibly the audience's—Prospero has colonized an island he stole from a native he first took advantage of and then enslaved.[2]

This view of Prospero and Caliban, however, can become one-sided and sentimental, overstating both Prospero's villainy and Caliban's victimization. It's complicated in the playscript in myriad ways. Most significant, as Caliban himself relates, Prospero trusted him and was kind to him until he attempted to rape Miranda (1.2.345-51).[3] In one sense, of course, Caliban is only following his natural instinct by trying to reproduce. On the other hand, Prospero wouldn't be much of a father if he didn't protect his daughter from rape or much of a man if he didn't expect civility from Caliban. Indeed, Prospero's assumption that Caliban will treat him and Miranda respectfully indicates his initial respect for Caliban, which Caliban's later actions invert. In regard to his unrestrained sexuality, Caliban is contrasted with Ferdinand, who, although tempted in the past by many courtly women, refrains from acting on his impulses with any of them, most especially Miranda, who, as both Ferdinand and Caliban attest, surpasses all women in desirability (3.1.39–48).

Repeatedly, Caliban comes across as an innocent—sometimes noble and pure and other times in dire need of education and a strong guiding hand. Although he lacks exposure to civilization, he is innately more astute and artistic than Stephano and Trinculo, clowns whose worldly experience counts for little. In his naïveté, Caliban accepts Stephano's liquor as a "celestial" elixir and Stephano (whose name, ironically, means "crown"), as a "god" (2.2.117). Yet before long Caliban's powers of perception clearly surpass those of Stephano and Trinculo, whom he's leading to murder Prospero so that they can seize the island. When his co-conspirators are attracted to the "*glistering apparel*" that Ariel has hung on a lime tree to tempt them, only Caliban discerns their true worthlessness (4.1.193 s.d.). "Let it alone," Caliban warns them of the flashy "wardrobe"; "it is but trash" (4.1.223–24).

In fact, Caliban's appreciation of real beauty, as opposed to "glister," approaches that of Prospero, Miranda, and Ariel (4.1.193 s.d.). It manifests itself in his recognition of Miranda's "beauty," although he has never seen any other woman but his mother, Sycorax, and it shows in his startling affection for the heavenly music Ariel releases on the island (3.2.100–03). "Be not afeard, the isle is full of noises," he tells Trinculo and Stephano when they all hear the mysterious music, "Sounds, and sweet airs, that give delight and hurt not" (3.2.135–36). That Caliban speaks these lines in verse further elevates him above his two companions, whose lines are consistently confined to prose.

Caliban's mastery of English, which may be his second language, belies Miranda's angry allegation that he can't learn, a speech so brutal it seems out of character. "Abhorred slave," she calls him, "Which any print of goodness wilt not take, / Being capable of all ill!" (1.2.351–53).[4] Prospero expresses similar impatience when Caliban conspires with Stephano and Trinculo to overthrow him. "A devil, a born devil," he fumes, "on whose nature / Nurture can never stick" (4.1.188–89). What accounts for this disparagement of Caliban, when he is clearly capable of learning? As susceptible to beauty as his counterpart, Ferdinand, Caliban is also disturbingly associated with belligerence, violence, and savagery—monstrosity, inside as well as outside.[5]

Although Caliban holds Prospero accountable for all the misery stemming from his servitude and says his only "profit" from learning Prospero's language is "know[ing] how to curse," the playscript resists such reductive interpretation (1.2.363–64). Ferdinand's easy acceptance of his servitude to Prospero in 3.1 purposefully contrasts with Caliban's unwillingness to submit to authority (although Ferdinand first opposes Prospero with a ferocity like Caliban's by drawing his sword), and Caliban has obviously learned more than how to curse in English, as his beautiful speech about the island's music reveals (1.2.467 s.d., 3.2.135–43).

At the same time, the audience suspects that Prospero's treatment of Caliban as a slave has become normative, intensifying Caliban's bad behavior. The slave/master and son/father paradigms recall Agassi's relationship with his father, who stoked his son's loathing of tennis and of himself by entrapping Agassi in ceaseless, nearly abusive training. Ironically, the harder Prospero bears down on Caliban, the more he himself resembles Caliban in his brutishness. Nowhere is this point clearer than when Prospero commands his spirits to track down and punish Caliban, Stephano, and Trinculo:

> Go, charge my goblins that they grind their joints
> With dry convulsions, shorten up their sinews
> With aged cramps, and more pinch-spotted make them
> Than pard or cat o' mountain [4.1.258–61].

Prospero's speech concerning Caliban is nearly indistinguishable from Caliban's for Prospero: "All the infections that the sun sucks up / From bogs, fens, flats, on Prosper fall, and make him / By inch-meal a disease!" (2.2.1–3).

In essence, Prospero and Caliban are at loggerheads. Each blames the other for his own abusiveness, and both are responsible for it. While projecting monstrosity onto each other, they ignore their own. Although Caliban remembers Prospero's initial kindness toward him, both have reached a point where neither can credit the other for any positive act or potential change (1.2.331–38). The upshot of this impasse for Caliban is his regrettable plot to assassinate Prospero and seize control of the island. The result for Prospero, whose magic will enable him to undermine Caliban's plot, is a counterproductive blindness to Caliban's potential goodness. Prospero's resulting despair over Caliban's inability to meet his perfectionist expectations is a form of pride every bit as monstrous in its own way as any of Caliban's attempted transgressions.[6]

Through such examples as Caliban, *The Tempest* joins many other Shakespearean plays in exploring the relationship between nature and nurture as they affect character development. At some points in the play, someone's character seems determined at birth, impervious to teaching or external influence. Of Antonio, Miranda says, "Good wombs have born bad sons," suggesting

A less than ducal Prospero (Raúl Juliá) and a tomboyish Miranda (Molly Ringwald) in a production of *The Tempest* for New York's Shakespeare in the Park, 1982.

that Antonio is simply a bad seed (1.2.120). At other points, a character seems malleable, capable of instruction and improvement, and subject to free will. When Ferdinand accepts the task of bearing logs for Prospero, he performs work unbefitting of a prince and yet key to winning Miranda's hand in marriage. His circumstances lead to decisions and actions that reward him for adapting. Ultimately, an enduring question in the play is whether the larger file of characters can reform, including Caliban, Prospero, and, most perplexingly, those who once usurped Milan from its rightful duke.

"Three men of sin"

Prospero's vexed relationship with Caliban is a frame for his relationship with his brother, Antonio. The villain and his two side-kicks, Alonso and Sebastian, are morally at least as monstrous as Caliban. One purpose of 2.1 is to demonstrate that, over 12 years, Antonio and Sebastian haven't changed for the better; they're now willing to murder Alonso in cold blood to capture rule of Naples, as Alonso once conspired with Antonio to usurp Milan from Prospero. The two characters' ridicule of Gonzalo is, like all juvenile bullying, funnier to them than to anyone else. Their insensitive and ill-timed blaming of Alonso for his son's presumed death at sea is unnecessarily hurtful, as Gonzalo points out (2.1.124–40).

When Prospero rescues Alonso from Antonio and Sebastian's intended execution, he's exercising his art in a morally responsible way: he's serving the higher, virtuous power from which his own, human power derives and upholding a greater good by preventing murder.[7] As Prospero proceeds to address the wrongs done to him by Antonio, Alonso, and Sebastian, however, his moral teetering between service and selfishness is evident. His goal is to bring these three men to penitence and conversion by making them vulnerable. But his temptation is to take advantage of their vulnerability and enact private revenge on them.

Alonso has been rendered vulnerable from the beginning through the supposed loss of his son, Ferdinand. Experiencing such loss will, by act 5, enable him to understand the loss he once inflicted on Prospero and Miranda. Antonio and Sebastian are tougher cases. Prospero works on them spiritually in one of the play's most spectacular scenes, 3.3, the "banquet scene." As 3.3 opens, the two hard-hearted conspirators are whispering about when they intend to kill Alonso (3.3.11–17). By the scene's end, they run off stage, "desperate," says Gonzalo, from "their great guilt" (3.3.104–06).

What's suddenly made them so prone to conscience? Prospero's presentation of the banquet works a kind of magic on them in stages. To prepare them, Prospero must first awaken their faith, their willingness to believe in what they see and hear, however alien and unthinkable. The sight of spirits bringing out the food, which would have been thought impossible, does just that. Sebastian, Antonio, and Gonzalo each, in turn, use the word *believe* to express their wonder at and receptiveness to the image (3.3.21, 24, 28).

Once the banquet has aroused the men's hunger and their willing belief, the food is abruptly removed and replaced with the threat of vengeance unless the men repent their wrongs.[8] In the shape of a harpy—a mythological figure, half bird, half woman, that snatches up criminals for punishment—Ariel appears amidst thunder and lightning to confront the transgressors with their crimes. Now they readily *believe* in Ariel as the voice of conscience. Ariel, in turn, pushes them to the brink, suggesting that they might kill themselves because he has made them "mad" and scoffing at Antonio and Sebastian for drawing their swords on him and his "fellows," who are untouchable "ministers of Fate" (3.3.59–61).

While Ariel's performance as a harpy is fearsome, his only real action is reminding the "three men of sin" of their "foul deed" (3.3.53, 72). Their activated imaginations do the rest. "But remember," intones Ariel as he recalls their cruelty toward Prospero and Miranda (3.3.68). Confronting them with their wrongs, he convinces them that their only escape from the "wraths" of the higher "pow'rs" is "heart's sorrow, / And a clear life ensuing"—penitence and conversion to a better future life (3.3.79, 73, 81–82). The alternative, "[l]ing-'ring perdition," is what they would bring on themselves if they remained unrepentant (3.3.77). All three men succumb to Ariel's suggestiveness, though Alonso, not surprisingly, is the most susceptible, since he believes Ariel's fabrication that Ferdinand has died as a result of his father's crimes (3.3.75–76, 100–02).

Alonso's admission that his past is "monstrous" uncouples monstrosity from appearance alone and portrays it as a spiritual state (3.3.95). Just a few speeches earlier, Gonzalo attests to the "gentle, kind" behavior of spirits who (to him) outwardly appear "monstrous" (3.3.29–34). While showing Prospero's magic to have worked upon these men as planned, Shakespeare continues to play with the concept of monstrosity as it also applies to Caliban and Prospero. At the scene's end, when Prospero observes, "mine enemies … now are in my pow'r," he raises the possibility of his own monstrosity, should he abuse his power over the others through revenge (3.3.89–90).

If Prospero's use of magic were to become about satisfying himself, rather than about leading the others toward enlightenment, then it would become tarnished by pride and lose legitimacy. But if Ariel truly is, as he says, a "minister of Fate," then, by extension, his service to Prospero in bringing the sinners to penitence serves a higher purpose than Prospero's personal vendetta (3.3.61). No doubt Prospero would like nothing better than to control his enemies much as he attempts to subjugate Caliban, and no doubt the audience can understand his urge toward vengeance. At this point, the audience waits to see whether a teetering Prospero will bear out Ariel's claim and tilt toward higher purposes.

Prospero's relationship with his brother, recapitulated in his relationship with Caliban, proves key to his self-discovery. Prospero, Antonio, and Caliban are a trio of secret sharers, all resembling one another in some respects. To deal with his feelings about Antonio, Prospero must come to terms with elements of himself reflected in his brother, as well as in Caliban. Specifically, Prospero must choose between forgiving Antonio or punishing him, giving him another chance to be trusted or doubting that he can ever be trusted again.

The rivalrous relationship between these brothers, though unique, also has universal application, as tension between any two people can lead either to irreconcilable differences or to greater self-knowledge and growth for each. In this regard, Andre Agassi's constant competition with tennis champion Pete Sampras, whom Agassi calls his "evil twin," parallels *The Tempest* (190). Although Agassi often felt that he couldn't escape Sampras, with whom he was matched in one finals round after another, the way Agassi learned to cope with Sampras' gift for beating him has much in common with how Prospero reconciles himself to a future with Antonio in it.

Letting Go

The process by which Prospero recovers his dukedom while dealing with moral issues progresses significantly in another of the play's spectacular scenes, 4.1. The Masque of Ceres, which he presents to Miranda and Ferdinand, celebrates their betrothal and warns repeatedly against premarital intimacy.[9] No matter how fervently Ferdinand promises not to sleep with Miranda before marriage, Prospero keeps reminding him not to (e.g., 4.1.14–31, 53–56). The content of the masque further discourages wanton sexuality through the assurance that Cupid, god of sexual love, is keeping a safe distance from the engaged couple.

The masque's moral lesson also involves the woe that can come to parents who aren't actively protecting their children's virginity. According to classical mythology, Dis (another name for Pluto), god of the underworld, kidnapped and raped Proserpina when her mother, Ceres, goddess of the harvest, wasn't paying attention. Ceres' concern in the masque over Cupid's whereabouts reflects her anxiety about having lost her daughter (4.1.86–91). When Iris, goddess of the rainbow, assures Ceres that Cupid has given up shooting his arrows to stir up illicit sexuality, she is also ensuring the chastity of the engaged couple who are a part of the masque's audience (4.1.91–101).

As a play-within-a-play, the masque mirrors concerns in the larger drama. The specific connection between the Masque of Ceres and *The Tempest* comes into focus once Juno and Ceres have blessed Miranda and Ferdinand's union and presented a *"graceful dance"* of nymphs (4.1.138 s.d.). When *"Prospero starts suddenly,"* he remembers "that foul conspiracy / Of the beast Caliban and his confederates," who aim to assassinate him and kidnap Miranda (4.1.138 s.d., 139–41). Just as suddenly, Prospero disrupts the masque and sends away the spirits who were acting and dancing in it (4.1.142). Apparently, the representation of Ceres' having lost her daughter out of inattention helps Prospero turn his focus from his artistic creation to his worldly duties—defending himself and his daughter. This seemingly small detail actually speaks volumes about Prospero's moral growth.

As Prospero has admitted to Miranda at the play's beginning (1.2), 12 years earlier he was oblivious to his own safety and to that of his child. He preferred the theoretical over the practical—a life removed from the worldly responsibilities of ruling and immersed in books. In 4.1, by contrast, he withdraws from the enticing world of art and fantasy in order to attend to his immediate, practical responsibilities. This is a marked change. Prospero's art remains as absorbing and inviting as ever, as is clear from Ferdinand's attraction to it. "Let me live here ever," says Ferdinand, about the island, the masque, or both. "So rare a wond'red father and a wise / Makes this place Paradise" (4.1.122–24). Ferdinand implies that the realm of imagination and entertainment is infinitely more enthralling than the mundane necessities entailed in ruling and surviving. But Prospero's interest in rescuing Miranda signals his having learned responsibility from his earlier mistake.

His paternal action also reveals his humility because it involves the artist's learning from his own art. Prospero's inclination to take control through his magic from behind the scenes can smack of the entitlement that breeds arrogance. An artist who thinks of himself as above the influence of his own art is a different sort from an artist who is subject to his own art's effects. Put another way, the moral artist understands he is an instrument of a higher good—an aid to Providence, or divine power. He also realizes that, while his art may encompass unchanging, enduring truths, it is human-made and therefore subject to the decay of the created, physical world. Prospero's famous speech about the transitoriness of this life, including "the great globe itself," reveals his awareness of his limitations. "We are such stuff / As dreams are made on," he tells Miranda and Ferdinand, "and our little life / Is rounded with a sleep" (4.1.156–58). Prospero's response to his own creation, the Masque of Ceres, intimates his strides toward inner reform.

Prospero makes more progress toward letting go in 5.1, but not without further teetering in 4.1. Here his cynical lines about Caliban's inability to learn, like his ugly commands to his spirits to punish Caliban, Trinculo, and Stephano physically, reveal his ongoing intolerance of other people and his temptation to abuse his power (4.1.188–93, 255–61). Prospero has trouble conceiving that he himself, as a human being, needs understanding and forgiveness. When Ariel informs him that he left the three clownish co-conspirators in a "filthy-mantled pool" with "Tooth'd briers, sharp furzes, pricking goss, and thorns" painfully stuck in their "frail shins," he paints a picture, not just of three battered characters, but of fragile humanity in general (4.1.180–82). Everyone has frail shins, and thus everyone needs compassion. But at the close of the scene, as he exits the stage to deal with the "three men of sin," Prospero could be intent on punishment. "At this hour," he tells Ariel, "Lies at my mercy all mine enemies," a line both ominous and yet noncommittal (4.1.262–63).

The decisive moment for Prospero occurs in his interaction with Ariel at the opening of 5.1. Ariel describes the men under Prospero's spell in movingly sympathetic terms:

> ARIEL: Your charm so strongly works 'em
> That if you now beheld them, your affections
> Would become tender.
> PROSPERO: Dost thou think so, spirit?
> ARIEL: Mine would, sir, were I human [5.1.17–20].

Ariel appeals to Prospero's sense of humanity, a humanity he shares with those who have wronged him, and coaxes him to view their frailty as grounds for mercy. Prospero does so:

> And mine shall.
> Hast thou, which art but air, a touch, a feeling
> Of their afflictions, and shall not myself,
> One of their kind, that relish all as sharply
> Passion as they, be kindlier mov'd than thou art? [5.1.20-24].

Not to be surpassed in compassion by an airy spirit, Prospero elects to show undeserved mercy to his transgressors: 'gainst my fury / Do I take part" (5.1.25-27). Refraining from lashing out, he settles on self-restraint. "The rarer action is / In virtue than in vengeance," he concludes, conceding to Ariel's promptings (5.1.27-28).

Andre Agassi writes in *Open* of equally instructive guidance from his second wife, German-born tennis prodigy Stefanie Graf (usually referred to as "Steffi" in the news media). Acting as his Ariel upon noting the repeated setbacks he suffered when he tried too hard to control his tennis game, she told him, "Stop thinking. Feeling is the thing. *Feeling*" (328). By over-intellectualizing his game, Agassi was choking. Neither was he enjoying himself. "You can't *try* to feel," Graf said. "You have to let yourself feel" (328). Stefanie's advice often came back to him during future competitions, steadying him and improving his play.

Prospero's options aren't exactly thinking or feeling, but, rather, two kinds of feeling: destructive "fury" or "tender" "affections" (5.1.26,19, 18). Still, Prospero aligns the compassion Ariel urges with his "reason," the faculty of thought (5.1.26). Ultimately, Stefanie and Ariel are encouraging something similar: letting go. The theme of freedom runs throughout *The Tempest*, whether it pertains to Ariel's and Caliban's desire to be free of Prospero's demands or to grace, the spiritual freedom bestowed through forgiving past sins. The mercy Prospero shows to those who wronged him will free them of obligation to him, but, more important, free him from the tyranny of his own hard feelings. Likewise, once Agassi could let go of the inhibitions, inherited from his father, that continually stifled his game, he could win more often, not feel devastated by losing, and take pleasure in the sport.

Before Agassi's career and personal life began turning around in the late '90s, he'd repeatedly tried to reverse his fortunes. In particular, he declared the summer of 1995, when he was reaching his low point, his "Summer of Revenge," during which he intended to pay back players who had beat him by winning a series of tournaments (211). What drove him during that summer was, he says, "rage. Endless, all-consuming rage" (213). He won matches according to plan—26 in all. Then, in the 27th—the finals of the U.S. Open—Pete Sampras beat him. By summer's end, his "rage," his "fury," felt ineffective. "All that work and anger and winning and training and hoping and sweating," he writes, "and it leads to the same empty disappointed feeling" (217). He finally couldn't let go of the one loss. Over the next few years, however, as he and Stefanie became close and his fortunes rose, losing no longer kept him down. He learned self-acceptance, meaning that he admitted to being human and therefore fallible.

"Return from the dead"

When Prospero chooses mercy over revenge, his explanation to Ariel introduces one final complication. "They being penitent," he says of the "three men of sin," "The sole drift of my purpose doth extend / Not a frown further" (5.1.28–30). Because his forgiveness has strings attached—the provision that Antonio, Alonso, and Sebastian are "penitent"—it's not truly grace, which is, by definition, unconditional. That one condition continues to give Prospero a shred of control over his adversaries, indicating his hesitation to let go thoroughly.

Prospero seems finally, completely, to forgo such control upon meeting the charmed men inside the magical circle he's drawn on the ground (5.1.57 s.d.). To Antonio he says, "I do forgive thee, / Unnatural though thou art" (5.1.78–79). Albeit with a hint of reluctance, Prospero offers his brother grace despite his evil past and also in view of his capacity to commit further wrongs. He recognizes Antonio's having "entertain'd ambition, / Expell'd remorse and nature," and having plotted to kill Alonso, yet forgives him nonetheless (5.1.75–78). This ultimate letting go involves huge risk for Prospero, since he's giving his brother freedom to hurt him again. Even so, his freeing of Antonio from moral obligation simultaneously frees Prospero from hatred, anger, and self-defeating, perfectionist expectations of others.

Shakespeare's last plays, including *The Tempest*, are often called "romances," sometimes "tragicomedies." All end with restoration resembling Prospero's. The protagonists of *Pericles, Cymbeline,* and *The Winter's Tale* also persevere to reach the other side of tremendous personal loss, such that all these plays have a fairy tale sheen and an idealistic, reassuring vision. Enjoying and appreciating these works depends upon an audience's inclination to adopt a favorable, flexible perspective. As problematic and objectionable as some of Prospero's behavior has appeared and as unrealistic as his redemption may seem, the genre of *The Tempest* draws the sort of faith from an audience that Prospero reposes in Antonio and, before the play's end, Caliban. That faith is hard-won.

When Prospero takes responsibility for Caliban with the line "this thing of darkness I / Acknowledge mine" and dangles "pardon" before Caliban as an enticement to his reformation, he is taking perhaps his biggest step toward humility (5.1.275–76, 293–94). Yet Prospero's changed attitude toward Caliban, far from absolute, is fraught with ambiguity. What does he mean when he "acknowledges" Caliban as his own? Is he admitting to making Caliban a monster? Is he saying, rather, that he possesses his own inner monstrosity? Different readings are possible. How reliable, furthermore, is Caliban's promise that "I'll be wise hereafter, / And seek for grace" (5.1.295–96)? Is he motivated by inner shame for having pledged allegiance to a "drunkard" and a "fool" or by the external threat of being "pinch'd to death" by Prospero (5.1.297–98, 276)?

Similar unresolved questions arise about the "three men of sin." Alonso's case, relying as it does on his reunion with the son he thought was dead, is the most straightforward, leaving no doubt as to his sincerity in begging his "child forgiveness" and rejoicing in Ferdinand's marriage to Miranda (5.1.197–98). The extent of Sebastian's change is more difficult to gauge. Although at first he doubts Prospero by muttering, "The devil speaks in him," the discovery of the children playing chess a few lines later seems to fill him with awe (5.1.129, 171 s.d.). When he responds to that sight with "A most high miracle!" he seems as transformed as Alonso (5.1.177).[10] Only Antonio lets no hint escape as to his disposition toward Prospero and recent events. His last line, a characteristically crude joke about Caliban's appearance, leaves the audience mystified as to whether he's willing to return the rule of Milan to Prospero, as Prospero "require[s]" of him (5.1.265–66, 130–34).

Miranda's innocence poses almost as much of a challenge to the play's closure as Antonio's wickedness. Throughout the play, her purity inspires love and admiration—especially from Prospero and Ferdinand—and yet, by analogy to Prospero's naïve conduct before he was usurped, it comes across as perilously limited. True, experience engenders the kind of cynicism that pervades Antonio's character and has soured Prospero, who remarks of the young lovers' passion, "So glad of this as they I cannot be, / … but my rejoicing / At nothing can be more" (3.1.92–94). But adult experience is double-edged in that, while it tempers happiness, it also teaches the hard lessons that enable someone like Prospero to defend against future ill will. This paradoxical relationship between childish innocence and mature experience is encapsulated in Miranda's exultation upon meeting the shipwrecked characters and Prospero's response to her:

MIRANDA: O wonder!
  How many goodly creatures are there here!
  How beauteous mankind is! O brave new world
  That has such people in't!
PROSPERO: 'Tis new to thee [5.1.181–84].

In the midst of such complications, *The Tempest*'s main thrust is still toward regeneration, not merely for the young, who are just beginning, but for the older generation, who have stumbled and are now given the opportunity to atone and redeem their losses. Antonio, Sebastian, and Alonso, along with Prospero, are looking ahead to a second chance, a "clear life ensuing" (3.3.82). Prospero's last lines make clear that he is about to free Ariel and to exchange his magic book and mantle for the grittier business of state (5.1.317–19, 50–57). Much as Ferdinand and Alonso have been miraculously resurrected to one another, so has Prospero seemingly come back from the dead to those who once wronged him and in respect to his second chance at ruling Milan and choosing to live socially. With wonderment echoing that in *The Tempest*, Andre Agassi writes about his "return from the dead" when he recovered his tennis game in mid-career (297).

Not all comebacks take years to arrive, and not all involve the kind of soul-searching and suffering that mark Agassi's and Prospero's. But even if they don't, they may strike the public as miraculous, on the order of a resurrection. Surely the New England Patriots' 2017 Super Bowl win fits this category. The Atlanta Falcons had a wide lead during most of the game—by as much as 25 points. With two minutes left, though, the Patriots had almost caught up to the Falcons 28–20, then won the game in overtime. In a video clip on the CBS sports web site, NFL columnist Nick Kostos calls the Patriots reversal "The greatest comeback in the history of the Super Bowl," to which Fox Sports commentator Brady Quinn responds, "No, no, no, it's the greatest comeback in the history of all time." Kostos quickly agrees. And nearly everyone with something to say about the seemingly impossible victory attributes it to the leadership and performance of quarterback Tom Brady.

In that game, Brady simply did more of what he always does by being an exceptional player and doing it in time to reverse the Patriots' fortunes. Although both Agassi and Prospero are also exceptional, neither comes back without setbacks or nagging weaknesses. But both figures make startling turnarounds. The athlete who once said of himself, "After decades of merely dabbling in masochism, I'm making it my mission," grew to value a good belly laugh as much as a major tournament victory and to write of his transformation, "I didn't alter my image, I discovered it. I didn't change my mind, I discovered it" (248, 342, 372). And the dramatic character who has at one point struggled to forgive others begs in the Epilogue for the audience's "mercy": "As you from crimes would pardon'd be, / Let your indulgence set me free" (Epilogue 18–20). Both men exemplify the rewards of not merely surviving, but continued striving.

Discussion Questions for *The Tempest*

- What are some notable examples of other comebacks in sports, whether individuals or teams?
- Does Prospero hold his brother, Antonio, too responsible for his ouster as Duke of Milan?

- Even if his exile is all Prospero's fault, is 12 years of suffering too much?
- Is Caliban more monster than human? What is the textual evidence?
- In view of this last question, how might Caliban appear on stage?
- Imagine a future for Caliban once *The Tempest* ends. What's the story's plot and outcome?
- What is Ariel's relationship to Prospero? How might Ariel appear on stage?
- Why isn't Ariel visible to anyone but Prospero?
- *The Tempest* focuses on the roles in human development played by both nature and nurture. Which is more influential?
- A related question is whether education works. Are people able to change for the better? Do you believe Caliban's promise to "be wise hereafter" (5.5.1.295)?
- How are Prospero and Sycorax, Caliban's mother, alike and different? Why is Sycorax dead before *The Tempest* begins?
- How can the play's two views on Prospero's books—which represent learning, magic, art—be reconciled: one, that his books save Prospero and enable him to come to terms with his past and, two, that his books lured him away from ruling in the first place, contributed to his exile, and must be rejected before he can resume his dukedom in Milan?
- What role does ambition play for the characters in *The Tempest*? Does ambition have both positive and negative sides?
- What sports examples best illustrate both the positive and negative aspects of ambition? How should an individual's ambition be weighed against a team's, if at all?
- What's the significance of the detail that Alonso's daughter, Claribel, has married the king of Tunis, in northern Africa (2.1.69–72)?
- How does Shakespeare make the love-at-first-sight between Miranda and Ferdinand more realistic than it might be?
- What's the significance of the game of chess that Miranda and Ferdinand are playing when they're revealed to the marooned characters in 5.1.171? How does their dialogue add to the game's significance?
- Clothes are a recurring metaphor in the play—from the mantel that Prospero dons to practice magic to the "*glistering apparel*" that Ariel hangs on the clothes line to entice Stephano and Trinculo (4.1.193). What's the significance of the metaphor?
- What themes from the play does Prospero's Epilogue pick up on and expand?

Inside Shakespeare: Over-Simplification in and of *The Tempest*

As a romance, *The Tempest* includes many elements of fantasy and fable that seem to invite allegorical readings. Prospero is God ... or Shakespeare. Caliban is brutishness ... or unbridled desire. Miranda is Wisdom ... or Art (Smith 1659). The whole play is an allegory for British colonialism. And so forth. In truth, however, the play resists such allegorical readings, which are two-dimensional and fail to account for the psychological and literary complexity within the play. Prospero, for example, has god-like power through his art and yet is essentially human in his un–god-like temptation to abuse his power. He is at once a colonizer and an exile who yearns to return to his native Milan, very probably without further associating with Caliban. *The Tempest* yields the most enjoyment and beauty when its contents aren't reduced to simple lessons, principles, or ideas.

Significantly, the characters in *The Tempest* provide negative examples of such over-simplification, which they regularly perform toward one another. When Caliban insists to Prospero that the only "profit" he has received from learning Prospero's English is that he now "know[s] how to curse," he is making a claim that he blatantly contradicts a few scenes later (1.2.363–64). In 3.2, when he explains to Stephano and Trinculo that the music they hear is common on the island, he expresses his appreciation for the music's beauty in some of the play's most musical poetry:

> Sometimes a thousand twangling instruments
> Will hum about mine ears; and sometime voices,
> That if I then had wak'd after long sleep,
> Will make me sleep again, and then in dreaming,
> The clouds methought would open, and show riches
> Ready to drop upon me, that when I wak'd
> I cried to dream again [3.2.137–43].

At the same time that he uses language for purposes other than cursing with these lines, he also disproves Prospero's assessment of his incivility and his inability to learn (e.g., 4.1.188–92). For one thing, Caliban has learned English well enough to shape it into lovely poetry. For another, his aesthetic sensibility appears quite civilized. Prospero is right about Caliban's attempted rape of Miranda: it was a brutish act. But he is also wrong: that act alone doesn't have to characterize Caliban. Neither does Caliban's depiction of Prospero as an abusive master reflect Prospero's efforts to protect and nurture Miranda, as he once nurtured Caliban, according to Caliban's own report (1.2.332–38).

The dramatic mechanism of this play, then, is to discourage the very over-simplification that its characters practice even while it portrays characters in such a way as to encourage an audience to over-simplify them and the play's meaning. Why this roundabout mechanism? How does it work?

One way to answer that question is to think of the play as a mental exercise—something for the mind akin to resistance bands for the body. Like a band, the text gives to an audience's reading, allowing a certain amount of simplistic interpretation. But it reaches a point where it can't stretch any farther and, in fact, pulls the audience back to the starting point—but not exactly. The text has taken audience members through an experience, allowing them to discover on their own—rather than being told or lectured to—about the inadequacy of hasty and shallow judgment. The play has its own brakes (to shift metaphors). It enables an audience to test a reading that quickly appears inadequate, requiring that another additional layer of interpretation and understanding be added to the others (to shift metaphors again).

Chapter 7 refers to the prevalence of paradox in *The Tempest*, a paradox being an apparent contradiction. The intellectual language of the play is indeed paradoxical: everywhere one truth subsides to or masks another. One of the ultimate paradoxes is that of freeing through imprisonment. Prospero forces Ferdinand to carry logs as he does Caliban, but rather than complain about his treatment by his master, as Caliban does, he accepts his burden lightly. He sees his log-carrying as "service," a reflection of his submission to Miranda, and he understands that service is willing labor—freely given—on the servant's part (3.1.65). Lest this discussion of Ferdinand commit the same over-simplification that it's about, however, it should acknowledge that Ferdinand isn't idealized, isn't reduced any more than, finally, is Caliban. For Ferdinand's first response to encountering Prospero is to draw his sword and threaten violence, the very reaction that the "three men of sin"—Antonio, Sebastian, and Alonso—have upon seeing Ariel as the harpy in 3.3 (1.2.467 s.d., 3.3.59 s.d.). No matter how capable of virtue, any character may resort to violence, and this possibility lends a frame in which Ferdinand and Caliban are not diametrically opposed. It also frames the story of Prospero's curbing his own urge to avenge the wrongs done to him with violence.

The paradox of freedom within bondage thus extends to the play's overarching exploration of sin and forgiveness. When a trespasser is in his victim's debt, the debt can be canceled either because the trespasser makes up for the trespass or because the victim simply lets the debt go. Setting a debtor free in *The Tempest* not only exonerates the trespasser; paradoxically, it also liberates the victim, whose obsession with vengeance can well prove its own psychological prison.

Appendix
Professional Actors Comment on Parallels Between Spectator Sports and Shakespearean Performance

What follows are brief thoughts from Shakespearean actors about how their theatrical performances parallel spectator sports events. Actor Graham Smith, who is interviewed for this book, graciously canvassed his network of fellow actors on Facebook.

Rival theaters such as the Rose may be compared to rival team organizations.

* * *

I once performed *Henry V* on a football field with the British and French armies in sports uniforms. One of the most moving and magical Shakespeare shows I have ever done. The audiences that saw it still talk about it. It immediately gave the audience a sense of place and stakes and situation. Conflict and competition are inherent in sports and theater.

* * *

When I taught college-level writing, I made my acting students attend at least one basketball game. They then wrote essays comparing their game experience with the theatrical experience.

* * *

We don't expect athletes to be able to perform in an electric way if they have not trained thoroughly and indeed are not in continual, intense training—over and above simply showing up for practices. I reckon no Shakespearean actor who actually ignites the play, the ensemble, and the audience can be any less diligent.

* * *

In our present theater landscape in the U.S., if you have the good fortune to be cast in a Shakespeare play at a regional theater, it's like being part of an "All Star Team" in sports. Everyone you are playing with comes from a different training and performance background, and you all have to be at the top of your game to come together and pull it off … in three weeks or less.

* * *

Both require the ability to manage emotions, handle the biggest moments, and synchronize the psychological and physical exertion they will need to excel.

* * *

It was hard (and still is) for women to break into both Shakespeare's roles and sports. Additionally, all-female Shakespeare productions and all-female sports teams are far less popular than their all-male counterparts.

* * *

Alcohol consumption by spectators.

* * *

This is pretty specific, but I'd add that the focus on breath is a real link. As an example, Malcolm's tough line "O, by whom?" requires intentional focus on the breath and that powerful vowel that begins the line (*Macbeth*, 2.3.100). Similarly, an athlete lifting weights will be intentional about breathing in and out at certain times during the lift to be able to make it happen.

* * *

I was in a touring Shakespeare repertory company in the early '90s doing *Midsummer*, *Romeo and Juliet*, and *Antony and Cleopatra*, and at one point *Midsummer* got 27 standing ovations in a row. I remember thinking that the way we played together, the way we "passed the (story) ball," must have been what a basketball team playing at the highest level would be like—feeding off of the moment, improvising, all of us "in the zone." It was a sublime experience.

* * *

I had a director once admonish the cast backstage during tech because they weren't listening to the play. He said the tragic wheel requires everyone's undivided attention and support in order to keep spinning to the end of the play. Most coaches will demand the same attention from the supporting players on the bench.

Chapter Notes

Introduction

1. Although King James' declaration specifically prohibited bear-baiting and certain dramatic performances (like interludes) on Sundays, they were popular on other days of the week. Queen Elizabeth I, the reigning monarch during Shakespeare's earlier career, refused to prohibit bear-baiting on Sundays, and in 1591 her privy council issued an order prohibiting theatrical activity on Thursdays so as not to interfere with bear-baiting on that day.
   The savage Renaissance sports of bear-baiting and bull-baiting are analogous to modern day dog-fighting and bull-fighting, the first of which is outlawed in some countries. But inhumane treatment of animals in Shakespeare's England paled in comparison to the barbarous public executions of religious heretics and traitors that, throughout the 16th century, were staged before a public who expected the utmost in torture and human suffering. The severed heads of those executed were displayed on poles lining the entrance to London as a warning against treason. On the other end of the entertainment spectrum, sermons were another form of mass entertainment that competed in their own way with theatrical productions.

2. Theater historians have written extensively on the interplay between popular sports, games, and entertainments and professional London theatrical performances. See, e.g., Lin.

3. Some contemporary productions seek to incorporate historical staging conditions that once made Shakespearean performance so vitally spontaneous. These restored conditions, known as "original practices," usually eliminate the "fourth wall" and include interaction between actors and audience members in a theater where the audience is well lit, rather than obscured in darkness, as is typical. Contemporary theaters where these practices are in place include London's Globe and Staunton, Virginia's Blackfriars. But not even most "OP" productions eliminate the director.
   For extensive information about what Elizabethan theatrical rehearsal was like, see Stern's history.

4. These groups included the Lord Admiral's Men, for whom Shakespeare's rival Christopher Marlowe wrote *The Jew of Malta*, whose success prompted Shakespeare's *The Merchant of Venice*, featuring the Jewish Shylock. Groups of child actors also offered competition to traditional adult troupes. Hamlet expresses concern that the "little eyases" are exploited by company owners (2.2.339, 345–51).

5. According to one study of fans' identification with sports teams, "the fortunes of affiliated sports teams can cause lavish displays of civic gratitude and pride in American cities, or 'sports riots' in Europe, or murders in South America of players and referees whose actions had caused a home-team defeat. Through their simple connections with sports teams, the personal images of fans are at stake when their teams take the field. The team's victories and defeats are reacted to as personal successes and failures" (Cialdini et al. 374).

6. Many books and audio-visual materials can help students get started in the area of

Shakespearean performance. See, for example, Barton's *Playing Shakespeare,* an older but invaluable book with accompanying videos, which, though dated, are useful. See also works by Daw, Palfrey, Pritner and Colaianni, and Rodenburg. The Complete Arkangel Shakespeare audio recordings of all 38 plays, performed by some of the most distinguished Shakespearean actors of the 20th century, offer a convenient introduction to performance (Brill).

7. Of all contemporary American sports, this statement is perhaps truest of baseball, whose intricacies seem to require a prolonged period of familiarization, if not an entire lifetime.

8. For an older, but still relevant, discussion of "Shakespeare and the Myth of Perfection," see Harbage.

Chapter 1

1. The association between speech and reason, distinguishing human beings from beasts, was commonplace in Shakespeare's culture. For a book-length study of the implications of this association to Shakespeare's plays, see Hawkes.

2. Sports journalist Jack McCallum elaborates on popular conceptions of the two teams' differences: "The dichotomy extended to the benches: L.A. coach Pat Riley, clothed in Armani and glistening with mousse, was a Hollywood foil to first Bill Fitch, an ex–Marine, and then K. C. Jones, a plain-speaking former defensive ace. It extended to the boardroom: Lakers owner Jerry Buss smoked cigarettes, stayed mostly hidden and chased young women (still does, as a matter of fact) while Red Auerbach, 17 years removed from coaching duties but retaining the title of team president, smoked smelly stogies and remained relentlessly irascible. And it extended to the stands: The Fabulous Forum had Jack Nicholson, be-shaded, leering, redolent of sin. Boston Garden had Tip O'Neill, the New Deal Democrat, and a lotta red-faced guys from Southie."

3. Technically, the sonnet is a Shakespearean, or English, sonnet, defined by its rhyme scheme of abab cdcd efef gg—that is, three quatrains and a couplet. The central, sustained, and elaborate metaphor, or "conceit," compares first the two characters' hands, then their lips, to pilgrims who pray to saints and to the saints themselves.

Shakespeare wrote *Romeo and Juliet* in 1595, a time in his career when he favored elaborate, formal verse and rhyme over either prose or blank (unrhymed) verse crafted to resemble familiar, common speech. Other plays from the same year that reflect the similarly formal verse include *A Midsummer Night's Dream* and *Richard II.*

4. The reference to Rosaline's being Capulet's "fair niece" in 1.2.68–69 may be too brief for most auditors to pick up, but it is a crucial detail for establishing the difference between Romeo's apparently intense, but passing interest in Rosaline and his true affection for Juliet.

5. The Nurse is emotionally close to Juliet by virtue of her having been her "wet nurse," the woman who breast-fed the baby Juliet instead of her mother (see 1.3.23–32). This practice was common among aristocratic women of the time; the Nurse would have had breast milk for her own baby daughter, Susan, who, as the Nurse explains, has died (lines 18–20).

6. Mercutio's name invokes Mercury, the messenger of the gods and tutor to tricksters and thieves. Some critics also detect in his name an allusion to Shakespeare's near contemporary, playwright Christopher Marlowe (see, e.g., Mary Rosenberg). Modern Shakespeare criticism is divided over Mercutio's appeal and his sexuality. Some audiences respond more to his wit and winsome flamboyance than to his aggression (see, e.g., Holland). Others find his vulgar edginess unsuitable to a tragedy that, after all, celebrates pure love (see, e.g., McArthur). Thomas Browne sees Mercutio's impulsiveness as the main cause of bloodshed in 3.1 (49). As to Mercutio's sexual identity, Joseph A. Porter argues that his homosexuality is deepened by his association with Marlowe, whose works include same-sex erotic love, perhaps reflecting his own sexuality. But, says Porter, recognition of Mercutio's homosexuality has been suppressed in a long-prevailing climate of general homophobia.

7. Compare the lamentations of Bottom/Pyramus and Flute/Thisbe in 5.1 of *A Midsummer Night's Dream,* melodramatic expressions of woe clearly intended to be comical.

8. For an extensive discussion of formal and informal pronouns in Shakespeare's work, see Penelope Freedman, *Power and Passion in Shakespeare's Pronouns: Interrogating "you" and "thou."*

Chapter 2

1. For an excellent, brief overview of the play's historical context, see Healy, whose book situates the play in the history of Shakespeare's own day. As Healy explains, Shakespeare's portrayal of political subversion two centuries earlier could be read as a threat to the Tudor Elizabeth I. It was, therefore, a risk on Shakespeare's part.
2. *Richard II* shares abundant rhyme and meter with other plays from around the same year, 1595, including *Love's Labor's Lost, Romeo and Juliet,* and *A Midsummer Night's Dream.*
   Richard's characterization is also rich, but probably less nuanced overall than Bullingbrook's. In the earlier acts, the King's thoughts and intents come across in either excessive dramatic display or private conversations the audience overhears. See the "Inside Shakespeare" discussion of subtext that follows this chapter for more on the issue of characterization.
3. For a fuller discussion of how Machiavellian political thinking informs Shakespeare's portrayal of Henry IV and Henry V, see Chapter 4.
4. This deposition scene, as Saccio points out, is "quite unhistorical" and in Shakespeare's day "was thought so inflammatory that it was censored out of the earliest editions of *Richard II*" (32).
5. For Machiavelli's view of a ruler's effective use of theatricality, see, for example, *The Prince,* Chapter 18, suggestively entitled "How Princes Should Keep Their Promises."
6. Because the play text also continues to refer to the character as "Aumerle," so will my discussion.
7. Historically, the Duchess was Aumerle's stepmother, but Shakespeare has endowed her with full maternal devotion.
8. That Herb Brooks was rejected from the 1960 U.S. hockey team gave him added incentive at the 1980 Olympics.

Chapter 3

1. For a fuller treatment of brotherhood in the play, as well as many other topics in Chapter 3, see Montrose.
2. The poet and literary critic Wendell Berry offers a provocative reading of the Duke's speech about living in the wild in "The Uses of Adversity" (213–16).
3. For a helpful discussion of how the setting of the play functions, see especially Daley.
4. The cross-dressing in *As You Like It* is of special interest because it involves four gender layers: the boy actor, who plays a female character, who cross-dresses as a boy, who then plays the role of a woman (Rosalind). Other instances of female-to-male cross-dressing in Shakespeare's plays typically involve just the first three of those four.
   The confusion of identity is difficult not only for the characters within the play, but also for the actor playing Rosalind and for the audience: just who is speaking, to the extent that it is clear, may vary from line to line. The Epilogue provides a particularly ambiguous example, in which the actor speaks directly to the audience as both male and female.
   My use of the names *Rosalind, Ganymed,* and *Rosalind/Ganymed* is intended to reflect something about this constantly shifting identity, though not with the promise of absolute consistency and clarity. When I'm writing from the audience's perspective, I'm likely to use *Rosalind,* since the audience is aware of her presence beneath the disguise. When referring to Orlando's or another character's perspective (often in combination with the audience's point of view), I'll often refer to *Rosalind/Ganymed* or simply *Ganymed.* "Rosalind" denotes Rosalind/Ganymed's posing as Rosalind during conversations with Orlando in the forest.
5. The history of feminist criticism concerning Rosalind, which includes interest in

her (and other Shakespearean heroines') cross-dressing, dates to the late 1970s and early 1980s and to pioneers in the field like co-editors Lenz, Greene, and Neely. Since that time, the overarching question about Rosalind and other strong comic women has been whether they are truly feminist portrayals. Do these heroines escape patriarchal confines and win lasting independence, or do they elude those confines only for a time, after which they must become reabsorbed by—contained within—traditional male social structures? See n. 8 below.

6. For discussion of the homoerotic interplay between Phebe and Rosalind/Ganymed, see, for example, DiGangi, Traub, and Whalen.

7. For fuller discussion of this scene (4.3), which is far richer than is represented in this chapter, see Montrose and Lewis.

8. One notable exception to the play's closure would be the question of Rosalind's independence. Having spent the better part of the play freely exercising power usually available only to men, she appears in the final scene restored to her feminine identity and submitting herself to Orlando and her father: "To you I give myself, for I am yours" (5.4.116–18). As her husband, however, Orlando could be expected to submit himself to her, as well.

9. Women have had obstacles to negotiate similar to those of minorities, a topic that Chapter 5 discusses at length.

Chapter 4

1. http://theselvedgeyard.files.wordpress.com/2010/01/broadway-joe-namath.jpg

2. Despite Prince Hal's deliberate exploitation of his wayward past, as well as his drinking companions, he can also appear sensitive about being judged as immature, as in the case of the Dolphin's insults. Even so, like Namath, he makes use of others' underestimation of his abilities and seriousness, most especially that of the Dolphin and, in *1 Henry IV,* of his rival Hotspur.

3. The city and cathedral of Ely are in Cambridgeshire, England. The name, deriving from the Anglo Saxon for *eel,* refers to the abundance of that creature in the area.

4. For a fascinating discussion of Namath's influence on American male culture, see John Bloom, "Joe Namath and Super Bowl III: An Interpretation of Style." Bloom's article partly addresses differences in interpretation of the game and Namath by analyzing the NFL film about the game, which, not surprisingly, is sympathetic to the Colts.

5. Most historians agree that close friends during this period commonly shared a bed without necessarily engaging in sexual relations. See, for example, Bray and Matz (Chapter 10). For another point of view on Hal's intimacy with Scroop, see Goldberg (174–75).

6. Views of Falstaff's character range more widely than can be justly represented here. The well known critic Harold Bloom is the character's most vocal apologist. In Chapter 17 of his book *Shakespeare: The Invention of the Human,* he promotes Falstaff as Shakespeare's supreme characterization, "a miracle in the creation of personality" (313). For Bloom, Falstaff represents the "freedom ... *from* society" that is the very life force (276).

7. Shakespeare takes some pains to create dialogue specific to each character's nationality. Fluellen, for instance, often pronounces his *b* sounds as *p* sounds, as in "I think he will *plow* up all, if there is not better directions," where he means *blow* up (3.2.63–64).

8. The essay was reprinted in *Shakespeare and the Problem of Meaning* as "Either/Or: Responding to *Henry V.*"

9. Holinshed writes: "When this dolorous decree, and pitifull proclamation was pronounced, pitie it was to see how some Frenchmen were suddenlie sticked with daggers, some were brained with pollaxes, some slaine with malls, other had their throats cut, and some their bellies panched, so that in effect, having respect to the great number, few prisoners were saved" (Bullough 397).

10. Historically, Henry clearly made the first of these two choices, since the killing of the luggage boys had happened long before the alarum sounded (Saccio 83–84). Here, as often, Shakespeare toys with historical events to enrich his exploration of his title character.

11. In 4.4, Pistol's holding Monsieur le Fer at knife-point for "Egregious ransom" forges one of many connections between this less than honorable character and his erstwhile companion, the present king (4.4.11). Such overlaying repeatedly raises the question of whether Pistol stands in contrast to or in some way mirrors Henry. That Henry nobly refuses to be ransomed throughout the play disassociates him from Pistol's ignoble bribery of the Frenchman. At the same time, Pistol's rough and underhanded treatment of le Fer while extorting payment from him savors of the generally exploitive English treatment of France, despite Henry's pronouncement that "when lenity and cruelty play for a kingdom, the gentler gamester is the soonest winner" (3.6.112–13).

12. Other references to the French preoccupation with their armor and their livery include the Constable's many references to the "fair show" the French will present in battle, in contrast to the ragged English troops, and his insistence on taking a "guidon" (or "banner") into battle (4.2.15–37, 60–62).

Chapter 5

1. Compare the reason that Rosalind and her cousin Celia give for disguising themselves as men in *As You Like It*—that they'll be less vulnerable to danger on the road (1.3.108–22). Also compare the relative amount of power and control that a male disguise gives women in both plays. Rosalind's disguise is discussed at length in Chapter 3.

2. Compare the transition in women's bodybuilding from the feminine Lisa Lyon to Bev Francis, who was often ridiculed as a "man in a bikini."

3. King's match with the 55-year-old Riggs, labeled "The Battle of the Sexes," attracted a crowd of approximately 30,500 at the Houston Astrodome and a television audience of about 48,000,000. Nancy E. Spencer's excellent article narrates the fascinating story in detail and analyzes its cultural significance—in particular, to the evolution of feminism in the U.S. In 2017, the contest between King and Riggs was dramatized in the film *The Battle of the Sexes*, with Emma Stone and Steve Carell.

4. As far as women have come in the arena of professional sports, they are far from integrated with men. Some women officiate alongside their male colleagues in the NBA, and a few women have successfully tried out for the position of kicker on college football teams. On August 31, 2001, Ashley Martin, playing for Jacksonville State, was the first woman ever to play on an NCAA Division I football team. Most sports, however, are still fully segregated according to gender.

5. From this point on, references to Viola's character will reflect the instability of her gender. Depending on the context and the point of view in question, Viola will also be referred to as Viola/Cesario, Cesario, she, and he.

Some classic studies of gender fluidity in *Twelfth Night* include those by Belsey, Shapiro, Callaghan, and, more recently, Schwarz.

6. An intriguing question, related to that of how gender is defined is whether Olivia falls for Viola or Cesario—for a female or a boy who isn't yet sexual. See note 7, below, for more on same-sex attraction in *Twelfth Night*.

7. The specific source for the Pauline concept of wise folly is 1 Corinthians 3:18–19: "Let no one deceive himself. If any one among you thinks that he is wise in this age, let him become a fool that he may become wise. For the wisdom of this world is folly with God. For it is written, 'He catches the wise in their craftiness.'" Renaissance humanists understood Christ to be the ultimate wise fool for forfeiting his worldly possessions and dying so that sinners could be forgiven.

Antonio's lavish expressions of love also suggest homoeroticism, a subject that, like Olivia's attraction to Viola/Cesario, has received much critical attention. See Chapter 3, n. 6. Additional sources on Antonio's professed "desire" for Sebastian include Hammond, Osborne, and Pequigney.

8. Having referred to Malvolio as a "kind of puritan," Maria retracts that label a few

lines later, probably because Shakespeare sought to avoid a term so politically charged (2.3.140–53). Even so, Malvolio's plain, dark clothing as a steward would have resembled Puritan dress, visually paralleling him with a religious group that detested theater on moral grounds, as Malvolio dislikes revelry. (Olivia's references to Malvolio as "sad" associates him with Puritans' somber clothing, referred to at the time as "sadd" [3.4.5, 18].) Malvolio's strained efforts to "make" the letter "resemble something in" himself, moreover, are often read as satirizing the Puritans' practice of carefully scanning the Bible for evidence of their election to God's salvation (2.5.119–20).

    9. In today's theater, Olivia's line always gets a laugh, since she seems to be rejoicing in having two Sebastians. But modern usage has lost the sense of true, otherworldly *wonder* implicit in the word *wonderful*.

    10. A spectrum of critical views on how the subplot affects the play's tone would be represented in the works of Ralph Berry, Hunt, and Kemper.

    11. The movie *She's the Man*, with Amanda Bynes and Channing Tatum, is an adaptation of *Twelfth Night* in which the character named Viola is a soccer player who disguises herself as her brother and joins the all-male soccer team at his high school. The movie's target audience appears to be young and predominantly female.

    12. My female students who participate in Division I athletics tell me that the spirit of Title IX is far from being fulfilled.

Chapter 6

    1. Not everyone agrees about the stigma attached to performance-enhancing drugs. Jose Canseco's book about his own drug use, *Juiced*, extols their effects. See especially Chapter 4, in which he writes of his success, "I can tell you now: Steroids were the key to it all. I was such an improved player, and I think it was because steroids not only give you a lot of physical strength and stamina, they also give you a mental edge" (51). In a related vein, reporter Malcolm Gladwell, having explored the inadequacy of testing to keep pace with the rapid invention of new, undetectable versions of drugs, concludes his essay "Drugstore Athlete" with a meditation on whether drugs truly provide advantages any less "legitimate" than nature's (59). Sidney Gendin, a professor emeritus of philosophy of law, fully develops a (non-satirical) argument in favor of steroid use and of banning non-users from competition.

    2. Some critics take a line from a speech by Lady Macbeth in 1.7 to suggest that Macbeth had proposed Duncan's murder to her earlier, perhaps before the action of the play begins:

> When you durst do it, then you were a man;
> And to be more than what you were, you would
> Be so much more the man. Nor time, nor place,
> Did then adhere, and yet you would make both [lines 49–52].

But many commentators and editors point out that Lady Macbeth may be referring to the letter from Macbeth in 1.5 (see especially Bradley 390–93, Note CC in Appendix). Others conjecture that this reference in 1.7 is to a now lost scene between 1.5 and 1.7 showing the couple conferring about the murder or to an off-stage conference that the audience is meant to imagine.

    3. L. C. Knights' *How Many Children Had Lady Macbeth?* dates to 1933. It rejects literary criticism (in particular, A. C. Bradley's) preoccupied with facts about characters' lives that a play simply doesn't yield. Sigmund Freud, on the other hand, thinks Lady Macbeth's childlessness is the key to her motivation (159–66). Bristol, Calef, and Chamberlain have each written distinctly about the textual suggestion that Lady Macbeth killed her child. Of relevance here is also the televised version of *Macbeth*, directed by Rupert Goold and starring Patrick Stewart, during which Lady Macbeth (Kate Fleetwood) opens a drawer in her vanity to reveal a glimpse of a baby's shoe, suggesting the loss, through whatever circumstances, of a child.

    Critics have long recognized the preoccupation in *Macbeth* with children. The classic essay originally dealing with this theme is by Cleanth Brooks, "The Naked Babe and the Cloak of Manliness."

4. Much has been written in recent decades on the issue of gender in *Macbeth*. Critical works that can give students some orientation to this area include those by Del Villano, Hirsch, Kimbrough, Mangan, and Rose. The New Casebook collection of essays on *Macbeth*, edited by Sinfield, includes many articles that pertain to the topic.

5. Roman Polanski's provocative film version of *Macbeth* concludes by suggesting that Macbeth isn't unusual in his susceptibility to the witches' influence. As Duncan's second son, Donalbain, rides by the witches' hut, they lure him inside, indicating that he is their next victim.

6. Some followers of this story believe that Hunter thought Jones' first autobiography, published in 2004 at almost precisely the time of his testimony about her, violated a nondisclosure agreement they had reached during their divorce. So, the reasoning goes, he may have taken revenge. Because Hunter never lied about his own drug use, he was never charged.

7. For example, Barry Bonds, a baseball star with the Pittsburgh Pirates and the San Francisco Giants until 2007, who holds the Major League record for home runs, told a grand jury that he understood that doses of "The Clear" and "The Cream" offered to him by his trainers were nutritional supplements, flaxseed oil, and lotion for pain. In April of 2011, Bonds was convicted on one count of obstruction of justice. Another three counts of perjury for lying to a grand jury about having taken steroids resulted in a mistrial when a jury couldn't agree on a verdict. In December of 2011, Bonds was sentenced to 30 days of house arrest, two years' probation, and 250 hours of community service. But the sentence was put on hold pending Bonds' appeal of his conviction, which was eventually overturned in 2015. These legal proceedings have done little to clarify Bonds' persistent claim that he didn't knowingly take steroids.

8. For a fuller treatment of Mantle's life and career, as well as his significance to American sports culture (and culture in general), see Leavy's *The Last Boy*.

9. Compare Christopher Marlowe's tragedy *Doctor Faustus*, in which the despairing hero finds himself being carried off to hell because he can't bring himself to repent his sins or believe in God's mercy.

10. In the early seventeenth century, a mother who bore a child, like Macduff, by Caesarian section would likely have already died in the birthing process.

11. Any annotated edition of *Macbeth* will explain the connection of this passage with the investigation into the Gunpowder Plot of 1605, whose purpose was the assassination of King James I.

12. A *Los Angeles Times* editorial on the allegations that Armstrong manipulated blood samples collected for drug tests no doubt speaks for many people's feelings on the matter before Armstrong surrendered: "We hope Armstrong is innocent—not only because we'd like to believe that his achievements were legitimate, but because his story as a testicular cancer survivor who went on to become one of the most successful athletes in history has inspired millions battling their own cancers. But if he's guilty, there are no good excuses" ("Chasing Lance Armstrong").

13. This is the conclusion of an independent report on the case conducted by former FBI Director Louis Freeh, published in 2012.

14. The NCAA's handling of the Penn State case reignited debate over whether and how to address collegiate athletic programs that have run amok because of greed. Can the ideal of the student-athlete ever be retrieved at a university whose athletic program now exists for the main purpose of generating income? Many analysts are doubtful. See, for example, Branch.

15. Critics of Marion Jones have expressed similar views of her post-conviction confessional, *On the Right Track*, viewing it was an attempt to profit without fully confessing.

16. *Macbeth* is, among other things, a tribute to James I of England, who was crowned in 1603 and had been King James VI of Scotland since 1567. Banquo was the legendary progenitor of James' royal line, the House of Stuart. In the show of kings presented by the witches in 4.1, Macbeth can see the regal "line stretch out to th' crack of doom"—that is, extending over eight generations from Banquo to James and far into the future (4.1.117).

17. Perhaps similar grief causes Rosse's almost cruel delay in telling Macduff about the murder of his family in lines 174–207.

Chapter 7

1. Ariel's gender in the text is clearly male, although some of his traits may strike a contemporary audience as female. Indeed, in many contemporary productions, Ariel is cast as a woman.

2. The colonialist reading of *The Tempest* originated in the mid-1970s with an essay, "Learning to Curse," by Shakespeare scholar Stephen Greenblatt. The essay was later anthologized in a book by the same title. Such interpretations of the play, which are also referred to as New Historicist readings, take a particularly dim view of Prospero that is perhaps darkest in Stephen Orgel's "Prospero's Wife."

3. Although rape seems every bit as heinous today as it did in Shakespeare's time, not everyone in our day values a woman's virginity the way Prospero's society would have. To take Miranda's "honor" by force would be to "violate" her and ruin her chances of marriage (1.2.348, 347). Prospero's monitoring of her courtship with Ferdinand is possibly another instance of his over-controlling tendency, and his choice of Ferdinand as her suitor involves self-interest because it will secure a dynastic connection between Milan and Naples. But his concern over finding a suitable match for his daughter and guiding the young couple toward wedded sexuality was a common expectation for patriarchs in the period.

4. Although this speech is assigned to Miranda in the Folio of 1623, some editors reassign it to Prospero on the grounds that it's too harsh for Miranda and it echoes other speeches by Prospero.

The point about Caliban's verbal facility is crucial from an early modern perspective. Regardless of whether Caliban already spoke a language (as Greenblatt has argued in "Learning to Curse") or was pre-verbal before Prospero's arrival on the island, his very ability to speak would classify him, to Shakespeare's original audience, as a rational creature, since language was the Renaissance marker between animals and human beings. Caliban's capacity to speak thus qualifies him as human, not monstrous.

5. The name *Caliban* is a near-anagram of *cannibal* and an exact anagram of the Spanish *canibal*. Christopher Columbus applied the word (interchangeably with *carib*) to man-eating natives of the West Indies ("Cannibal").

6. Despair in the early modern period is often depicted as a form of pride, as in the case of *Macbeth* (see Chapter 6) and Christopher Marlowe's *Doctor Faustus*. Faustus' lack of faith in his ability to be saved by God's grace is, in effect, an arrogant over-estimation of his sinfulness, which he deems greater than Satan's: "Faustus' offence can ne'er be pardoned. The serpent that tempted Eve may be saved, but not Faustus" (13.15–16).

7. How much influence does Prospero exert over Antonio and Sebastian's plotting? The scene opens itself to a number of interpretations. One is that the co-conspirators act completely on their own; they're not susceptible to Ariel's music, which puts the others to sleep, perhaps because their immorality inoculates them against appreciating such beauty. Another is that Prospero, by guaranteeing that everyone will doze off except Antonio and Sebastian, sets up conditions that encourage the sinister plotting. The most negative readings of Prospero argue that, without his involvement through Ariel, the villains' plotting wouldn't have happened and, thus, Prospero is responsible for their moral lapse.

8. Frank Kermode, editor of the Arden edition of the play, traces the disappearing banquet to a possible biblical source, the book of Job 20:23, 27 (n. to 3.3).

9. A masque was a formal, ritualized kind of theater performed mainly at court in the late 16th and 17th centuries. It emphasized spectacle over plot, and its characters typically wore masks (hence the name).

10. Many students today hear cynical irony in Sebastian's line, but a textual basis for that reading isn't evident.

Bibliography

Allen, Kevin. "College Kids Perform Olympic Miracle." *USA Hockey: A Celebration of a Great Tradition*, Triumph, 1997. *ESPN Classic Selections*, www.espn.com/classic/s/miracle_ice_1980.html.
———. "The First Miracle on Ice." *USA Hockey: A Celebration of Great Tradition*, Triumph, 1997. *ESPN Classic Selections*, www.espn.com/classic/s/1960_ice_mircle_1226.html.
Bach, Rebecca Ann. "Tennis Balls: *Henry V* and Testicular Masculinity, or, According to the OED, Shakespeare Doesn't Have Any Balls." *Renaissance Drama*, vol. 30, 1999–2000, pp. 3–23.
"Ball Talk: On the Finals, Old, Soft and the Best There Is." *Latest Headlines—NBA News*, 2 June 2010, https://web.archive.org/web/20100606090552/http://www.nba.com:80/2010/news/features/06/02/balltalk/index.html?ls=iref:nbahpt1.
Barton, Anne. Introduction to *Twelfth Night*. *The Riverside Shakespeare*, edited by G. Blakemore Evans and J.J.M. Tobin, 2nd ed. Houghton Mifflin, 1997, pp. 437–41.
Barton, John. *Playing Shakespeare*. London/Methuen: Channel Four Television Company, 1984. Book and DVD.
The Battle of the Sexes. Directed by Jonathan Dayton and Valerie Faris. Performed by Emma Stone and Steve Carell, Fox Searchlight, 2017.
Belsey, Catherine. "Disrupting Sexual Difference: Meaning and Gender in the Comedies." *Alternative Shakespeares*, edited by John Drakakis. Methuen, 1985, pp. 166–90.
Berry, Ralph. "*Twelfth Night*: The Experience of the Audience." *Shakespeare Survey*, vol. 34, 1981, pp. 111–19.
Berry, Wendell. "The Uses of Adversity." *Sewanee Review*, vol. 115, no. 2, 2007, pp. 211–38.
The Bible. Edited by Herbert G. May and Bruce M. Meetzger, Oxford Annotated Edition, Revised Standard Version, Oxford UP, 1962.
Bloom, Harold. *Shakespeare: The Invention of the Human*. Riverhead Books/Penguin Putnam, 1998.
Bloom, John D. "Joe Namath and Super Bowl III: An Interpretation of Style." *Journal of Sports History*, vol. 15, no. 1, Spring 1988, pp. 64–74.
Borden, Sam. "The Remarkable Rise of Leicester City." *New York Times*, 29 Apr. 2016, www.nytimes.com/2016/05/01/sports/soccer/how-leicester-city-went-right-side-up.html?_r=0.
Boyer, Peter. "Changing Lanes." *New Yorker*, vol. 86, no. 15, 31 May 2010, pp. 52–61, www.newyorker.com/magazine/2010/05/31/changing-lanes-2.
Bradley, A.C. *Shakespearean Tragedy: Lectures on* Hamlet, Othello, King Lear, Macbeth. 1904. Meridian/World, 1963.
Branch, Taylor. "The Shame of College Sports." *Atlantic Magazine*, Oct. 2011, www.theatlantic.com/magazine/archive/2011/10/the-shame-of-college-sports/308643/.
Bray, Alan. "Homosexuality and Male Friendship." *Queering the Renaissance*, edited by Jonathan Goldberg, Duke UP, 1994, pp. 40–61.

Brill, Clive, director. *The Complete Arkangel Shakespeare Preview CD*. Audio Partners, 2003.
Bristol, Michael D. "How Many Children Did She Have?" *Philosophical Shakespeares*, Routledge, edited by John J. Joughin, 2000, pp. 18–33.
Brooks, Cleanth. "The Naked Babe and the Cloak of Manliness." *The Well-Wrought Urn*, Harcourt, 1947, pp. 22–49.
Browne, Thomas. "Mercutio as Mercury: Trickster and Shadow." *Upstart Crow*, vol. 9, 1989, pp. 40–51.
Bull Durham. Directed by Ron Shelton, performed by Kevin Costner and Susan Sarandon, The Mount Company, 1988.
Bullough, Geoffrey. *Narrative and Dramatic Sources of Shakespeare*. Vol. 4. Columbia UP, 1966. 8 vols.
C. C. & Company. Directed by Seymour Robbie, performed by Joe Namath and Ann-Margret, Embassy Pictures, 1970.
Cahn, Susan. *Coming on Strong: Gender and Sexuality in Twentieth-Century Women's Sport*. Harvard UP, 1995.
Calef, Victor. "Lady Macbeth and Infanticide or 'How Many Children Had Lady Macbeth Murdered?'" *Journal of the American Psychoanalytic Association*, vol. 17, no. 2, 1 Apr. 1969, pp. 528–48.
Callaghan, Dympna C. "'And all is semblative a woman's part': Body Politics and *Twelfth Night*." *Shakespeare Without Women: Representing Gender and Race on the Renaissance Stage*. Routledge, 2000, pp. 26–48. Accents on Shakespeare.
"Cannibal." Def. 1.a. *The Oxford English Dictionary*, 2nd edition. 1989.
Canseco, Jose. *Juiced*. HarperCollins/Regan Books, 2005.
Cayleff, Susan E. "The 'Texas Tomboy': The Life and Legend of Babe Didrikson Zaharias." *OAH Magazine of History*, vol. 7, no. 1, Summer 1992, pp. 28–33.
Chamberlain, Stephanie. "Fantasizing Infanticide: Lady Macbeth and the Murdering Mother in Early Modern England." *College Literature*, vol. 32, no. 3, Summer 2005, pp. 72–91.
"Chasing Lance Armstrong." *Los Angeles Times*, 15 June 2012, http://articles.latimes.com/2012/jun/15/opinion/la-ed-armstrsong-clemens-20120615.
"Charm." Def. 1. a. *The Oxford English Dictionary*, 2nd edition, 1989.
Cialdini, Robert B., et al. "Basking in Reflected Glory: Three (Football) Field Studies." *Journal of Personality and Social Psychology*, vol. 34, 1976, pp. 366–75.
Daley, A. Stuart. "Where Are the Woods in as *You Like It*?" *Shakespeare Quarterly*, vol. 34, 1983, pp. 172–80.
Daw, Kurt. *Acting Shakespeare and His Contemporaries*. Heinemann, 1998.
Deford, Frank. "The Game's the Thing: The Super Bowl as Seen Through Shakespeare's Eyes." SI.Com, 30 Jan. 2008, www.si.com/more-sports/2008/01/30/superbowlxlii.
Del Villano, Bianca. "The Weird Sisters: Truth and Identity in Shakespeare's *Macbeth*." *English Studies 2003*, edited by R.A. Henderson, Turin, Trauben, 2004, pp. 25–43.
DiGangi, Mario. "Queering the Shakespearean Family." *Shakespeare Quarterly*, vol. 47, 1996, pp. 269–90.
Do You Believe in Miracles? The Story of the 1980 U.S. Hockey Team. Written by Bernard Goldberg, performed by Liev Schreiber, Craig R. Whitney, Walter Mondale, and John Powers, HBO, 2001.
Dodd, Mike. "Recognizing 'I'm 14 years late,' Rose Admits He Bet on Baseball." *USA Today*, 5 Jan. 2004, usatoday30.usatoday.com/sports/baseball/2004-01-05-rose_x.htm.
Dowd, Maureen. "JoePa Sold His Soul. As for Jerry Sandusky, He Didn't Have One to Sell." *Pittsburgh Post-Gazette*, 23 July 2012, www.post-gazette.com/opinion/Op-Ed/2012/07/23/Maureen-Dowd-JoePa-sold-his-soul-As-for-Jerry-Sandusky-he-didn-t-have-one-to-sell/stories/201207230127.
Duerr, Charlie. "A Brief History of the Lakers-Celtics Rivalry." *Time Arts*, 16 June 2010, http://content.time.com/time/arts/article/0,8599,1996810,00.html.
Evans, G. Blakemore, and J.J.M. Tobin, editors. *The Riverside Shakespeare*. 2nd edition, Houghton Mifflin, 1997.

Forgotten Miracle. Directed by Tommy Haines and Andrew Sherburne, performed by John Mayasich, Bill Cleary and Jack McCartan, Golden Puck Pictures, 2009.

Freedman, Penelope. *Power and Passion in Shakespeare's Pronouns: Interrogating "you" and "thou."* Ashgate, 2007.

Freud, Sigmund. *Writings on Art and Literature*. Stanford UP, 1997.

Frost, Robert. "Mending Wall." *The Poetry of Robert Frost*, edited by Edward Connery Latham. Holt, Rinehart, and Winston, 1969.

Garner, Joe. *And the Crowd Goes Wild*. Sourcebooks, 1999.

Gendin, Sidney. "Non-Steroid Users Should Be Barred from Athletic Competition." *MESO-Rx*, CEM/MESO, Fall 2000. http://people.bridgewater.edu/~rhammill/Word%20Documents/Non-steroid%20users%20should%20be%20barred%20from%20athletic%20competition.pdf.

Gibson, Kirk. "Kirk Gibson—Interview." *YouTube*, SteinerSports, 15 Oct. 2008, www.youtube.com/watch?v=8PlWhQ6gaPY.

Gladwell, Malcolm. "Drugstore Athlete." *New Yorker*, 10 Sept. 2001, pp. 52–59.

Goldberg, Jonathan. *Sodometries: Renaissance Texts, Modern Sexualities*. Stanford UP, 1992.

Goudsouzian, Aram. "'My Impact Will Be Everlasting': Wilt Chamberlain in History and Memory." *Journal of Sport History*, vol. 32, no. 2, Summer 2005, pp. 235–48.

Greenblatt, Stephen J. "Learning to Curse: Aspects of Linguistic Colonialism in the Sixteenth Century." *First Images of America: The Impact of the New World on the Old*, edited by Fredi Chiappelli, J.B. Michael, and Robert L. Benson. U of California P, 1976, pp. 561–80. 2 vols.

———. *Learning to Curse: Essays in Early Modern Culture*. Routledge, 1990.

Gruver, Ed. *Baltimore to Broadway: Joe, the Jets, and the Super Bowl III Guarantee*. Triumph, 2009.

Hammond, Paul. "Shakespeare's Male Utopias." *Etudes Anglaises*, vol. 61, no. 3, 2008, pp. 266–78.

Harbage, Alfred. "Shakespeare and the Myth of Perfection." *Shakespeare 400: Essays by American Scholars on the Anniversary of the Poet's Birth*, edited by James G. McManaway. Holt, Rinehart and Winston, 1964, pp. 1–10.

Hass, Nancy. "Love Me, Hate Me, Just Don't Ignore Me." *GQ*, vol. 82, no. 2, Feb. 2012, pp. 48–54, 119, www.gq.com/story/terrell-owens-nfl-football-wide-receiver.

Hawkes, Terence. *Shakespeare's Talking Animals: Language and Drama in Society*. London, Arnold, 1973.

Hazlitt, William. *Characters of Shakespeare*. Oxford UP, 1952.

Healy, Margaret. *William Shakespeare, Richard II*. Plymouth, UK, Northcote House/British Council, 1998. Writers and Their Work.

Henry V. Directed by Kenneth Branagh, performed by Kenneth Branagh and Derek Jacobi, Renaissance Films, 1989.

Hirsch, Brett D. "'What are these faces?': Interpreting Bearded Women in *Macbeth*." *Renaissance Poetry and Drama in Context: Essays for Christopher Wortham*, edited by Andrew Lynch and Anne M. Scott. Newcastle, Cambridge Scholars, 2008, pp. 91–113.

Holland, Norman N. "Shakespeare's Mercutio and Ours." *Michigan Quarterly*, vol. 5, Spring 1996, pp. 115–23.

Hunt, Maurice. "Malvolio, Viola, and the Question of Instrumentality: Defining Providence in *Twelfth Night*." *Studies in Philology*, vol. 90, Summer 1993, pp. 277–97.

Jackson, Phil, and Charley Rosen. *More than a Game*. Fireside/Simon & Schuster, 2001.

Jones, Marion. Interview on *Oprah*. WLS-TV, Harpo Studios, 29 Oct. 2008.

———. *On the Right Track*. Howard, 2010.

"June 17, 1994." *30 for 30*, directed by Brett Morgan, vol. 1, episode 15, ESPN, 16 June 2010.

Kemper, Becky. "A Clown in the Dark House: Reclaiming the Humor in Malvolio's Downfall." *Journal of the Wooden O Symposium*, vol. 7, 2007, pp. 42–50.

Kermode, Frank, ed. *The Tempest*. Arden 6th edition, Methuen, 1964.

Kilduff, Gavin J., Hillary Anger Elfenbein, and Barry M. Staw. "The Psychology of Rivalry:

A Relationally Dependent Analysis of Competition." *Academy of Management Journal*, vol. 53, no. 5, 2010, pp. 943–69.

Kimbrough, Robert. "Macbeth: The Prisoner of Gender." *Shakespeare Studies*, vol. 16, 1983, pp. 175–90.

King, Billie Jean. Personal interview by Erica Hill. *CBS This Morning*, CBS, 22 June 2012.

Klosterman, Chuck. *Sex, Drugs, and Cocoa Puffs: A Low Culture Manifesto*. Scribner's, 2003.

Knights, L.C. *How Many Children Had Lady Macbeth? An Essay in the Theory and Practice of Shakespeare Criticism*. 1933. Haskell, 1973.

Lasorda, Tommy. Personal Interview. 1 Dec. 2011.

A League of Their Own. Directed by Penny Marshall, performed by Geena Davis and Madonna, Columbia, 1992.

Leavy, Jane. *The Last Boy: Mickey Mantle and the End of America's Childhood*. HarperCollins, 2010.

Lenz, Carolyn R.S., Gayle Greene, and Carol Thomas Neely, eds. *The Woman's Part: Feminist Criticism of Shakespeare*. U of Illinois P, 1980.

Levy, Ariel. "Trial by Twitter." *The New Yorker*, vol. 5, Aug. 2013, pp. 38–49.

Lewis, Cynthia. "Emphasis Added: Reading Shakespeare's Language Clearly." *Early Modern Culture*, vol. 12, 2017, tigerprints.clemson.edu/cgi/viewcontent.cgi?article=1027&context=emc.

———. "Horns, the Dream-Work, and Female Potency in as *You Like It*." *South Atlantic Review*, vol. 66, no. 4, 2001, pp. 45–69.

Lin, Erika T. "Popular Festivity and the Early Modern Stage: The Case of George A. Greene." *Theatre Journal*, vol. 61, 2009, pp. 271–97.

Macbeth. Directed by Roman Polanski, performed by Jon Finch and Francesca Annis, 1971.

Macbeth. Directed by Rupert Goold, performed by Patrick Stewart and Kate Fleetwood, 2010. Great Performances.

Machiavelli, Niccolò. *The Prince*. 1513. *Machiavelli: The Chief Works and Others*, translated by Allan Gilbert. Vol. 1. Duke UP, 1965.

Macur, Juliet. "How Armstrong's Wall Fell, One Rider at a Time." *New York Times*, National edition, 21 Oct. 2012, A1+.

Mangan, Michael. *Staging Masculinities: History, Gender, Performance*. Palgrave Macmillan, 2003.

Mantle, Mickey. "Time in a Bottle." *Sports Illustrated*, 18 Apr. 1994, pp. 66–77.

"Marion Jones: Press Pause." *30 for 30*, directed by John Singleton, vol. 2, episode 28, ESPN, 2 Nov. 2011.

Marlowe, Christopher. *Doctor Faustus*. Edited by Roma Gill, 2nd edition, Norton/New Mermaids, 1989.

———, and James R. Siemon. *The Jew of Malta*. London: Black [u.a.], 1994.

Marrero, Mercedes. "Nancy López." *Latino Legends in Sports*, 2003, http://www.latinosportslegends.co/Lopez_Nancy-bio.htm.

Matz, Robert. *The World of Shakespeare's Sonnets: An Introduction*. McFarland, 2008.

McArthur, Herbert. "Romeo's Loquacious Friend." *Shakespeare Quarterly*, vol. 10, no. 1, Winter 1959, pp. 35–44.

McCallum, Jack. "The Rivalry." *Sports Illustrated*, vol. 108, no. 23, 9 June 2008, pp. 36–42. https://www.si.com/vault/2008/06/09/105700886/the-rivalry#.

Miracle. Directed by Gavin O'Connor, performed by Kurt Russell and Patricia Clarkson, 2004.

Montrose, Louis Adrian. "'The Place of a Brother' in as *You Like It*: Social Process and Comic Form." *Shakespeare Quarterly*, vol. 32, 1981, pp. 28–54.

O'Neil, Paul. "The Great Broadway Joe Is Brash, Arrogant, and Lives It Up But ... He Gets Away with It." *Life*, 24 Jan. 1969, pp. 24–29.

Osborne, Laurie E. "Antonio's Pardon." *Shakespeare Quarterly*, vol. 45, 1994, pp. 108–14.

Orgel, Stephen. "Prospero's Wife." *Representations*, vol. 8, 1984, pp. 1–13.

Padawer, Ruth. "The Humiliating Practice of Sex-Testing Female Athletes." *New York Times*

Magazine, 28 June 2016, www.nytimes.com/2016/07/03/magazine/the-humiliating-practice-of-sex-testing-female-athletes.html.

Palfrey, Simon. *Doing Shakespeare*. The Arden Shakespeare, London, Thomson Learning, 2005.

Pat and Mike. Directed by George Cukor, performed by Katharine Hepburn and Spencer Tracy, MGM, 1952.

Pequigney, Joseph. "The Two Antonios and Same-Sex Love in *Twelfth Night and the Merchant of Venice*." *English Literary Renaissance*, vol. 22, 1992, pp. 201–21.

Porter, Joseph A. "Marlowe, Shakespeare, and the Canonization of Heterosexuality." *Displacing Homophobia: Gay Male Perspectives in Literature and Culture*, edited by Ronald R. Butters, John M. Clum, and Michael Moon. Duke UP, 1989, pp. 127–47.

Pritner, Cal, and Louis Colaianni. *How to Speak Shakespeare*. Santa Monica P, 2001.

Rabkin, Norman. *Shakespeare and the Problem of Meaning*. U of Chicago P, 1981.

Rodenburg, Patsy. *Speaking Shakespeare*. Palgrave Macmillan, 2002.

Romeo and Juliet. Directed by Carlo Carlei, performed by Hailee Steinfeld and Douglas Booth, Amber Entertainment, 2013.

Romeo and Juliet. Directed by Franco Zeffirelli, performed by Olivia Hussey and Leonard Whiting, BHE Films, 1968.

Rose, Mary Beth. *Gender and Heroism in Early Modern Language*. U of Chicago P, 2002.

Rose, Pete. *My Prison Without Bars*. Rodale, 2000.

Rosenberg, Mary. "Marlowe and Mercutio." *Shakespeare Newsletter*, vol. 58, no. 2, Fall 2008, pp. 55–56, 79.

Rosenberg, Michael. "Lakers-Celtics: The Good, Old Days." *Detroit Free Press*, 1 June 2010, http://www.freep.com/.

Saccio, Peter. *Shakespeare's English Kings: History, Chronicle, and Drama*. Oxford UP, 1977.

St. Onge, Peter. "Getting the 'W' Without Winning." *Charlotte Observer*, 25 Aug. 2012, p. 14 A.

Schwartz, Larry. "Namath Was Lovable Rogue." *ESPN Classic*, n.d., espn.go.com/classic/biography/s/namath_joe.html.

Schwarz, Kathryn. *What You Will: Gender, Contract, and Shakespearean Social Space*. U of Pennsylvania P, 2011.

Shakespeare, William. *Antony and Cleopatra*. Edited by Evans and Tobin, pp. 1395–1439.

———. *As You Like It*. Edited by Evans and Tobin, pp. 403–36.

———. *Cymbeline*. Edited by Evans and Tobin, pp. 1569–1611.

———. *Hamlet*. Edited by Evans and Tobin, pp. 1189–1245.

———. *Henry IV*, parts 1 and 2. Edited by Evans and Tobin, pp. 889–972.

———. *Henry V*. Edited by Evans and Tobin, pp. 979–1020.

———. *King Lear*. Edited by Evans and Tobin, pp. 1303–54.

———. *Love's Labor's Lost*. Edited by Evans and Tobin, pp. 213–50.

———. *Macbeth*. Edited by Evans and Tobin, pp. 1360–90.

———. *The Merchant of Venice*. Edited by Evans and Tobin, pp. 288–319.

———. *A Midsummer Night's Dream*. Edited by Evans and Tobin, pp. 256–83.

———. *Pericles*. Edited by Evans and Tobin, pp. 1531–64.

———. *Richard II*. Edited by Evans and Tobin, pp. 847–83.

———. *Romeo and Juliet*. Edited by Evans and Tobin, pp. 1104–45.

———. *The Taming of the Shrew*. Edited by Evans and Tobin, pp. 142–75.

———. *The Tempest*. Edited by Evans and Tobin, pp. 1661–88.

———. *Twelfth Night*. Edited by Evans and Tobin, pp. 442–75.

———. *The Winter's Tale*. Edited by Evans and Tobin, pp. 1617–54.

Shakespeare in Love. Directed by John Madden, performed by Gwyneth Paltrow and Joseph Fiennes, Universal Pictures, 1998.

Shapiro, Michael. *Gender in Play on the Shakespearean Stage: Boy Heroines and Female Pages*. U of Michigan P, 1994.

She's the Man. Directed by Andy Fickman, performed by Amanda Bynes and Channing Tatum, Dreamworks, 2006.

Sinfield, Alan. *Macbeth. New Casebooks*, St. Martin's, 1992.
Smith, Hallett. Introduction to *The Tempest*. Edited by Evans and Tobin, pp. 1656–60.
Spencer, Nancy E. "Reading Between the Lines: A Discursive Analysis of the Billie Jean King Vs. Bobby Riggs 'Battle of the Sexes.'" *Sociology of Sport Journal*, vol. 17, 2000, pp. 386–402.
Stern, Tiffany. *Rehearsal from Shakespeare to Sheridan*. Oxford, Clarendon, 2000.
Thompson, Carmen Renee. "Repaying by the Hour." *ESPN the Magazine*. ESPN, 20 May 2011, www.espn.com/espn/news/story?id=6570816.
Traub, Valerie. "Desire and the Difference It Makes." *The Matter of Difference: Materialist Feminist Criticism of Shakespeare*, edited by Valerie Wayne, Cornell UP, 1991, pp. 81–114.
"U.S. Women's Soccer, Water Polo Team Go for Gold." *Morning Edition*, hosted by Renee Montagne, Natl. Public Radio, 9 Aug. 2012. Radio.
Van Natta, Don. *Wonder Girl: The Magnificent Sporting Life of Babe Didrikson Zaharias*. Little, Brown, 2011.
Whalen, Denise A. *Construction of Female Homoeroticism in Early Modern Drama*. Palgrave Macmillan, 2005. Early Modern Cultural Studies.
Zaharias, Babe Didrikson, and Harry Paxton. *This Life I've Led: My Autobiography*. A.S. Barnes, 1955.

Index

Numbers in **bold italics** indicate pages with illustrations

A-10 Conference (NCAA) 74, 77
Abram (*Romeo and Juliet*) 13
Ackland, Joss ***125***
Adam (also old Adam) (*As You Like It*) 58, 59, 67, 71, 73
Adam and Eve 56
Adams, Abigail 138
AFL (American Football League) 84, 86, 89; merger with NFL 84, 89, 99
Agassi, Andre: achievements 169; challenges 166, 167, 173; competition with Pete Sampras 176, 179; marriage to Brook Shields 169; marriage to Stefanie ("Steffi") Graf 179–80; *Open* 166, 167, 179; perfectionism 168–69; pride 169–70, ***170***; rage 179; recovery 179–80, 182; as teeterer 169–71
agency (free will) *see* Lady Macbeth, influence over Macbeth; Macbeth (character), agency of; *Macbeth*, tragic cause in; *Romeo and Juliet*, tragic cause in
Agincourt, Battle of 10, 84, 87, 94, 95, 102; decisive factors 97, 193n12; English victory over France 52, 84, 98; parallels with Leicester City triumph 99; parallels with Super Bowl III 98
Aguecheek, Sir Andrew 122, 123–26, ***125***, 130, 134, 135
Alexander the Great 102
Alice, Dame (*Henry V*) 92
Aliena *see* Celia
All-American Girls Professional Baseball League 128
Allen, Kevin 37, 51
Allen, Ray 17
Allen Wranglers 157
Alonso 168, 180, 183; redemption 181; resurrection 182; "three men of sin" 174–76, 181, 185
American Football League *see* AFL

Andrew Aguecheek, Sir *see* Aguecheek, Sir Andrew
Angell, Roger 10
Ann-Margret ***93***
Antetokounmpo, Giannis 72
Antonio (*The Tempest*) 166, 180, 182, 196n7; compared to Pete Sampras 176; evil 168, 173–74, 181; question of penitence 181; "three men of sin" 174–76, 181, 185
Antonio (*Twelfth Night*) 126, 129, 130; complexity of character 120; homoeroticism 193n7; as wise fool in love 119–21, 122, 123, 130, 131, 193n7
Antony, Mark *see* Mark Antony
Antony and Cleopatra 11, 188
Apothecary (*Romeo and Juliet*) 20, 29
Appalachian State University 38
Archbishop of Canterbury (*Henry V*) 86, 88–89, ***88***, 96
Arden *see* Forest of Arden
Arenas, Gilbert 22
Ariel 166, ***167***, 172, 180, 182, 183, 196n7; as agent of mercy 176, 178–79; gender 196n1; as harpy 175–76, 185; nature 170; relationship with Prospero 170–71, 183
Armstrong, Lance 94, 143, 148, 150, 154, 160, ***161***, 195n12
Arsenal soccer team (England) 106
Arsenal Stadium 110
A's *see* Oakland Athletics
As You Like It 12, 55, 56, 57, 67, 68, 73, 74, 131, 193n1; bloody napkin 65; brotherhood 91ch3n1; chain 60, 66; gender identity 60–63, 74, 191ch3n4, 193n1; homoerotic play 192ch3n6; jealousy 56–57; male fear of betrayal, commitment 60, 64, 65; narration 73–74; nature 57–58, 73; Phebe/Silvius subplot 62–63, 73; resolution 7–68, 74, 192ch3n8; as romantic comedy 59, 74;

snake 63, 66; sudden changes 66, 74; symbolism 66–67
Association of Tennis Professionals (ATP) 169
Athletics *see* Oakland Athletics
Atlanta Braves 23
Atlanta Falcons 182
Atlanta Olympics (1966) 169
Audrey (*As You Like It*) 74
Auerbach, Red **15**, 190*n*2
Augustus (Octavius) Caesar 11
Aumerle, Duke of 41, 45, 47, 48, 52, 54, 191*n*6, 191*n*7
Australian Open 169
Ayatollah Khomeini 50

Bach, Rebecca Ann 101
"Bad Boys of the NBA" *see* Detroit Pistons
Bagot, Sir John (*Richard II*) 39, 41, 45
Baldwin, Alec **147**
Balthasar (*Romeo and Juliet*) 13, 29
Baltimore Colts 84, 87, 89, 98, 192*n*4
Banks, Dick 133
Banquo 144, 145, 146, 163, 195*n*16; ghost 148, 163; as Macbeth's foil 150, 155
Bardolph 89, 90, 94, 95, 102
Barton, Anne 122
Barton, John 136, 190*intro.n*6
Baseball Hall of Fame 71, 72, 143, 158
Bassett, Angela **147**
Bates, John (*Henry V*) 95, 96
The Battle of the Sexes (film) 193*n*3
"The Battle of the Sexes" (tennis match) 193*n*3; *see also* King, Billie Jean; Riggs, Bobby
Bear-baiting 5, 189*n*1
Belch, Sir Toby 120, 123–27, **125**, 130, 134–35
Belsey, Catherine 193*n*5
Benvolio 17, 20, 21, 31, 32
Berkeley, Lord (*Richard II*) 41
Berlin Olympics (1936) 69–70, **70**
Berry, Ralph 194*n*10
Berry, Wendell 191*ch*3*n*2
Bias, Len 17
Bird, Larry 13, 14, 17, 20, 30
Bishop of Carlisle (*Richard II*) *see* Carlisle, Bishop of
Bishop of Ely (*Henry V*) 86, 88–89, **88**
Blinebury, Fran 13
Bloom, Harold 192*ch*4*n*6
Bloom, John 192*n*4
Boar's Head Inn 86
Bonds, Barry 143, 195*n*7
Booth, Douglas **19**
Borden, Sam 99
Boston Celtics **15**, 28, 190*n*2; rivalry with L.A. Lakers 1, 10, 13, 14, 16–17, 30; "Three Amigos" 17
Bosworth Field 103
Bottom (*A Midsummer Night's Dream*) 190*ch*1*n*7

Bournemouth soccer team (England) 105
Boy (*Henry V*) 90, 91, 95, 102
Boyer, Peter 117
Bradley, A.C. 150, 194*n*2, 194*n*3
Bradley, Bill 80–81
Brady, Tom 137, 182
Branagh, Kenneth **88**, 92
Branch, Taylor 195*n*14
Bray, Alan 192*ch*4*n*5
Bristol, Michael D. 194*n*3
Brokaw, Tom 4
Brooklyn Dodgers **71**, 72
Brooks, Cleanth 195*n*3
Brooks, Herb 34–35, 37, 40, 191*n*8; loss at 1960 Olympics 191*ch*2*n*8
Browne, Thomas 190*ch*1*n*6
Bryant, Kobe 13, 17, 20, 28, 30, 94
Buck, Jack 55–56
Buffalo Bills 156
bull-baiting 189*n*1
Bull Durham 12
Bullingbrook 35, 44, 45, 47, 49, 103; characterization 40, 44, 50, 191*ch*2*n*2; exile 36, 37, 39, 45, 46, 49, 53; as Lord Appellant 53; motives 36, 40, 42; overreaching 40–42, 46, 48, 50, 52; as politician 40–41, 43, 44, 45; popular support 34–35, 39, 46; verbal ambiguity 40, 42, 43, 45, 46, 47, 53–54; *see also* Henry IV
Bullough, Geoffrey 192*ch*4*n*9
Burbage, Richard 7
Bushy, Sir John (*Richard II*) 39, 41
Buss, Jerry 190*n*2
Bynes, Amanda 194*n*11

Caesar, Augustus (Octavius) *see* Augustus (Octavius) Caesar
Cahn, Susan 121, 128
Cain and Abel 56–57
Calef, Victor 194*n*3
Caliban 166, 171, 174, 177, 178, 179, 181, 183, 184; complexity of character 172, 184, 196*n*4; contrasted with Ferdinand 172, 173, 185; name 196*n*5; relationship with Prospero 171–74, 176, 180–81, 184, 196*n*4
Callaghan, Dympna 193*n*5
Cambridge, Earl of (*Henry V*) 89
Canseco, Jose 67, 143; *Juiced* 194*n*1
Canterbury, Archbishop of *see* Archbishop of Canterbury
Captain (*King Lear*) 136
Capulet, Lady *see* Lady Capulet
Capulet, Lord *see* Lord Capulet
Capulets 10, 17, 18, **19**, 21, 23, 28, 30; monument 29; rivalry with Montagues 1, 13, 14, 18, 23, 29, 30–31
Carell, Steve 193*n*3
Carlesimo, P.J. 22
Carlisle, Bishop of (*Richard II*) 35, 39
Carolina Panthers 81

Index

Carson, Johnny 101
Cawdor, Thane of *see* Thane of Cawdor
Cayleff, Susan E. 114, 115
C.C. & Company **93**
Celia 74, 193n1; as Aliena 63, 64, 193n1; devotion to Rosalind 57; role of as priest 64–65
Cesario 113, 117, 119, 122, 123, 126, 193n5, 193n6; *see also* Viola
Chamberlain, Stephanie 194n3
Chamberlain, Wilt 13, 14, **16**, 17
Champions League (soccer) 108–9
Chand, Dutee 128–29
Charles the Wrestler (*As You Like It*) 56, 60, 65, 73
Chastain, Brandi 130
Chelsea soccer team (England) 106, 108
Chicago White Sox 23
Chorus (*Henry V*) 89, 91, 95, 99, 101
Chorus (*Romeo and Juliet*) 20
Christian, Dave 37
Cialdini, Robert B. 189n5
Cincinnati Bengals 156
Cincinnati Reds 143, **157**, 158
Claribel (*The Tempest*) 183
Clemente, Roberto 72
Cleveland Cavaliers 82
Colaianni, Louis 164, 190*intro*.n6
Cold War 50
Connors, Jimmy 166
Constable (*Henry V*) 193n12
Cordelia 136
Court, Alexander (*Henry V*) 95
Cowell, Simon 99
Craig, Jim 37
Crécy, Battle of 89
Crittenton, Javaris 22
Crouchback, Edmund 42
Cukor, George 128
Curry, Dell 80
Curry, Sonya 80
Curry, Stephen 74, 76, 80–83
Cymbeline 180

Daley, A. Stuart 191*ch*3n3
Dallas Cowboys 156, 157
Dauphin (*Henry V*) *see* Dolphin
Davidson College 74, **75**, 76
Davis, Geena 128
Davis, Mike 55, 66
Daw, Kurt 190*intro*.n6
Declaration of Sports (1617) 4, 189n1
Deford, Frank 10
Del Villano, Bianca 195n4
Dench, Judi **125**
Detroit Pistons 17
Detroit Tigers 67
DiGangi, Mario 192*ch*3n6
Do You Believe in Miracles? 37, 50, 51
Doctor (*Macbeth*) 154
Doctor Faustus *see* Marlowe, Christopher

Dodd, Mike 158, 161
Dodger Stadium 55
Dodgers *see* L. A. Dodgers
Dolphin (Dauphin) (*Henry V*) 85–86, 92–93, 95, 97, 101, 102, 192n2
Donalbain 195n5
Douglas, Buster 99
Dowd, Maureen 155–56
Drake 83
Duchess of Gloucester 36, 51
Duchess of York 48, 54, 191n7
Duerr, Charlie 13, 16
Duke Frederick 59, 131; animus toward Duke Senior 57, 58; conversion 67, 74; court 73; jealousy 57; shame 57
Duke of Gloucester *see* Woodstock, Thomas of
Duke of Lancaster *see* Bullingbrook; Gaunt, John of
Duke of Norfolk *see* Mowbray, Thomas
Duke of Northumberland *see* Northumberland, Duke of
Duke of York *see* York, Duke of
Duke Senior 57, 67, 73, 131; exile 57, 58; popularity 57; positive attitude 57, 58, 59, 73; skepticism toward Jaques 59; usurpation of by Duke Frederick 57
Duke University 7
Duncan: murder 144, 146, 147, 148, 153, 155, 194n2
Durocher, Leo 72

Earl of Worcester *see* Worcester, Earl of
early modern staging *see* Original Practices
Eckersley, Dennis 55–56, 66
Edgar (*King Lear*) 4, 51
Edmund (*King Lear*) 4, 136
Edward the Confessor 158
Elfenbein, Hillary Anger 14
Eliot, T.S. 137
Elizabeth I 7, 52–53, 84, 85, 189n1, 191*ch*2n1; as Machiavellian monarch 101
Ely, Bishop of *see* Bishop of Ely
Ely, England 192n3
Epiphany/epiphany 122–23
Erpingham, Sir Thomas (*Henry V*) 95
Eruzione, Mike 37
Escalus, Prince (*Romeo and Juliet*) 13, 14, 22, 31, 32
Essex, Earl of 53
Essex Rebellion 52–53
Exeter, Duke of 89
Exton, Sir Pierce of 48–49, 50, 54

Fabian 124, 126, 127, 130, 135
Falstaff, Sir John 86, 90, 91; character 192*ch*4n6
fate *see* *Macbeth*, tragic cause in; *Romeo and Juliet*, tragic cause in; Weïrd Sisters
Ferdinand 166, 170, 171, 174, 175, 176, 181, 183,

196n3; contrasted with Caliban 172, 173, 185; resurrection 182; temptation 177–78
Feste 118, 120, 124, 126–27; final song 128–29; name 127; as Sir Topas 126–27
Fitch, Bill 190n2
Fitzwater, Lord 45, 48
Fleance 144
Fleetwood, Kate 194n3
Flint Castle 41, 46, 53
Fluellen 92, 95, 99–100, 102; dialect 102, 192ch4n7
Flute (*A Midsummer Night's Dream*) 190ch1n7
Fool (*King Lear*) 131
football *see* soccer in England
Football Association Challenge Cup (FA Cup) (England) 105
Football Bowl Subdivision (FBS) 38–39
Football Championship Subdivision (FCS) 38–39
"football hooliganism" 23
Forest of Arden 56, 57, 58, 60, 66; correspondences with baseball field 57, 59
Forgotten Miracle 50
Fort Riley, Kansas 72
Foster, David T., III **75**
Francis, Bev 193n2
free will (agency) *see* agency (free will)
Freedman, Penelope 191ch1n8
Freeh, Louis 195n13
Freeman, Freddie 23
French Princess (*Love's Labor's Lost*) 51
Freud, Sigmund 194n3
Friar Lawrence 14, 18, 20, 25, 27, 31, 32, 134; compared to athletic coach 27–28, 29; desperation 27, 28–29, 30; illiteracy 27

Gallico, Paul 114
Ganymed: as Rosalind's disguise 60–62, **61**, 63, 64, **63**, 191ch3n4; *see also* Rosalind; Rosalind/Ganymed
Gardener (*Richard II*) 44, 49–50
Garnett, Kevin 13, 17, 20
Garvin, Mark **132**
Gaunt, John of (Duke of Lancaster) 36, 37, 46, 49, 53
Gendin, Sidney 194n1
Genesis, biblical book of: Adam and Eve 56; Cain and Abel 56
Gentlewoman (*Macbeth*) 154
Gibson, Kirk 65, 66; changed mind 55–56, 65; heroism 67–68; home run 55–56, 67; humility 58, 68; marriage 67
Gladwell, Malcolm 150–51, 194n1
Globe Theater 84
Gloucester, Duke of (*Richard II*) *see* Woodstock, Thomas of
Gloucester, Earl of (*King Lear*) 4
Goldberg, Jonathan 192ch4n5
Golden State Warriors 22, 74, 77, 82

Gómez, Carlos 23
Gonzalo 131, 166, 174–75, 176
Goold, Rupert 194n3
Goudsouzian, Aram 14
Gower (*Henry V*) 95
Graf, Stefanie ("Steffi") 179–80
Gratiano (*The Merchant of Venice*) 131
Great Depression 69
Green, Sir Henry (*Richard II*) 36, 39, 41
Green Bay Packers 10
Greenblatt, Stephen 196n2, 196n4
Greene, Gayle 192ch3n5
Gregory (*Romeo and Juliet*) 13
Grey, Sir Thomas (*Henry V*) 89
Groom (*Richard II*) 49–50
Gruver, Ed 87, 98
guards (*Macbeth*) 153
Gunpowder Plot (1605) 195n11

Hal *see* Prince Hal
Hamlet (character) 133, 143, 189n4
Hamlet (play) 4, 6, 96, 133, 189n4
Hammond, Paul 193n7
Harbage, Alfred 190n8
Harfleur ("Harflew") 11, 91–92
Harper, Bryce 23
Hass, Nancy 157
Hatcher, Mickey 23
Hawkes, Terence 190n1
Hazlitt, William 94
Healy, Margaret 191ch2n1
Hecate 144
Hefner, Hugh 99
Henry IV (character) 34, 35, 44, 45, 46, 47, 52, 54, 89, 103; as politician 40–41, 42, 43, 45, 191ch2n3; pride 50; testing 48; theatricality 46; verbal ambiguity 42, 47, 48–49, 54; *see also* Bullingbrook
Henry IV, parts 1 and 2 (plays) 41, 45, 47, 49, 53, 86, 89, 90, 192n2
Henry V (character) 10, 11, 12, 35, 84–88, **88**, 102–103; at Agincourt 52; complexity of character 94, 95–96, 99–101, 192n10; conquest of Princess Katherine 92–94; death 98–99; dubious morality 90–92, 95, 96, 100, 192n10, 193n11; masculinity 101; parallels with Joe Namath 94, 98, 101, 192n2; and Pistol 102, 193n11; as politician 41, 42, 191ch2n3; rhetorical skills 87, 91, 100; sensitivity to insults 192n2; sympathy for 97; treatment of Montjoy 102; trustworthiness 87–91, 96–97, 99–100; as victor 97; wooing of Princess Katherine 100–1; *see also* Prince Hal
Henry V (1989 film) **88**, 92
Henry V (play) 11, 35, 52, 53, 84, 86, 94, 98, 187, 192ch4n8; brother in 102; dialects 102, 192ch4n7; England's invasion of France 11, 85–86, 88–89, **88**, 90; England's loss of France 99; French ridicule of English 85–86,

Index

95, 101, 102–3, 192n2; male rivalry 85–86, 92–93, 101–2; masculinity 101; *mock* in 102–3; *reckoning* in 96, 103; ridicule of French 85, 95, 102–3; St. Crispin's Day speech 87, 97, 100, 102
Henry VI 35
Henry VII 53, 103
Henry VIII 53
Hepburn, Katharine **61**, 128
Herford, Duke of (Henry) *see* Bullingbrook; Henry IV (character)
Hirsch, Brett D. 195n4
Hitler, Adolf 69–70
Hofstra University 74
Holinshed, Raphael 95, 192ch4n9
Holland, Norman N. 190ch1n6
Holtz, Lou 10
Hotspur 47, 192n2
Houston Astrodome 193n3
Houston Rockets 72
Hugh Capet 88
Hunt, Maurice 194n10
Hunter, C.J. 151, 195n6
Hussey, Oliva 32
Hymen 67

Illyria: name 120
Indoor Football League 157
IndyCar 117
International Association of Athletics Federations 129
International Olympic Committee (IOC) 142
"intersex" identity *see* sex-testing
Iowa University 39

Jackson, Phil 27, 30; *More Than a Game* 30
Jacksonville State University 193n4
James I (also James VI of Scotland) 4, 7, 189n1, 195n11, 195n16; *Daemonologie* 163
Jamy (*Henry V*) 92
Jaques 59, 131; hypocrisy 59; indirect introduction 58; as "melancholy malcontent" 57–58; realism 58; seven ages of man speech 58
Jesuits 155
The Jew of Malta see Marlowe, Christopher
Johnson, Magic (Earvin), Jr. 13, 14, 17, 20, 30
Johnson, Mark 37
Johnson, Vinnie 17
Jones, Marion 142, 143, 144, 151, 152, **152**, 161, 195n6; *On the Right Track* 195n15; Take a Break 161
Juliá, Raúl **149**, **174**
Juliet 18, 19–20, **19**, 22, 23, 24–25, 26, 27, 28, **28**, 29, 30, 31, 32, 33, 134, 143, 164, 190n4, 190n5; desperation 26, 27; maturation 19–20, 24–25, 28

Kahn, Michael **43**
Kanté, N'Golo 108

Katherina (*The Taming of the Shrew*) 51
Katherine, Princess of France (*Henry V*) 92, 100; wooing by Henry V 100–1
Kemper, Becky 194n10
Kermode, Frank 196n8
Kilduff, Gavin J. 14
Kimbrough, Robert 195n4
King, Billie Jean 116–17, **116**, 121, 193n3; political activism 116–17
King Harry *see* Henry V
King Lear (character) 131, **132**, 134, 136, 143
King Lear (play) 4, 51, 131, 136
King of England *see* Edward the Confessor; Henry IV; Henry V; Henry VI; Henry VII; Henry VIII; Hugh Capet; James I; Lewis the Tenth; Pepin; Richard II; Richard III
King of France (*Henry V*) 92
King of Scotland *see* Duncan, Macbeth, Malcolm
King's Men 7
Klosterman, Chuck 16
Knacke-Sommer, Christiane 150–51
Knights, L.C. 194n3
Kostos, Nick 182
Ku Klux Klan 69

Ladies Professional Golf Association *see* LPGA
Lady Capulet 18–19, 20, 25, 26, 29, 33
Lady Macbeth 53, 142, 151, 160, 163, 165, 194n2; crisscrossing with Macbeth 153–54, 163; death 154, 165; despair 153–54; disease (insanity) 154; gender traits 146; guilt 148, 163; influence over Macbeth 142, 144, 146, **147**, 148, 150, 160, 162; insecurity 144; introduction 145; possible lost child 146–47, 194n3; theatrical role 163; *see also* Duncan: murder of
Lady Macduff 159, 160
Laertes 133
Laimbeer, Bill 17
Lake Placid (NY) Olympics (1980) 34, **38**, 42; political shadings 51
Lamont, Gene 23
Lancaster, Duke of *see* Bullingbrook; Gaunt, John of
Lancaster, House of 35, 53
Landis, Floyd 148, 160
Lasorda, Tommy 55–56, 65; advice to players 57; as encouraging coach 59; parallel of with Gibson 68; strategy 66
Lawrence, Friar *see* Friar Lawrence
League Cup (England) 105
A League of Their Own 128
Leavy, Jane 195n8
Le Beau (*As You Like It*) 73
Leicester, England 103, 104
Leicester City football (soccer) team 99, 103–12; League Cup wins 105; parallels with Battle of Agincourt 99

Leicester City King Power Stadium **112**
Leicester City Premier soccer team 52
Lennox (*Macbeth*) 131, 153, 156
Lenz, Carolyn R.S. 192*ch*3*n*5
Levy, Ariel 156
Lewis, Cynthia 192*ch*3*n*7
Lewis the Tenth 88
Lombardi, Vince 10
London Olympics (2012) 3
Lopez, Nancy 115
Lord (*Macbeth*) 156
Lord Admiral's Men 189*n*4
Lord Capulet 13, 14, 15, 17, 20, 23, 24, 28, 31, 33, 131, 134, 190*n*4; aggression 24, 25–26, 29–30, 134
Lord Chamberlain's Men 7
Lord Montague 14, 30, 31, 32
Los Angeles (L.A.) Dodgers 55, 58, 59, 66, 67
Los Angeles (L.A.) Lakers 27, 28, 30, 190*n*2; rivalry with Boston Celtics 1, 10, 13, 14, **16**, 17, 30
Los Angeles Olympics (1932) 114
Louis, Joe 68–69; loss to Schmeling (1936) 68; as pioneer in integrating golf 69; rematch with Schmeling (1938) 68–69, **69**
Love's Labor's Lost 51, 191*ch*2*n*2
LPGA (Ladies Professional Golf Association) 114, 115
ludus see play (the act of playing)
Lyon, Lisa 193*n*2

Macbeth (character) 53, **147**, 154, 156, 158, 159, 160, 163, 165, 194*n*2, 195*n*16; agency 144–46, 149–51, 162, 195*n*5; ambition 142, 145; crisscrossing with Lady Macbeth 153–54, 163; despair 153–54, 158, 165; disease 154; equivocation 153–55; influences 142, 144, 145, 148–51, 149, 160, 162; insecurity 144; loss of conscience 153–54, 161, 163; motives 145–46, 160; murder of Macduff's family 144, 159; off-stage beheading 143; soliloquies 142, 163; temptation 142, 143, 144–46, 150, 162, 195*n*5; as tyrant 143, 148, 154, 156, 160; *see also* Duncan: murder of
Macbeth (1971 film) 195*n*5
Macbeth (play) 131, 142, 162, 163, 165, 188, 196*n*6; addiction in 43–44; children in 195*n*3; despair in 196*n*6; disease in 154, 158; emphases in verse 164–65; "England scene" 158–59; equivocation in 153–58; gender in 146–48, 195*n*4; good kingship in 163; Gunpowder Plot (1605) 195*n*11; higher power in 154; manliness in 159–60; parallels between characters and athletes 142, 143, 144, 146, 148, 150–52, 154, 155, 156–57, 158, 160–61, 164; religious framework 155; rhyme in 163; safety in 144, 154; soliloquies in 142, 163; stage properties in 146, 163; temptation in 142, 143, 144–46, 150; tragic cause (fate and free will / agency) in 142, 144–46, 149–52,

162; as tribute to James I 163, 195*n*16
Macbeth (2010 film) 194*n*3
Macduff 143, 153, 154, 155, 156, 195*n*10, 196*n*17; flight to England 144, 156, 159; loyalty to Scotland 158, 159, 160, 163; manliness 160; moral choices 159, 163; testing of Malcolm 158–59
Machiavelli, Niccolò 85, 101; political advice in *The Prince* 42, 45, 90–91, 94, 191*ch*2*n*5; source of characterization for Lancastrian kings 191*ch*2*n*3
Macmorris (*Henry V*) 92
Macur, Juliet 148, 160
Madonna 128
Mahrez, Riyad 108
Major League Baseball (MLB) 71, 72, 143, 195*n*7
Malcolm 131, 146, 154, 158, 188; on manliness 160; testing of Macduff 158–59; virtue 143, 158
Malvolio 11, 118, 119, 129, 130, 134; foolish love 120–21; injuries 127; name 120; plot against 123–27; as Puritan 193–94*n*8
Manchester City soccer team (England) 106
Manchester United soccer team (England) 106
Mangan, Michael 195*n*4
Manning, Peyton 6, 137
Mantle, Mickey 143, 151–52, 153, 161, **162**, 195*n*8
Maria 120, 124–27, **125**, 130, 134, 135
Mark Antony 11
Marlowe, Christopher: *Doctor Faustus* 195*n*9, 196*n*6; *The Jew of Malta* 189*n*4; and Mercutio 190*ch*1*n*6
Marrero, Mercedes 115
Martin, Ashley 193*n*4
masque: defined 196*n*9
Masque of Ceres (*The Tempest*): as play-within-a-play 177; *see also The Tempest*
Massey, Raymond **167**
The Matchmaker 138
Matz, Robert 192*ch*4*n*5
Maynard, Don 87
McArthur, Herbert 190*ch*1*n*6
McCallum, Jack 190*n*2
McCoy, Hal 158
McDowall, Roddy **167**
McGwire, Mark 67, 143, 155
McKillop, Bob 74–83, **75**; background 74; on basketball as improvisation 78; on a basketball court's resemblance to a stage 78, 79; challenges 77; coaching strategies 78, 82, 83; goals 77; on referees 78–79; on relationship between college academics and athletics 74–76; response to disappointment 79–80; on role of fans during a game 80; on Stephen Curry 76, 80–83
McPhee, John (*A Sense of Where You Are*) 81
"melancholy malcontent" *see* Jaques

The Merchant of Venice 131, 189*n*4
Mercutio 17, 20, 24, 31, 32; aggression 20–22; name 190*ch*1*n*6; Queen Mab monologue 20, 31
Messick, Andrew 148
Miami Heat 17
A Midsummer Night's Dream 11, 131, 133, 188, 190*n*3, 190*ch*1*n*7, 191*ch*2*n*2
Milwaukee Brewers 23
Milwaukee Bucks 72
Ming, Yao 72
Minnesota Timberwolves 23
Miracle (movie) 40
"Miracle" (1960 Olympics) 50
"Miracle on Ice" (1980 Olympics) 34, 50, 103
Miranda 166, 168, 170, 171, 172, 173, **174**, 175, 177, 178, 183, 184, 185, 196*n*3, 196*n*4; innocence 181
Mirren, Helen **63**
Monsieur Le Fer (*Henry V*) 193*n*11
Montague, Lord see Lord Montague
Montagues 10, 17; rivalry with Capulets 1, 13, 14, 18, 23, 29, 30–31
Montana, Joe 137
Montjoy (*Henry V*) 102
Montrose, Louis Adrian 191*ch*3*n*1, 192*ch*3*n*7
Morgan, Wes 108
Moscow Olympics (1980) 150–51
Mowbray, Thomas (Duke of Norfolk) 36, 45, 53
Muir, Kenneth 165
murderers (*Macbeth*) 150
Murray, Jim 4
My Prison Without Bars see Rose, Pete
Myshkin, Vladimir 37

Namath, Joe 84–87, **85**, **93**, 192*n*4; athletic ability 98; Bachelors III 86, 94; as "Broadway Joe" 86, 87, 94, 101; cultural significance 87; Hanes Beauty Mist advertisement 86; humble beginnings 97; as "Joe Willie" 86; maturation 97–98; parallels with Henry V/Prince Hal 94, 98, 101, 192*n*2; as victor 98
NASCAR 117
National Basketball Association see NBA
National Collegiate Athletic Association see NCAA
National Football League see NFL
National League (baseball) 68, 71
Nazism 68–70
NBA (National Basketball Association) 72, 74, 80, 193*n*4; aggression and violence 22–23; 2017 championship playoffs 82; rivalry 1, 10, 13, 14, 16, 17, 30
NCAA (National Collegiate Athletic Association) 193*n*4, 195*n*14; 2008 championship playoffs 77
Neely, Carol Thomas 192*ch*3*n*5
Neville, John **125**
New England Patriots 10, 182

New Historicism 196*n*2
New York Giants 10
New York Jets 6, 10, 84, **85**, 87, 89, 92, 94, 98
New York Knicks 14, 23
New York Mets 99
New York Yankees 72, 143, **162**
Newton, Cam 81
NFL (National Football League) 84, 87, 89, 94, 99, 157, 192*n*4
Nicholson, Jack 190*n*2
Norfolk, Duke of see Mowbray, Thomas
North Dakota State University 39
Northumberland, Duke of 41, 46, 47
Norwich soccer team (England) 105, 109
Nurse (Angelica) (*Romeo and Juliet*) 15, 19, 20, 21, 24, 25, 27, 28–29, 33, 190*n*5; compared to athletic coach 29; self-interest of 26–27
Nym 89, 90, 95, 102

Oakland Athletics 55, 66, 67
Ohio State University 69–70
Olbermann, Keith 10
Oliver 56, 59, 67, 74, 131; conversion 65–67, 74; jealousy 56–57; mistreatment of Orlando 56–57, 60; as narrator (4.3) 65–67, 73–74
Olivia, Countess 113, 117, 118–19, 120, 121, 123, 124, 127, 135, 193*n*6, 193*n*7, 193–94*n*8, 194*n*9; mad (wisely foolish) love 119, 122, 131
Olympics: amateurism in 51, 52; see also Atlanta; Berlin; Lake Placid; London; Los Angeles; Moscow; Rio; Rome; Squaw Valley; Sydney
On the Right Track see Jones, Marion
O'Neal, Shaquille 30
O'Neil, Paul 98
O'Neill, Della 52, 103–12, **104**, **112**
O'Neill, Kevin 52, 103–12, **104**, **112**
O'Neill, Martin 105
O'Neill, Tip 190*n*2
Open see Agassi, Andre
Orgel, Stephen 196*n*2
Original (early modern staging) Practices (OP) 5, 6, 189*n*3
Orlando 56, 57, 58, 60, 71, 74, 191*ch*3*n*4, 192*ch*3*n*8; as critic of Jaques 59; fear of betrayal, commitment 60, 64, 65–66, 73; as Ganymed's student 60–65, 73; growth 59, 65–66; heroism 67, 68, 73–74; naiveté 60, 63–65; overcoming adversity 60, 65–66; perseverance 57; positive attitude 59; wrestling victory 56, 60, 73
Orsino, Duke 113, 117, 118, 119, 120, 128, 129; as lover 121–22, 123
Osborne, Laurie E. 193*n*7
Osric (*Hamlet*) 133
Owens, Jesse 69–71, **70**

Owens, Terrell 156–57
Padawer, Ruth 129
Palfrey, Simon 190*intro.n*6
Papelbon, Jonathan 23
Parham, the Rev. Robert 158
Paris, Count (County) 18, 19, 23, 24, 25–26, 27, 28, 29, 30, 31, 32, 33
Pat and Mike 128
Paterno, Joe 155–56
Patrick, Danica 117
Pauline wise folly (concept) 120, 123, 193*n*7
Pennsylvania State University (Penn State) 155–56, 195*n*14
People's Light (Theater) *132*, 134, 138, 139
Pepin 88
Pequigney, Joseph 193*n*7
Percy, Henry *see* Hotspur
Pericles 180
Peter (*Romeo and Juliet*) 20
Phebe 62, 65, 73; attraction of to Ganymed 62–63; awakening 63; deception of Silvius 62–63
Philadelphia Eagles 110, 156
Philadelphia 76ers 74
Philadelphia Warriors 14
Pierce, Paul 17
Pistol 89, 90, 91, 95, 101, 102; parallels with Henry V 193*n*11
Pittsburgh Pirates 72, 195*n*7
play (the act of playing) 5–6, 8, 10–12
Plimpton, George 10, *11*
Plunkett, Sherman 86
Polanski, Roman 195*n*5
Polonius 139
Pomfret Castle 49, 52
Porter (*Macbeth*) 154–55
Porter, Joseph A. 190*ch*1*n*6
Premier League (England) 99; 2016 championship 103–12
The Prince see Machiavelli, Niccolò
Prince Escalus *see* Escalus, Prince
Prince Hal 41, 47, 86, 99, 192*n*2, 192*ch*4*n*5; trustworthiness of 86; *see also* Henry V
"Prince of Cats" *see* Tybalt
Pritner, Cal 164, 190*intro.n*6
Prospero 166, *167*, *174*, 182, 183, 184, 196*n*2, 196*n*4, 196*n*7; abuse of power 176, 178, 184, 185; books 168, 177, 182 183; collaboration with Providence 170, 175, 176, 178; complexity of character 170–71, 184; despair 169, 173; mercy 178–81, 185; perfectionism 168–69, 173, 180; pride 170–72, 173, 176; as protector of chastity 172, 177–78, 196*n*3; redemption 180–82; relationship with Ariel 170–71, 178, 183; relationship with Caliban 171–74, 176, 180–81, 184, 196*n*4; as teacher 175; as teeterer 168–69, 175, 176, 178; temptation 175, 178, 184
Puck 11, 133
Puritans 5; *see also* Malvolio, as Puritan

Queen Mab monologue *see* Mercutio
Queen of England *see* Elizabeth I; *Richard II*, Queen (Isabel) in
Quickly, Hostess (*Henry V*) 90
Quinn, Brady 182

Rabkin, Norman 94
Ranieri, Claudio 99, 109–11
Reynard the Fox 21
Richard II (character) 45, 48, 49, 51, 53; abuse of power 49; Bullingbrook's (Henry IV's) disrespect 41; characterization 191*ch*2*n*2; claim to divine right 34–35, 39; corrupt court 40, 49; decline from power 42; deposition 34–35, 40, 42, *43*, 44, 47, 50, 52, 191*ch*2*n*4; over-confidence 34–35, 39, 52, 103; overreaching 36–37, 50; role in Thomas of Woodstock's death 36, 53; self-pity 39; soliloquy (5.5) 49, 52; sympathy for 46–47, 49–50, 52, 54; theatrical behavior 36
Richard II (play) 34, 46, 47, 50, 103, 190*n*3, 191*ch*2*n*2; censorship 191*ch*2*n*4; divine right in 34–35, 39, 51; humor in 52; parallel quarrels in 45; Queen (Isabel) in 39, 44, 46, 47, 50, 51; rebellion in 47–48; stage properties in 43, 51–52; subtext in 40, 53–54; trust in 47, 49; *un-*words in 35; verbal ambiguity in 40, 42, 43–44, 47, 48–49, 52–54; women's roles in 51
Richard III: corpse 103–4, 110; as Shakespearean character 103
Richmond, Earl of *see* Henry VII
Riggs, Bobby 116, 193*n*3
Riley, Charles 71
Riley, Pat 190*n*2
Ringwald, Molly *174*
Rio Olympics (2016) 31
Rivera, Mariano 72
Robinson, Jackie 71–72, *71*; civil rights activism 71–72; induction into Baseball Hall of Fame 71; racial prejudice toward in MLB 72; support of by Joe Louis 72
Rodenburg, Patsy 190*intro.n*6
Rome Olympics (1960) 115
Romeo 15, 17, 18, *19*, 20, 21, 22, 24, 25, 26, 27, 28, 29, 30, 31, 32, 33, 143, 164, 190*n*4; aggression 22, 29–30, 31, 32, 33; desperation 25, 27, 29; immaturity 22
Romeo and Juliet (1968 film) 32
Romeo and Juliet (play) 31, 32, 131, 134, 164–65, 188, 190*n*3, 191*ch*2*n*2; aggression and violence in 20–22, 24, 25–26, 29–30, 31, 32; desperation in 25, 27–28, 29, 30; human reason in 14–15; humanity and beasts ("grace" and "rude will") in 14–15, 16, 20, 21–22, 24–25, 28–29, 30–31; literacy (reading) in 14–15, 22, 27, 28; parental responsibility and irresponsibility in 22, 23–24, 25–27, 29, 30–31; prolonged narration in 32; rivalry in 1, 10, 13, 14, 18, 21–22, 29, 30–31;

Index

tragic cause (fate and free will) in 20, 31, 32, 143; young love in 18–20, 25
Romeo and Juliet (2013 film) **19, 28**
Rondo, Rajon 13
Roosevelt, Franklin Delano 69–70
Rosalind 57, **61, 63**, 67, 68, 74; chain 60, 65, 66; control over others 62–63, 73; disguise as Ganymed 60, 191*ch*3*n*4, 191–92*ch*3*n*5, 193*n*1; exile 57; feminism 73, 191–92*ch*3*n*5, 192*ch*3*n*8; intervention in Phebe and Silvius' courtship 62–63; marriage to Orlando 64–65; as Orlando's teacher 60, 61, 62, 63–66; perseverance 57; popularity 57; positive outlook 59; as Silvius' teacher 62–63
Rosalind/Ganymed **61**, 62, **63**, 64, 65, 66, 67, 191*ch*3*n*4, 192*ch*3*n*6; *see also* Ganymed; Rosalind
Rosaline (*Love's Labor's Lost*) 51
Rosaline (*Romeo and Juliet*) 18, 190*n*4
Rose, Mary Beth 195*n*4
Rose, Pete 94, 143, 157–58, **157**, 161; *My Prison Without Bars* 151
Rose Theater 187
Rosenberg, Mary 190*ch*1*n*6
Rosenberg, Michael 13
Rosse (*Macbeth*) 159, 160, 196*n*17
Rote, Kyle **85**
Rozelle, Pete 94
Rudolph, Wilma 115–16
Russell, Bill 13, **15**, 17, 28
Russell, Kurt 40
Rutland, Earl of *see* Aumerle, Duke of
Ryan, Nolan 23

Saccio, Peter 42, 191*ch*2*n*4, 192*n*10
St. Crispin's Day speech 10, 87, 97, 100, 102
St. Louis Cardinals 72
St. Onge, Peter 155
Saint Paul 120; *see also* Pauline wise folly (concept)
Salic ("Salique") law 88, 96
Sampras, Pete 179; comparison to Antonio (*The Tempest*) 176
Sampson (*Romeo and Juliet*) 13
San Francisco 49ers 156
San Francisco Giants 195*n*7
Sandusky, Jerry 155–56
Sasaki, Norio 3
Saunders, Flip 22
Schaap, Dick 1
Schmeichel, Kasper 108
Schmeling, Max 68–69, **69**
Schneider, Buzz 37
Schwartz, Larry 87, 94
Schwarz, Kathryn 193*n*5
Scroop, Lord 89, 90, 192*n*5
Seattle Mariners 72
Sebastian (*The Tempest*) 180, 196*n*7; question of penitence 181, 196*n*10; "three men of sin" 174–76, 181, 185

Sebastian (*Twelfth Night*) 113, 119–20, 122, 123, 126, 129, 131, 193*n*7, 194*n*9
sex-testing (of female athletes) 129–30
Shakespeare, Craig 105, 109, 110
Shakespeare, William 96, 156; acting the plays 131–41, 187–88; meter and emphasis in plays 164–65; pronouns (*you, thou*) in plays 32–33, 191*ch*1*n*8; in role of old Adam (*As You Like It*) 58–59, 73; in role of William (*As You Like It*) 73; subtext in plays 52–54; *see also* Williams, Michael
Shakespeare in Love 20
Shapiro, Michael 193*n*5
She's the Man 194*n*11
Shields, Brooke 169
Shylock 131, 189*n*4
Sidney, Sir Philip ("An Apology for Poetry") 73
Silk, David 51
Silvius 65, 73; naiveté 62–63
Simpson, Nicole Brown 4
Simpson, O.J. 4
Sinfield, Alan 195*n*4
Sir Topas *see* Feste
Siward (young) (*Macbeth*) 160
Smith, Graham 130, 131–41, **132**, 187; advice to aspiring actors 138; on parallels between theater and sports 136–37, 139–41; on playing King Lear 136, 137; on rehearsing Shakespeare 133; on roles in *Twelfth Night* 134–35
Smith, Hallett 184
soccer in England 104, 105, 108, 110, 111
Solo, Hope 31
sonnet: defined 190*n*3
Southern Conference (NCAA) 74
Soviet Olympic hockey team (1980) **38**, 39, 40, 42, 50, 51, 103; humbling 47; overconfidence 34–35, 37, 44, 46; shaming 51
Spanier, Graham 156
Spencer, Nancy E. 117, 193*n*3
sports: parallels with theater 1, 3–12, 111, 133, 134, 136–37, 187–88
Sprewell, Latrell 22–23
Squaw Valley (CA) Olympics (1960) 50
Staw, Barry M. 14
Steinfeld, Hailee **19, 28**
Stephano (*The Tempest*) 131, 172, 173, 178, 183, 184
Steubenville, Ohio 156
Stewart, Patrick 136, 194*n*3
Stocksbridge Park Steels soccer team (England) 107
Stoke soccer team (England) 106
Stone, Emma 193*n*3
Streep, Meryl 136
Streisand, Barbra 77
Stuart, House of 195*n*16
Super Bowl III (1969) 84, **85**, 87, 94, 192*n*4; parallels with Battle of Agincourt 98

Super Bowl LI (2017) 182
Suzuki, Ichiro 72
Sycorax 171, 172, 183
Sydney Olympics (2000) 142

The Taming of the Shrew 51
Tatum, Channing 194n11
Team USA Olympic hockey team (1980) *see* U. S. Olympic hockey team
Tebow, Tim 6
The Tempest 11, 131, 139, 166, **167**, **174**, 176, 182, 183; ambition in 183; "banquet scene" 175–76; clothes 172, 183; despair in 169, 173, 175, 196n6; epilogue 182, 183; faith (belief) in 175, 180; freedom in 179, 180, 182, 185; game of chess in 183; innocence experience in 181; love-at-first-sight in 183; Masque of Ceres 177–78; memory in 175–76; mercy in 178–81, 182, 185; monstrosity in 171–74, 176, 181, 183; nature/nurture in 172, 173–74, 183; New Historicist (colonialist) reading 184, 196n2; over-simplification of and in 184–85; paradox in 168, 181, 185; pride in 170–71, 173, 196n6; protection of chastity in 172, 177–78, 196n3; Providence in 170, 175, 176, 178; redemption in 180–82; resurrection in 182; as romance 180, 184; service in 170, 171, 175, 176, 185; slavery in 166, 171, 172, 173; "three men of sin" in 174–76, 181, 185; as tragicomedy 180
Texas Rangers 23
Thane of Cawdor (character) 148, 155
Thane of Cawdor (title) 143, 145
theater: parallels with sports 1, 3–12, 110, 133, 134, 136–37, 187–88
This Life I've Led see Zaharias, Babe Didrikson
Thomas, Isiah 17
"Three Amigos" *see* Boston Celtics
"three men of sin" *see* Alonso; Antonio; Sebastian; *The Tempest*
Tikhonov, Viktor 34–35, 37, 39, 40
Title IX 117, 128, 194n12
Tottenham soccer team (England) 106, 111
Touchstone 63, 65, 68, 73, 74; ridicule of Jaques 59; wise folly 59
Tour de France 148, 155
Tour of California 148
Tracy, Spencer 128
tragic cause *see* Macbeth; Romeo and Juliet
Traub, Valerie 192ch3n6
Tretiak, Vladislav 37, 40
Trinculo (*The Tempest*) 172, 173, 178, 183, 184
Tudor, House of 53, 84, 85
Tulsa Shock 161
Twelfth Night 11, **125**, 134–35; alternative (sub-) title 130, 131; barriers to love in 113, 117, 118–19, 121, 122; epiphany in 122–23; gender in 113–14, 117, 121–22, 128–29, 130, 193n5, 193n6; homoeroticism in 193n6,

193n7; identity in 117, 123; "letter scene" (2.5) in 120–21, 124, 126, 127, 134; letters in 131; mad (wisely foolish) love in 119–22, 128; parallels with female athletes 114, 117, 121, 128; "prison scene" (4.2) in 126–27; resurrection in 123; roles in 134; social class in 113, 120, 127, 130; tone of subplot 123–27, 130
Tybalt 17, 24, 25, 29, 30, 31, 32; aggression 21–22, 24; as "Prince of Cats" 21
Tyson, Mike 99

unconditional love *see* Pauline wise folly (concept)
Unitas, Johnny 87
U.S. Olympic hockey team (1980) 34–35, 37, **38**, 39, 40, 42, 44, 46, 51, 103, 191ch2n8
U.S. Open (1994) **170**
University of Louisville 7
University of Michigan 38
University of North Carolina at Chapel Hill 151
University of North Carolina at Charlotte **75**

Van Natta, Don 114–15
Vardy, Jamie 106, 107
Vaughters, Jonathan 160
Ventura, Robin 23
Viola 117, 118, 119, 120, 121, 193n5, 194n11; disguise as Cesario 113, 114, 117, 119, 121, 122, 128–29; gender of 113, 117, 128–30, 193n5, 193n6; identity 123, 128–29, 130; mad (wisely foolish) love 123, 128; as Orsino's teacher 121–22; resistance to love 121; wooing of Olivia 118–19; *see also* Cesario Viola/Cesario 118–19, 120, 121, 122, 123, 193n5, 193n7; *see also* Cesario; Viola
Virginia Tech University 80

Ware, Kevin 7
Wars of the Roses 35
Washington Nationals 23
Washington Wizards 22
Weïrd Sisters (witches, *Macbeth*) 142, **149**, 158, 163, 195n16; association of name with fate 144; control over characters 145, 149–50, 162, 195n5; equivocal prophecies 153, 154; gender 146
Westmerland, Earl of 89
Westminster Abbey 86
Whalen, Denise A. 192ch3n6
Wilkinson, Tom 20
Will, George 10
William, Prince: and Princess Kate 100
Williams, Matt 23
Williams, Michael (*Henry V*) 95, 99–100; as Henry V's adversary 96–97, 100; representing William Shakespeare 96
Winfrey, Oprah 151
The Winter's Tale 180

wise folly *see* Pauline wise folly (concept)
Witches (*Macbeth*) *see* Weïrd Sisters
Women's National Basketball Association (WNBA) 161
Woodstock, Thomas of (Duke of Gloucester) 35, 45, 48, 53
Worcester, Earl of 47
World Series (1988) 55, 67

York, Duke of 37, 39, 41, 45, 46, 48, 54
York, House of 35, 47

Zaharias, Babe Didrikson 114–15, *115*, 121, 128; accomplishments 114; as "Texas Tomboy" 114; *This Life I've Led* 114
Zaharias, George 115
Zeffirelli, Franco 32